Off-White

Off-White

Yellowface and Chinglish by Anglo-American Culture

Sheng-mei Ma

BLOOMSBURY ACADEMIC
NEW YORK · LONDON · OXFORD · NEW DELHI · SYDNEY

BLOOMSBURY ACADEMIC
Bloomsbury Publishing Inc
1385 Broadway, New York, NY 10018, USA
50 Bedford Square, London, WC1B 3DP, UK

BLOOMSBURY, BLOOMSBURY ACADEMIC and the Diana logo are trademarks of
Bloomsbury Publishing Plc

First published in the United States of America 2020

Cover design by Eleanor Rose |
Cover image: Katharine Hepburn as Jade Tan in Dragon Seed (1944) © MGM /
Mary Evans / AF Archive

For legal purposes the Acknowledgments on p. xi constitute an extension
of this copyright page.

Bloomsbury Publishing Inc does not have any control over, or responsibility for, any
third-party websites referred to or in this book. All internet addresses given in this
book were correct at the time of going to press. The author and publisher
regret any inconvenience caused if addresses have changed or sites have
ceased to exist, but can accept no responsibility for any such changes.

Whilst every effort has been made to locate copyright holders the publishers
would be grateful to hear from any person(s) not here acknowledged.

Library of Congress Cataloging-in-Publication Data
Names: Ma, Sheng-mei, author.
Title: Off-white : yellowface and chinglish by Anglo-American culture / Sheng-mei Ma.
Description: 1. | New York : Bloomsbury Academic, 2019. | Includes bibliographical
references and index. | Summary: "Critiques the representation of Chinese characters and
perspectives in English-language fiction and film."– Provided by publisher.
Identifiers: LCCN 2019025898 (print) | LCCN 2019025899 (ebook) | ISBN 9781501352201
(hardback) | ISBN 9781501352188 (epub) | ISBN 9781501352195 (pdf)
Subjects: LCSH: Chinese in motion pictures. | Motion pictures–United States–History
and criticism. | China–In motion pictures. | Stereotypes (Social psychology) in
motion pictures. | Chinese in literature. | Stereotypes (Social psychology) in literature. |
American fiction–History and criticism.
Classification: LCC PN1995.9.C48 M33 2019 (print) | LCC PN1995.9.C48 (ebook) |
DDC 791.43/6529951–dc23
LC record available at https://lccn.loc.gov/2019025898
LC ebook record available at https://lccn.loc.gov/2019025899

ISBN: HB: 978-1-5013-5220-1
    ePDF: 978-1-5013-5219-5
    eBook: 978-1-5013-5218-8

Typeset by Integra Software Services Pvt. Ltd.

To find out more about our authors and books visit www.bloomsbury.com
and sign up for our newsletters.

CONTENTS

FIGURES

ACKNOWLEDGMENTS

I wish to thank Bloomsbury Academic's Haaris Naqvi and the two readers. The readers' insightful critiques helped me refine my argument immensely. MSU's College of Arts and Letters and the English Department have supported *Off-White* with a summer fellowship. A short excerpt of Chapter 6 is published in *The Ephemera Journal*, vol. 21, no. 3, May 2019.

Introduction

How do English-speaking novelists and filmmakers tell stories of China from a Chinese perspective? Given their motives of earnest curiosity and empathetic identification as well as of materialistic gain and psychological projection, how do they keep up appearances of pseudo-Sino immanence while ventriloquizing solely—soullessly?—in the English language? Anglo writers and their readers join in this century-old game of impersonating and dubbing Chinese. Each printed page, like its filmic adaptation on-screen, becomes Stanislavski's fourth wall, through which Anglo-America espies a Chinese drama unfold with the surround sound in Chinese simultaneously interpreted, as it were, into the white sound of English. Throughout this wish fulfillment, writers lean on grammatical and conceptual frameworks of their mother tongue to represent an alien land and its yellowface aliens. Off-white or yellow-*ish* characters and their foreign-sounding speech—Chinglish, Konglish, and Japlish—are thus performed in Anglo-American fiction and visual culture; both yellowface and Chinglish are of, for, by the (white) people. The off-white race and tongue, as Americanism has it, come off of the whites. Off-white is the shadow of whites, having very little to do with Asia, which is but a phantom tail sewn to the West's soles, a tale of phantom pain and pleasure.

Suppose some gentle readers were taken aback by the unsettling portmanteaus of "yellowface" and "Chinglish." The off-white fictitious universe, however, is nothing if not disturbingly uncanny. One may even be so shocked by the agent provocateur opening as to demand: "Define the white people!" Indeed, white, yellow, brown, and black are misnomers for skin color—much like binaries of East/West, North/South, Old/New, Masculine/Feminine, and Self/Other—but who can deny they remain powerful social constructs that shape people's minds, institutions, and traditions! That said, pray that the gentle reader in consternation takes a good hard look into the mirror for self-reflection on white or white-ish privilege over the Other in English-language discourse, a privilege that never has to see itself, remaining as invisible and inviolable as God, which is why one can afford to be at ease, ever so gentle until provoked. To flip the proverbial "I know it when I see it," one knows not even when one sees oneself in the looking-glass of these pages. Those keywords of yellowface and Chinglish are Anglo-America's dirty little secret hiding in plain sight on the page and on the screen, a secret that elicits knee-jerk denial. Such a feeling of being offended may well be a self-defensive recoil. Rather than *Off-White* playing the race card, white or white-ish indignation stems from the majority culture's trump card of self-styled objectivity and dispassionateness, unhinged whenever the bluff is called.

To borrow from Krystyn Moon's *Yellowface* (2005), yellowface in theater "describe[s] the ways in which white actors portrayed Asians, manifest[ing] degrading images of Chinese immigrants on the stage" by means of "dialect, makeup, posture, and constuming" (6). Moon shrewdly links physical and vocal performances by underlining "dialect" or "a combination of pidgin English and gibberish" (42). These yellowface characters, as a result, come to speak with an unwittingly forked tongue, decidedly English yet laced with a defamiliarizing register at the fringes of Standard English, a doublespeak that can only be called Chinglish. The challenge Chinglish poses is exactly how to parse Western writers' good intentions to touch, even to bond with the Other and the stereotypes that invariably ensue, which further distance the Other. If Chinglish is necessary, even a necessary evil, for English to reach beyond itself, how do we heirs of airy Chinglish, particularly those of us most afflicted, those who look nonwhite, off-white, transubstantiate it for the greater good, not only for ethnic communities but also collectively for millennial Sino-US, and Anglo-Asian by extension, relationships? The necessary evil of Chinglish can be turned in time: Anglo-America's Asian turn need not be a return to Orientalism, nor must our new millennium revert to neo-Orientalism, as in Neo's Orientalism in *The Matrix* (1999), techno-Orientalism, that is.

This Chinglish is formulaically flat, wooden, weirdly chiseled, with little or no correlation to the Chinese language, a classic case of Edward Said's *Orientalism* (1978). If a Chinglish grammar, a primer, were ever to be written, contractions, the active voice, strong verbs and conjugations, mot juste, rhetorical economy, and most other features of good English would have been banished. This stylization based on exclusion culminates in a narrative so repetitive yet so mystifying as to be half-dead, half-divine, a narrative of allegorical types rather than round characters, whose voices oscillate between omniscience and silliness, cosmic and comic. This grammar must make sense of Chinglish nonsense, which swings dialectically to an über-superlative sense or at least a sixth sense no longer retained by the "rational, scientific" West since the Enlightenment. Nevertheless, Chinglish is highly volatile, inconsistent, and willfully mercurial as it enjoys a discursive impunity, a creative jouissance of kneading clay figures and putting words into their mouths. Accordingly, Chinglish shifts to colloquialism and Americanism, literary belles lettres and fine turns of phrase, proverbs and biblical archaism, among other shades of English, no different from American actors forgetting to do their characters' Irish brogue, guttural German, or other foreign accent halfway through their film.

For instance, Pearl S. Buck, the matriarch who weds Western rhetoric's two powerful genetic strands—China missionary pidgin and Anglo-American yellowface fiction—drifts imperceptibly midway through *The Good Earth* (1931) out of the orbit of her Chinglish-inflected style to a biblical tone of voice, easing back to her more natural speech. Albeit quaint by the standards of modern English, the King James half of "Mrs. Chinahand Buck," as William Faulkner mercilessly derides, at least dispenses with the pretense of atrocious grammatical errors. The discourse of English, exemplified by the Nobel laureate Buck, thus enacts this imaginary Chineseness as if it were a foreign object, an invasive species, while, in reality, Chinglish is the subconscious "backtalk" "badtalk" from the Janus-faced Anglo-American literature. Buck, in this case, assumes a narrative voice in a backhanded manner; her stereotypical yellowface characters uncannily double back to her Orientalist given name Pearl. This mainstream regression in fallacy would in time progress to the minority, the "Chinks," pardon my French, consciously talking back, parodying, deconstructing fake oldies—definitely not fake news—of Chinglish. This evolution is in line with Bakhtin's carnivalesque elevating of the low, with postcolonial subversion of the "mimic man," and with glocalization's center-margin reappropriation. What unites these insurgent movements, the study of Chinglish included, is the "repo" of one's history of pain, from the Devil's Standard English in William L. Lorimer's *The New Testament in Scots* (1983)[1] to Gangsta Rap's N-word to Taiwan and Hong Kong gays' appropriation of the communist term *tongzhi* (comrade).

Let me briefly demonstrate by way of a contrast between two novels' openings, nearly a century apart. Buck's *The Good Earth* opens with "It was Wang Lung's marriage day" instead of the customary "wedding day" (1). Buck's awkward, un-English phrase opens a novel of, for lack of better words, Chinglish spoken by yellowface characters to, on the one hand, defamiliarize readers from English, although they are reading English and English only, and to, on the other, transport readers to a faraway land where dialogue and narrative descriptions are magically translated, in a manner of speaking, from Chinese to English. Buck switches to the "wedding day" (22) in *The Living Reed* (1963), on Korea, and appears to have generally outgrown the affectation of garbled Chinglish. In Buck's 1930s, however, the common expression "wedding day" comes across almost like a misnomer. The right phrase sounds wrong, whereas the wrong phrase "marriage day" sounds about right because it is China. Given that wedding pinpoints the ceremony on a specific day, marriage expands from that moment of union to the entire span and even institution of two individuals forming a family.

Buck's intelligible, if unintelligent, sentence only deteriorates henceforth into near unintelligibility, such as Wang Lung's father looking forward to a grandson "to warm my bones in my age" (3), until a stylistic resurrection in the King's (King James's) English in midstream. Are Chinese patriarchs more heartened by the prospect of male heirs who reach deeper emotionally, all the way to the "bones," than for Westerners? This allusion to "bones" is the first of many that consistently portray the Chinese as a people apart, who feel with the body's extremities or interiorities to the extent that they appear primordial, in touch with elemental forces and atavistic memory, but out of touch with modern concepts of self. Pathological self-alienation turns mystical; depersonalization personifies a national character. Instead of the first-person "me," Wang Lung's father expects a grandson to "warm my bones," a third-person polarization of one specific body part. This warming would occur "in my age," a strange downsizing of "in my old age." Overall, Wang Lung's father is a character who generalizes, essentializes the Chinese as if they were, at any point in the course of their lives, hardwired with skeletal nerve endings to be quickened by, to borrow the title of Buck's 1941 novel, *Dragon Seed*. The Chinese gene is made to jump species between its organic functions and its stand-alone affect, with indiscernible intermediary of self-consciousness. This is just one of Buck's strategic jumps or Sino-splits over the first-person voice divorced from biological groundings, of the third-person transcendence over body parts.

The American children's game of "Dig a hole to China" is germane to the study of Chinglish, for China has long been viewed as the opposite to the Western Self, as the Other that does things in a diametrically different way from "us," including our language. The English expression "Chinese Whispers" for another children's game, "Telephone" in the US, eerily sums up Buck's doctored trans-Pacific missives. Received on this shore, Buck's word choice sounds foreign, shifting away from the idiomatic, familiar English language and the English-speaking world where a festive celebration would be in order for the "wedding day." In place of all the happy associations evoked by the "wedding day," Anglo readers are displaced onto an Orient of stereotypical Orientals speaking wooden, stilted Chinglish and behaving accordingly. Far from dynamic, evolving, and organic Chinese voices, what readers hear instead is Basic or Remedial English, spoken by beginning learners of English as a Second Language (ESL). Moreover, these ESL speakers seem to have been drilled on one textbook only, the King James Version, their speech marred by archaism, by endless run-ons with "ands," by a tone-deaf, brain-dead rhetorical flatlining, by the total absence of colloquial contractions, just to name the most egregious. Almost by default, Chinese en masse are made to parrot Christian converts' faulty English. Rather than the "marriage day" for Wang Lung and O-lan, Buck's protagonists, it turns out to be "the beginning of a beautiful friendship" for Buck and the Western readership eager for news from afar, which is really same old, same old within the West's own mind. Buck's Pulitzer and Nobel Prizes crystalize the mid-twentieth-century Western dreams over that other world.

In direct opposition to Buck, the second paragraph of Asian American Patricia Park's *Re Jane* (2015) gives an establishing shot of Koreatown in Flushing, New York, where Konglish, Chinglish's sound-alike to Western ears, is "perpetrated":

> Flushing. The irony was that none of its residents could pronounce the name of their adopted hometown; the Korean language lacked certain English consonants and clusters. The letter *F* was assimilated to an *H* or a *P*. The adults at church would go *Hoo* before they could form the word, as if cooling it off their tongue. My uncle and aunt's rendition: Poo, Rushing. It could've been poetry. (3)

Irony lies at the heart of the immigrant condition, or any bicultural (mis) communication as in the case of Buck. In Park, that parenthetical "mis" registers not only the ambiguity of new arrivals with mounting nostalgia but also that of (un)naturalized "new" Americans who remain perennial aliens to "old" Americans. As such, Korean expatriates in Flushing fail to articulate where exactly they reside in the United States owing to linguistic interference. The "f" in Flushing eludes Korean speakers, morphing into either "h" or "p." "Hoo" puns with Who, as if uprooted Korean immigrants are questioning who they are or are being so questioned by English speakers since they cannot identify their residence properly. "Hoo" also sounds like blowing on spicy food such as the quintessential Korean side dish kimchi in an attempt to "cool[ing] it off their tongue." Pungent and spicy food stimulates, even overstimulates, the tongue's taste buds. The momentary stinging, numbing sensations cause displeasure before they are absorbed into the system and lead to gustatory joy. The tongue's initial shock and discomfort turn into pleasure.

Generationally, Park's first-generation Korean immigrants labor in working-class professions—grocers, short order cooks, beauticians, hairdressers, laundromat workers, and whatnot—in order for their second- or 1.5-generation children to attend schools and become Americans. Immigrants' pain mellows into American-born children's pleasure. The concluding sentence of the quote epitomizes this transubstantiation. Korean immigrants' pidgin or atrocious English is alchemized by the protagonist Jane Re's narrative voice into poetry. Note that the contraction of "could've" in fact closes this paragraph in a most American, most conversational tone. Despite its casual understatedness, the subjunctive mood intimates immigrant and, to some extent, minority tentativeness, a precarious existence unsure of its own worth. Park the novelist has traversed in a short paragraph immigrant Konglish and Standard English, the alien speech and Americanism, internalized ethnic erring and grounded majority entitlement.

Other than a generational evolution, the h and p polarization can be construed in terms of the human body. The sound of "f" in Flushing bifurcates into, at the "top" end, the entry into the human body via the tongue and the mouth over "who/hoo" and, at the "bottom" end, the exit from the human body as "poo" or fecal matter. Indeed, if one eats, then one poos. As immigrants eke out a living in Flushing, they slowly age and their lives turn into body (as) waste and are flushed out of America in a place aptly called Flushing. This figure of speech of the human body can become America's body politic. The undesirable aliens resemble waste matter expelled from America by the power of the state during the Chinese Exclusion Act (1882–1943), the wartime internment of Japanese Americans, US-born notwithstanding (1942–1945), the acquittal of Vincent Chin's baseball bat-swinging killers (1982–1987), and other racial purging.[2] Currently, the aliens in us (US) are secreted in ethnic closets of Koreatown and such until outed; until one of their own talks back in the poetry of Konglish.

Chinglish—or Konglish, for that matter—is English in a minor key, affecting a pentatonic, Oriental feel. Whereas English flows with the greatest of ease, Chinglish frustrates as it seizes the act of reading or viewing like spasms of neural, synaptic misfiring. The body's smooth movement and speech convulse into involuntary tics, irrepressible hiccoughs, be it Buck's Orientalizing or Park's poeticizing. To draw from Ezra Pound's ideographic splitting in *The Cantos* (1970), *chin* (親 or *qin* in the People's Republic of China's *pinyin* rendering) means to kiss, to endear, among a plethora of homophones. Chin-glish or "kiss English" is precisely what Anglo-American artists put Chinese characters up to, namely, submitting them to speaking in tongues, in a stylization of the global lingua franca in which few of them are adept. If "every dialect, every language, is a way of thinking. To speak means to assume a culture" is valid, as Frantz Fanon argues in "The Negro and Language" (1967), then Chinglish-speakers are grafted with an alien tongue from the underbelly of English whenever they are made to role-play the Other. Chinglish is English playacting, feigning the Other. While Fanon seeks to give credence and voice to non-standard speaking communities, Chinglish is English writing communities'—more so of Buck's buddies than Park's—voice-over for mandarins-cum-marionettes.

Nonetheless, puppeteers and puppets, masters and slaves, tend to coexist symbiotically. The American slang "kiss my ass" for "go to hell," say, on rear bumper stickers, suggests the counterforce of repulsion implicit in any attraction, and vice versa, between two parties. Embedded in "kiss my ass," the upper orifice that pooches out to smooch is the partner to the out-of-sight lower orifice that blooms downward to poop. English is what Anglo-America speaks; Chinglish is what it shits. The hole on top is the "front man" to the corporeal and cultural circulation of entry into and exit out of the self and non-self, into and out of Anglos and "Chinks," a circulation vital to any organism's and culture's sustainability. Ang Lee's *Crouching Tiger, Hidden Dragon* (2000) enacts this yin-yang circle in the archvillain Jade Fox's dying words while reaching out to Jen, her disciple who betrays her and whom she tries to poison: "My only family [*qin*], my only foe [*chou*]." "Foe" (*chou*) or vengeance used to be written in classical Chinese as 讎, two short-tailed birds (*zhui*) cuddling the middle radical for talk, dialogue (*yan*). In the politically incorrect ancient China, twittering birds, some even pecking for blood, embody doppelgangers' duet/duel.[3] The parallelism of the ideogram *chou* and of Jade Fox's last words conjures up the hidden love–hate, *qin–chou* (affection–vengeance) symmetry between facial cheeks and butt cheeks, and, in this case, English and Chinglish. This Chinese swordplay genre's conundrum evinces a common repetition compulsion, well-nigh universal in mythology, fantasy, and children's stories.

Apologies for the string of *chin/qin* associations and mixed metaphors from mouth to anus to Ang Lee to short-tailed birds, which, nonetheless, befit Chinglish that is both mixed and metaphorical, both random and predetermined. A Chinaman's "spitch," to quote Frank Chin's pidgin for "speech" in "The Year of the Dragon" (1974: 131), is genetically programmed in the West's will to power. And the very mixing of Chinglish is metaphorical: Chinglish cannot possibly be literal, unless bilingual writers code-switch steadily between Chinese ideograms and English letters— an ideal even Spanglish writers from the same Indo-European family of languages as English fail to achieve, an ideal that is but living reality for millions of bilingual immigrants. This dream in Chinglish does come true partially in polyphonic filmmaking with bilingual actors undergirded by English subtitles on the bottom of the screen. At best in literature of printed words, however, a few Romanized, italicized, and barely pronounceable Chinese words slouch in a sea of English alphabet. To English-only artists enamored with creatures they have cooked up and cut up, Chinglish is but Chinks' English, a juicy rare, bloody fare on the platter. Dialectically in any codependency, however, Chinglish can also be recalibrated to chip away the master tongue and white sound, as in the case of Patricia Park.

Like snow, white sound, originally an acoustic term for white noise or ambient surround sound, shrouds the Anglo-centric English-language discourse, the whole world thus muffled and muzzled, except strewn here and there with some light tracks of Chinglish and the like—Park's Konglish, Milton Murayama's Hawaiian creole Japlish, Louis Chu's Cantonese-inflected English—from fictional characters of Asian extraction. Their accents are but off-white, Standard English with a touch of yellow covered apace by snowfall, barely making a dent. Before the tracks vanish altogether, let us trace Chinglish and the like for, as racists say, they all look alike. Chinglish et al. means how English speakers, of white and Asian descent alike, do foreigners, how they do foreign-language dialogue and narratives in English. The most competent wordsmiths among them double-tongue, as inflected, stylized as a flutist's two-note double-tonguing or a violinist's double-stop. Many of these wordsmiths are Asian Americans tuned to both their native-speaking English and their erstwhile home languages, now regressed and foreign. The least competent simply saw away on their fiddle rhapsodically to the delight of those deaf to all sounds save Standard English. Many of the latter—creators and fans—hail from the monolingual majority group. Between the ethnic wordsmiths and others "full of passionate intensity," white sound envelops exotic lands, whitewashes alien brains, an omnipresence taken for granted and scarcely registered.

Chinglish, by definition, is a bit off, off-kilter from mainstream English. To borrow from Maxine Hong Kingston's memorable description of immigrant FOBs (fresh off the boaters) in *Tripmaster Monkey* (1989), Chinglish sounds "offu" (5). One cannot help associating offu with the awful word offal, gutted matter, even fecal matter, expelled by proper English. If English enlivens the desirable, useful white body, Chinglish seems its dropping, disavowed anon precisely because it is produced by that body—that body's guts, its visceral emotion, its gut feeling repressed and purged. This unseemliness of Chinglish springs from its hybridity—a duality taken for duplicity, a hetereoglossia lapsing into unreadable aphasia. The linguistic doubleness harks back to W. E. B. Du Bois's double consciousness as both Americans and Black Americans. Instead of the invisible whiteness that possesses America, peoples of color and their speech patterns are marked by deviations from the norm, hence mongrelized. To represent a foreign land and foreigners in the midst of Anglos and English, such as Chinatowns and Chinese descendants, English is slanted like stereotypical slant eyes, as if it were capturing a strange world in a disorientingly tilted Dutch angle. Its collective, age-old practices and habits—grammatical rule, idiom, colloquialism, slang, even Americanism—are transgressed. Chinglish both repulses for being anomalous and attracts for being exotic.

Conceptually, the study of Chinglish opens by insisting on the former of the "Form-Content" divide. Rather than looking past the medium of language—both dialogue and narrative descriptions—for the content or subject matter on China and Chinese, an exegesis of Chinglish looks at the words, non-transparent, even opaque by definition and oftentimes deceptive, Machiavellian by design. We must not look past yellowfaces with slant eyes and all to see yellows or Chinese behind them: those yellowfaces are masks worn by whites; they are off-white, of whites. Think of Chinglish as water, or Lewis Carroll's looking-glass. Water is far from absence, a non-entity through which we spy marine life; on the contrary, it reflects the lookers and their world, refracting them, distorting them. The *unheimlich* (un-home-like) Chinglish is a Freudian displacement and substitution of the English speaker's self and home. Admittedly, this parsing of form may be counterintuitive for English speakers: what comes naturally to them is not so much a neutral, taken-for-granted means of representation as an extension of Anglophone privilege. One such flagrant abuse of power lies in Chinglish, which, in the worst-case scenario, constitutes disinformation on China, yellowface characters mistaken for the Other's authentic face and voice. Let us disabuse ourselves of medieval religiosity of looking through the penitent's body for the soul: Chinglish gives not the Chinese soul; it gives away, instead, the likeness of the English language, whose twisted self-image is a confession from Anglo-America's own soul.

Nevertheless, like the subject of God, it is easier to describe what Chinglish is not than what it is. Although Chinglish reads like translation, it is not. Chinglish does not negotiate between the source and the target language, only the pretense of rendering a source culture. Chinglish is not a mainstream, majority language anywhere in the world, nor is it a minor language. It resembles but does not amount to a contact language, such as pidgin or creole, which thrives in contact zones of borders and trading ports. Nor has it risen to the valorized constellation of "minority American languages" (7) envisioned by Shu-mei Shih and colleagues' *Sinophone Studies* (2013) in the wake of Werner Sollors's *Multilingual America* (1998). On the thin crust of top soil left behind by nineteenth- and early twentieth-century Western traders, native compradors, and Christian missionaries, English-language writers and artists raise the specter of Chinglish, sprouting a tongue foreign even to Lazaruses, its reputed speakers. Theoretically, Chinglish could have been a living, evolving organism from bilingual, bicultural communities of Chinese and Asian diaspora, had novelists tapped into such populations. Salient examples of ethnic performance abound, albeit largely ignored by mainstream society: Louis Chu's New York bachelor community in *Eat a Bowl of Tea* (1961); Joy Kogawa's Japanese-speaking Second World War internees in *Obasan* (1982); Alice Wu's code-switching émigrés in Flushing, New York, in *Saving Face* (2004); Mira Nair's characters speaking Bengali in Calcutta and accented English in New York in *The Namesake* (2006); Hong Khaou's Mandarin and English interface in *Lilting* (2014); Patricia Park's Konglish morphing between Flushing's Koreatown and Seoul's Itaewon in *Re Jane*; and even Gene Luen Yang's graphic novels *Boxers and Saints* (2013) and *The Shadow Hero* (2014).

By comparison, white Chinglish writers are decidedly not insiders of vibrant yet non-mainstream bilingualism in Flushing; Monterey Park, Los Angeles; and the International District, Seattle. Even in the microcosm of each immigrant family across the United States and elsewhere, Chinglish animates the tension between home and work languages, between that which immigrant parents feel most at home and that which American-born children gravitate to in the course of assimilation. If only more white and off-white writers listen with their heart, yellow birds sing in authentic Chinglish right in their backyard, although slightly out of (white) tune. This is easier said than done, though, evidenced by the émigré, bilingual writer

Ha Jin's *A Good Fall* (2009) on New York's Chinese immigrant enclave, where characters speak in self-assured vernacular English that reflects the author's enviable command of English rather than his characters'. Keenly aware of his language "alien to [his Chinese] subject-matter," Ha Jin still chooses to write in American English that de-alienates his characters for the reader, contrary to his avowed "literary principle" of "translatability and similarity" ("Exiled to English" 112). Ha Jin surely knows that bilingual switching or heteroglossia defy translation, and bear little resemblance to monolingual American English. After all, having come from outside the host language, Ha Jin feels compelled to prove that he is in, no longer off-white linguistically. For the US-born Patricia Park, Ha Jin's erstwhile Boston University creative writing master mentee whose "birthright" includes the language, the creative impulse drives her to venture out of monolingualism by playing with English. Her master thesis advisor must be pleased to see how Park has outplayed white writers' Chinglish as well as his own English-only stories, notwithstanding the largely Chinese setting from *Waiting* (1999) to *Nanjing Requiem* (2011). As the saying goes, *qingchuyulan shengyulan* (Out of blue comes green that surpasses blue). The disciple bests the master because the color green, punning with "the young" in Chinese, mixes blue and yellow serendipitously, as does Park in cross-breeding blue-blooded Englishes with yellow-stained Konglishes.

Alas, for Chinglish-spewing creatures, many a writer latches onto the deadened discourse of Orientalism, mummifying characters, metastasizing speech patterns within an intertextual alternate universe of comic book Dragon Lady, pulp fiction Charlie Chan and Fu-Manchu, and other usual suspects of the East dreamed up by the West. The yellowface constellation shines with Katharine Hepburn (*Dragon Seed*), Bela Lugosi (*The Mask of Fu Manchu*), Anna May Wong (*Shanghai Express*), Jennifer Jones (*Love Is a Many-Splendored Thing*), Mickey Rooney (*Breakfast at Tiffany's*), Nancy Kwan (*The World of Suzie Wong*), and many more stars. This alternate universe resembles the virtual reality of the screens that we have come to favor. We millennial Bartlebys, the copyists, prefer not the frameless, amorphous reality lying just beyond the reach of our fingertips. Heads Up, Head-Bowed Tribe (低頭族 or *ditouzu*, Mandarin term for those of us—all of us?—glued and bowing down to our electronic devices)! Belonging to such Head-Bowed Tribes are Chinglish writers so wont to Orientalist stereotypes that they are oblivious to diasporic communities' true Chinglish in our midst.

Off-White proceeds to interrogate seminal Anglo-American fiction and film on off-white bodies and voices, or Yellowface and Chinglish. It commences with one Nobel laureate, Pearl Buck, and ends with another, Kazuo Ishiguro, almost a century later. The trajectory in between illustrates that Anglo-American culture does not so much relinquish its old habits over the Orient and Orientals as repurpose them. The old British imperial wine of W. Somerset Maugham is thus rebottled with ethnic spices and Chinglish by Maxine Hong Kingston. The detective and mystery genres revolving around Sherlock Holmes and Hannibal Lecter also continue unabated their stock yellowface characters, who exude a magnetic charge so powerful as to, further afield, pull in Japanese anime and sci-fi imaginary in *Ghost in the Shell*. Representations of the Other invariably teeter on the knife edge of good and bad, the well known and the unknown. Hence, opposite to such extraordinary aliens as Dr. Fu-Manchu lie lowly Chinese laundrymen whitewashed from collective memory. Given the polarization, the attempt to harmonize drives a comparative juxtaposing of Taoist *Monkey* and Nordic *Beowulf*. Yet the universal urge to fashion a foil is ingrained in any will to power, so much so that even the millennial China creates an "off-yellow," darker-hued Orient in minorities and neighbors in Huallywood films to silhouette its global ascent. This tension between Self and Other, America and China, is played out close to home in the two MSUs: my home school Michigan State University and its Mandarin-speaking *u*ndergraduates. Ishiguro concludes this study, where his English-only whiteface characters repress any impulse of ethnic double-tonguing that has energized Asian North American cultural production. A short coda buttonholes a number of Asian American artists in *Crazy Rich Asians* (2018) as they perform an ethnic "show and tell" for Anglo-America.

1

Pearl and Jade and Yellowface and Chinglish

The question hides in plain sight and deserves reiteration: how do English-speaking novelists and filmmakers tell stories of China from a Chinese point of view? Anglo writers have routinely fashioned in English an alien land and its aliens. Their yellowface characters, as a result, come to "speak in tongues," in an English estranged by, for lack of a better term, Chinglish. Chineseness is integrated into the discourse of English, while remaining, to some extent, as foreign objects in the body of Anglo-American literature. The Anglo-Self and the Sino-Other are made to fraternize discursively from the genesis of Christian missionaries and Old China Hands of the nineteenth century, all the way down to the twenty-first. Indeed, yellowfaces and their Chinglish must be traced back to ancestors over a century ago: Western missionaries, colonialists, Orientalists, on the one hand, and, on the other, their Chinese mates of compradors, missionary school graduates, and Western wannabes. Such a mixed genetic makeup has been inherited by contemporary Anglo-American writers dabbling in things Oriental and by Westerners of Asian descent looking homeward, ancestrally, that is. A key transitional figure in this entrenched style of representation is Pearl S. Buck, whose career spans the middle decades of the twentieth century.

Despite or because of her Nobel and Pulitzer Prizes for literature, Pearl S. Buck is the Orientalist mother-of-pearl, secreting a host of yellowface characters spewing Chinglish, one of whom is Jade, the protagonist in *Dragon Seed* (1941). Both the Creator's and her creature's Christian names, pun intended, are darlings within the Orientalist discourse. This argument's title with three "ands" further emulates Buck's favorite run-on sentences with endless additions. With the wisdom of hindsight from postcolonial and cultural studies, we may look askance at Buck's body of works, such as *Dragon Seed* and the eponymous 1944 film featuring Katharine Hepburn as Jade with slant eyes (Figure 1.1). In the vein of what

FIGURE 1.1 *Katharine Hepburn as Jade with slant eyes in* Dragon Seed.

Prince Philip described as Orientals with "slitty eyes," these novels and films appear outdated, of historical interest mainly.[1] From Great Britain's royalty to Anglo-American popular culture, Buck inherits as well as perpetuates Orientalist representations of Asians. By taping shut, half-closing, and dimming Hepburn's big bright eyes, the film in fact commands an "Open Sesame!"—a sesame seed in the shape of a horizontal keyhole—to a faraway, war-torn China. Hepburn's epicanthic or single-folded eyelids offer the American audience a narrow window, as it were, to a sick China under the Japanese yoke, a pitiable victim worthy of American support. That narrow window carries, however, an odious ring of the racial epithet "chink," which gives access to China as much as defaces it. This is the Nobel laureate's best intentions, albeit patronizing, which continues the trajectory of *The Good Earth* (1931) fraught with stereotypes yet proving itself a surprising primer on turn-of-the-last-century Chinese culture, on the one hand, and, on the other, a playbook on Chinglish. In concert with the yellowface makeup of the Western cast, Hepburn's eyes are a marker of difference, even of disability, compared to Western eyes, round, wide open, "unobstructed." This sense of disability stems from the downright unnatural, stereotypical look of halved, upturned eyes all the Western actors assume, except Hepburn's husband played by Turhan Bey, son of a Turkish father and Czechoslovakian-Jewish mother. Bey's half-Asian ancestry and exotic appearance somehow guarantee Asianness, rendering cosmetics a moot point.

Akin to blackface minstrelsy, the yellowface is a performance tradition that authenticates otherness by reprising widely accepted stereotypes of Asians. While the West fixates on the racial other as a decorative and functional fixture in its own mental palace, yellowface taps into a highly destabilizing discourse on identity, culture, and power. There is no such thing as the particular skin tone of yellow, just as there are multiple eye shapes amongst Asians, not to mention Caucasians. The neologistic grafting of yellow onto faces, or Asianness onto white bodies, begs the question of both elements. Cauc-asians get under the Asian skin—to become as well as to irritate Asians—once their eyelids are "caulked," glued, complemented by such trite body language as bowing, bodies which mouth trite concepts of honor and shame in the speech pattern of pidgin Chinglish as mangled as taped eyes. Yellowfaces affect a Chinglish accent just as they sport slant eyes, a slant in physical and vocal representations to effect Chineseness.

Indeed, Hepburn's *Dragon Seed* manifests the double entendre of "getting under someone's skin" and, by implication, spilling out of someone's lips. That a yellowface feigns an Asian is already problematic in our cosmopolitan global village, particularly to our neighbors from Asia. On the other hand, a yellowface also points to the West's abiding obsession to superimpose the erstwhile, phantasmagoric Orient onto Asia of our own time. As seeds come from crops and generations of yesteryears, Buck inherits as well as sows the seeds for a dragon look and dragon talk. Her yellowface bodies come to sprout an archaic, near-biblical Chinglish, so uncanny à la Freud that it denotes a foreign tongue that is one's own, only estranged and repressed. To shed light on the role of Buck in our Western tradition of yellowface speaking Chinglish, this argument flashes back to where Buck came from in terms of her Chinese roots in that language and culture, of her magnum opus *The Good Earth*, and of Katharine Hepburn's *Dragon Seed* as well as the discourse swirling around the film.

Buck's Chinese

Born in 1893 to her Chinese missionary parents in West Virginia, Pearl Sydenstricker Buck was taken to China when she was three months old. She grew up "fully bilingual, speaking and reading both languages," as Peter Conn puts it in his 1996 biography *Pearl S. Buck: A Cultural Biography* (25). Jaime Harker in *America the Middlebrow: Women's Novels, Progressivism, and Middlebrow Authorship between the Wars* (2007) concurs that Buck was "fluent in both written and spoken Chinese" (91). Harker goes so far as to assert that "Buck composed her novels in Chinese and then translated them into English ... This produced a style that many readers could only recognize as scriptural; it carried authority and the aura of authenticity" (102). Kenneth Eble echoes Harker: "the narrative formed itself mentally into the Chinese language, and she then translated this material into English. She asserted that her prose was based on idiomatic Chinese and that she was often uncertain about the English qualities of the style" (33). None of these critics who has made similar claims produced any shred of evidence of Buck's drafts in Chinese. Contrary voices emerged amongst Chinese scholars. Kang-hu Kiang's scathing review of *The Good Earth* called into question "Buck's expertise on China and even her linguistic command of Chinese," but such critiques were routinely dismissed as Chinese literati's elitism, as Vanessa Kunnemann has done in *Middlebrow Mission* (qtd. in Kunnemann 2015, 173).

The family visited the United States in their furlough year of 1901 to 1902. Buck did not return to the United States until her first year in college at Randolph-Macon Woman's College in Lynchburg, Virginia, fairly close to her West Virginia home, in 1910. After graduation, she rejoined her family in China. She married John Lossing Buck, an agricultural economist and missionary, in 1917. Carol was born to the Bucks in 1920 and developed profound mental retardation, a disability recurring in Buck's characters throughout her career. Carol and Buck's physical condition prompted a quick trip back to the United States. With her stream of articles on China in American magazines and journals, Buck had obtained the status of an in situ witness to a chaotic and mysterious land. She went back to the United States a number of times, but China remained her home for the next decade or so, until the Bucks's homecoming in 1932. Before that, she had launched her literary career with *The Good Earth* in 1931, expertly edited and marketed by Richard Walsh of John Day, who was to become Buck's business partner and second husband after her divorce with Lossing in 1935. She traveled to Shanghai in 1933 in part to offer advice on the MGM filming of *The Good Earth* near the metropolis. In 1934, she made the transoceanic journey back to North America with Walsh, fully intending to return to China. But she never did. Her subsequent writing and professional career in the West rose not only to garner Nobel and Pulitzer Prizes but also to establish her as an Asian expert in the first half of the twentieth century, all on the "raw materials" she collected in her childhood and youth.

This alleged Chineseness—both Buck's command of the language and her in-depth understanding of Chinese culture—is key to her professional success. Chineseness inspired her work and became her foil against any criticism, conspicuously displayed in her December 12, 1938 acceptance speech of the Nobel Prize in Literature entitled "The Chinese Novel." It is an argument she resorted to throughout her long and prolific career. Buck attributed her literary output to "the Chinese and not the American novel which has shaped my own efforts in writing" (11). She asserted that "The Chinese novel has an illumination for the western novel and for the western novelist" (11). Rather than parsing that insight from her study of the Chinese novel, Buck offered a laundry list of key works in the name of egoless creation of the common folk. "A great novelist, or so I have been taught in China, should be above all else 'tse ran,' that is, natural, unaffected, and so flexible and variable as to be wholly at the command of the materials that flows through him" (31). Then why is the language of Buck's novels so stylized, affected, and imitative of the Scriptures? Buck's Chinglish mixes the King James Bible and American pop culture's Orientalist pidgin. The Nobel lecture culminates in a lengthy recap of the three classics of Chinese novels: *Romance of the Three Kingdoms*, *The Outlaws of the Marsh*, and *The Dream of the Red Chamber*. Akin to a tourist's hastily snapped photos, the Nobel laureate gave an account worthy of today's informative Wikipedia entry. She did pause long enough to put in a plug for her translation of Shi Nai'an's fourteenth-century classic *Shui Hu Zhuan* as *All Men Are Brothers*, whose "original title, *Shui Hu Chuan*, in English is meaningless, denoting merely the watery margins of the famous marshy lake which was the robbers' lair. To Chinese the words invoke instant century-old memory, but not to us" (44). A translator between us and them, Buck opts for "our" "century-old memory." Accordingly, Buck's choice of title conjures up the biblical association of "my brother's keeper," a religious connotation neither in keeping with the novel's secular human relationships valorizing *yi* or camaraderie nor with its Taoist/Buddhist folk belief system. In her defense, apologists would no doubt cite the proverb from *The Analects of Confucius* used on several occasions in the novel: "Within the four seas, all men are brothers" (四海之內，皆兄弟也 Shi Nai'an's original Chinese 47; Sidney Shapiro's translation as *The Outlaws of the Marsh* 44). However, to Buck's readers, it goes without saying that the biblical "brother" is closer than the Confucian one. Buck strategically ended her Nobel speech with a bang from the outer space of China: "In this tradition of the novel have I been born and reared as a writer ... so I have been taught in China" (55, 59).

Out of her voluminous output, Buck left behind nothing that testified to her Chinese proficiency. At best, the only indirect evidence lies in Buck's

All Men Are Brothers (henceforth *Brothers*), also rendered by Sidney Shapiro as *The Outlaws of the Marsh*. Although this translation fails to provide direct proof, a scrutiny of key characters suggests not so much Buck's firm grasp of the Chinese language and source materials as her infelicities in both the source and the target language. Her knowledge of Chinese vocabulary and phrases is as shaky as her idiomatic English. Buck's lifelong chicanery of playing a Chinese insider justifies the weakness of her English prose style. Furthermore, Buck's self-professed insider identity is not substantiated at all by her one and only dabbling in Chinese literature. Buck is no Gladys Margaret Tayler Yang, British translator of missionary parents and wife of Hsien-yi Yang. Gladys Yang was the University of Oxford's first graduate in Chinese language in 1980. For decades, even during the dark ages of political struggles and campaigns, including the Cultural Revolution, the Yangs had collaborated in producing seminal translations of classics and contemporary literature.

Brothers is Shi Nai'an's fourteenth-century historical novel that harks back to twelfth-century outlaws, a book subsequently edited and possibly expanded from seventy-one to one hundred chapters by Luo Guanzhong. It draws from the rebellion led by Song Jiang chronicled in *The History of Song* and other historical documents. Song Jiang and his gang had long become a legend inspiring folklore, stories, and plays over the centuries, culminating in Shi's and Luo Guanzhong's novel. The novel traces how 108 hero-rebels are forced by corruption and injustice into outlawry in the marsh areas at Liangshan (Mount Liang) in the province of Shandong. In chapter 3 or Buck's chapter 2, the hero Shi Jin tattooed with nine dragons demonstrates loyalty in not giving up his sworn brothers to the authority. Instead, he leads the getaway after being informed that his servant-messenger betrayed him. The servant confesses to misplacing his master's confidential correspondence with the outlaws: "It is because this humble one, who am I, was drunken" (Buck, *Brothers* 47). Buck's awkward, foreign-sounding line is rendered in idiomatic English by Sidney Shapiro: "I was drunk. I forgot about it" (31). Given the servant's lowly status, Shapiro's colloquial speech is far more apt than Buck's contorted rhetoric. Low-level officers (都頭 *dutou*) in pursuit of the outlaws are better rendered as "constables" (32) than the nonsensical "small officers" (Buck, *Brothers* 48). Readying themselves to break out of the siege, Shi Jin calls for "pack[ing] all his portable valuables" (Shapiro 33), which in Buck turns into a wordy, loose translation of "all the silver and gold and the good clothing he had and all that was of value" (48). Arming themselves, "Shih Chin and the three chiefs had on no armor and they had no bows and arrows, but on the weapon rack each person had hung a girdle knife and there were swords too" (48). Buck's translation is opposite to the original, which should have been "He and the bandit chiefs put on their armor and took the halberds and swords from the weapons rack" (Shapiro 33). Bemoaning the loss of his property, Shi Jin is made by Buck to mouth:

"After a year and a few days had passed ... Although I have some fine silken clothing and some valuables, yet all the furniture of my house is gone" (49). Buck has somehow lengthened the passage of time from several days to over a year and has unduly itemized Shi's loss. Shapiro's translation is closer to the original (細軟家財，粗重什物 miscellaneous household items, heavy bulky items): "Shi Jin remains for several days ... Although I managed to keep small valuables, my larger property is gone completely" (33).

As Buck moves from Shi Jin to the tattooed monk Lu Zhishen, the suspicion of her shaky grasp of Chinese is confirmed. Enraged by the ravishment of a woman in the hand of a local butcher Zheng with the nickname of the Lord of the West, Lu deliberately detains the butcher by a series of labor-intensive orders. Lu places the orders of, in Shapiro, "ten catties of lean meat, chopped fine, to be used for filling"; "ten catties of fat meat with no speck of lean in it"; and "ten catties of gristle, chopped fine" (39). The key phrase is *sàozǐ* (臊子), local dialect for minced or well-diced meat. Manually minced meat would be the equivalent of today's ground meat. In the context of Lu's instruction and the butcher's understanding that the meat is filling "to put in dumplings" (39), *sàozǐ* clearly points to meat minced rather than diced in cubes. Buck is thus way off: "ten catties of lean meat cut into strips"; "ten pounds of fat and it must be cut into shreds too"; "ten pounds of gristle and it also must be shredded" (*Brothers* 58, 59). Neither strips nor shreds correspond to Lu's order. Buck even casually flips between the Chinese unit of weight, "catty," to the Anglo-American one, "pound." With the last order, the butcher catches on, as minced gristle is unheard of. By then, Lu "landed a punch on Zheng's nose and flattened it to one side and brought the blood flowing like the sauces in a condiment shop—salty, sour and spicy" (Shapiro 40), vivid sensations with all three tastes from the original. Buck, instead, takes great liberty in proliferating the senses and interjecting the butcher's third-person perspective: "Cheng's nose was broken and bent to the side and of a sudden he smelled as many smells as though he opened a condiment shop—soy bean sauce, salt, sour, sweet, and hot—all in a second he smelled them all" (Buck, *Brothers* 59).

On the run after having beaten the butcher to death, Lu reunites with the butcher's victims, who proclaim their gratitude: "even though I killed my body I could not repay you for your mercy to us" (66). This echoes Buck's eerie obsession with the "Chinese body" in her subsequent novels, which I will revisit. In Chinese, the reference to one's body resembles that to one's self, hence, Shapiro's aptly worded "even if I gave my life I could never repay your benevolence" (Shapiro 43). With officials in hot pursuit, Lu's patron laments that "things might turn out badly if I kept you here, Major" (45), whereas Buck translates it literally "If I let the captain stay here it will be as dangerous as mountains too high and waters too deep" (*Brothers* 69). *Shangao shuishen* (literally, mountain high, water deep) denotes dangerous terrains, or danger in general. If Buck intends to broaden English expressions, she could have written "as dangerous as high mountains and deep waters." But then this implies a high level of self-consciousness and an in-depth understanding of both languages. Rather, Buck's quirky fixation on Chinese bodies, perhaps a displacement of missionary asceticism, persists: "Take good care of your [Lu's] body. What you need for clothing I will bid someone bring you" (74). Shapiro renders it as "Take good care of yourself. I'll send you warm clothing from time to time" (47–48). The well-wishing *baozhong baozhong* (保重保重 50) simply means "take care" or, in view of the Chinese refrain, "take good care of yourself," and has absolutely nothing to do with "your body."

Willful wild cards though they are, Shi Jin and Lu Zhishen point to heroes who have fallen on hard times and withdrawn into banditry at the heart of the brotherhood. Lin Chong the Panther Head and the arms instructor of the imperial guards exemplifies the persecution that turns some heroes against the authorities. The adopted son of the commander of the imperial guards, Marshall Gao Qiu, lusts after Lin's wife. Lin is framed for the attempted assassination of Marshall Gao, tattooed on the face as a criminal, and exiled to a military outpost in the remote frontier. On the eve of his exile, Lin wishes to dissolve his marriage for fear of "tying her [both] down" (84), fairly close to the Chinese original of *wangzi liangxiang danwu* (枉自兩相耽誤 99). Buck gives a confusing gloss of sorts: "Certainly we are in each other's way—we are in each other's light" (*Brothers* 142). One is hard pressed to figure out where Buck's "light" comes from—the Book of Genesis, perhaps, decidedly not Shi Nai'an's original. In his exile, Lin fails to find a local lord famed for feasting downtrodden hero-criminals. Lin regrets that "But my luck was poor and I was unable to find him" (Shapiro 93). Buck turns it into "But my reason for seeing him was so slight I could not hope to see him" (*Brothers* 157). Buck manipulates the Chinese text at will and with impunity, a trait that continues throughout the next two key characters.

Situated between the unbounded, explosive heroism of Shi and Lu, on the one hand, and, on the other, the reluctant revolt of Lin, Wu Song is known as the Pilgrim-Slayer of Tiger and Adulteress. Drunken, Wu pounces a man-eating tiger to a pulp. Getting increasingly inebriated before slaying the tiger, Wu orders the tavern waiter to "Bring me another two catties of beef" (Shapiro 220), which doubles back to Buck's neurosis over the flesh: "Bring two catties more of the flesh" (*Brothers* 380). Outside the tavern, Wu reads the official proclamation on the menace of a tiger because "Wu Song could read quite well" (Shapiro 221–222). The original's *poshejizi* (頗識幾字 259) is dissected and rendered almost word for word: "Now Wu Sung knew some few scattered letters," far from the intended meaning that Wu can read (Buck, *Brothers* 382). The self-denigrating phrase *xiaoren* (小人 literally, little person) is Buck's "my poor childish ability," strangely literal (a little or insignificant person turning into a child) and figural ("childish ability" 388) at once. Yet it really means Shapiro's "I have no talents" (226).

Subsequently, Wu avenges his half-brother poisoned to death by slaughtering the culprits. The guilty party comprises his sister-in-law Pan Jinlian (Pan Golden Lotus, who metamorphoses into the protagonist of a late sixteenth-century erotic novel *The Plum in the Golden Vase*), her lover Ximen Qing, and their matchmaker or pimp Mistress Wang. The cowardly, unsightly half-brother wishes Wu Song were nearby for protection: "If you were home, which of them would have dared to so much as fart?" (Shapiro 226). Such vulgarity brings alive the voice of the working class, but Buck sees fit to elevate the discourse, as if intended for the ear of a polite society: "When you were at home, who dared to come near and pass his wind?" (*Brothers* 391). Buck's predilection for respectability flies in the face of the original's earthy tone for the lower stratum of dynastic China. The plot thickens as Mistress Wang schemes to bring together the lovers behind the back of Wu Wong's brother. She questions Ximen Qing if he has what it takes, the second prerequisite for a successful liaison being "Second, you need a tool as big as a donkey's" (Shapiro 240). The crudeness over the male organ becomes an abstract quality in Buck: "Second, he must be as lusty as an ass," inevitable perhaps given Buck's times and missionary background (*Brothers* 413). Both Shapiro's "you" and Buck's "he" are the translators' additions to supply subjects to a Chinese language with no such need under most circumstances. Yet the second-person "you" gives a more direct tone than the detached, third-person "he." Buck consistently leans toward an abstract, wooden, scriptural style, abandoning her source's animated, colloquial voice. To James J. Y. Liu in *The Chinese Knight-Errantry* (1967), this voice is the novel's greatest achievement, "the first masterpiece written in colloquial Chinese"—not without a smattering of classical Chinese, though (114). While donkey and ass may be interchangeable, the association of ass with stupidity, idiocy is ill-fitting, in view of the meticulous planning for the adultery and murder. An ass evokes inanity rather than lust, nor does Buck bother with the original's precision in the size ("as big as") of a donkey's penis.

The fourth requirement, according to Mistress Wang, is "You must be as forebearing as a needle plying through cotton wool" (Shapiro 240). In Buck, it turns into a non sequitur of sorts: "Fourth, he must have a temper patient on the outside and as soft as shreds of cotton but inwardly as sharp as a needle" (*Brothers* 413). Long and convoluted, Buck does a disservice to *mianlizhen* (綿裡針, literally, cotton inside/hiding needle), which suggests not only the patience required to seduce Pan Jinlian, stitch by stitch, so to speak, but also his hard-on secreted within the niceties of the lovers' "arranged" chance encounter. Orchestrated by Mistress Wang, their rendezvous begins with Pan sewing, with a needle, of course, Mistress Wang's funeral dress funded by Ximen Qing. A Chinese cotton duvet keeps the sleeper warm; Mistress Wang's funeral dress figuratively shrouds the poison victim, dispatching Wu Song down the road of revenge.

The leader of the rebels, Song Jiang, appears throughout the novel as, true to his nickname, Timely Rain, aiding friends far and near. Song's official career is cut short when he kills his adulterous wife, similar to Wu Song's revenge. Tattooed and exiled to the frontier, Song is pestered by the prison superintendent who demands bribes, to which Song objects: "Gifts must be given willingly. They can't be forced. You're very petty" (Shapiro 377). Buck manages to produce awkward, unwieldy, and foreign-sounding English, taking leave of the smooth, vibrant dialogue in Chinese: "A favor should be given according to one's own desire, and will you compel a man's money by force? How mean a likeness of a man!" (*Brothers* 651). The last phrase reminds one of today's Google Translate. Threatened by the superintendent, Song retorts, "What crime have I committed that you want to beat me?" (Shapiro 377). Buck continues with her well-nigh non-English translation: "If you beat me for what fault is it?" (*Brothers* 651). The superintendent rejoins: "if I wish to kill you it will not be hard to do it, either. It will be but killing a fly" (652). Buck's translation ought to be retranslated, as in Shapiro: "I can take your life as easily as I swat a fly, if I feel like it" (377). As Song and other heroes converge in Liangshan Marsh, they refer to their home base as *shanzhai* (mountain barracks). Shapiro adroitly renders it as the neutral "stronghold," but Buck chooses "lair." The negative connotations associated with brigandage and wild animals in "lair" stand in stark contrast to the hero's image as victims of injustice and corruption. Buck's *Brothers* illustrates her self-professed grounding, one that is severely circumscribed, possibly amateurish, in the Chinese language and culture.

Buck's yellowface and Chinglish in *The Good Earth*

Her dubious Chinese notwithstanding, Buck's writings pivot on yellowface and Chinglish, amply illustrated by her most renowned novel *The Good Earth*. This 1931 novel opens with the peasant protagonist Wang Lung buying a slave O-lan for his wife from the House of Hwang. The Wang couple prosper owing to the proverbial "sweat of their [both his and hers] brow," purchasing farmland from the decadent landlord Hwang. During a famine, they have no choice but to flee south. Thus begins the novel's biblical paradigm of the exodus and Wang Lung the Moses figure surviving the string of natural disasters—drought, locusts, and flood. Luck strikes when they join the mob looting a southern landlord's mansion, the spoil enabling them to return home. As Wang Lung rises to become a property owner himself, he grows discontent over O-lan's plain looks and takes a singsong girl Lotus as his concubine. Wang Lung's eldest son grows enamored with Lotus, a recurring pseudo-incestuous motif in *The Good Earth*, and is expelled.

O-lan conveniently dies. Wang Lung comforts his old age by taking a young maid Pear Blossom barely past puberty, of his granddaughter's generation. Buck's missionary upbringing has colored her gaze at the erstwhile practice of polygamy, the transgressiveness of which harks back to biblical patriarchs with multiple wives—the lot of Abraham, Moses, and, in particular, Lot. The latter committed the sin of mating with his daughters. The incestuous motif runs deeper than Wang Lung's two concubines Lotus and Pear Blossom, so much so that it suggests a psychological complex. In the pleasure quarter, Lotus used to have a grain dealer customer, who felt inhibited from having intimacy with Lotus as a result of her physical resemblance to his daughter. His daughter is then married to Wang's eldest son, who had developed an amorous relationship with Lotus, his stepmother. The circuitous flow of affection and inhibition, attraction and repulsion, defines Freudian incest taboo. This Orientalist projection manifests not only the Judeo-Christian paradigms but the very wording is Scriptural. Catching his son in Lotus's bedroom, Wang Lung accuses her: "So must you ever be a whore and go a-whoring after my own sons" (244). "A-whoring" stems from "they have gone a-whoring after their god" (Exod. 34.15–16). Is it a Freudian slip when Buck writes "sons" since only the eldest is involved? After all, the third son goes "a-soldiering" after his intended Pear Blossom becomes Wang Lung's concubine.

Strategically after the demise of O-lan, the pitiable character plucking the heartstring of middlebrow readers, Pear Blossom functions as an O-lan substitute to sustain reader interest. Pear Blossom, however, is bound to come across as an object of pity and of horror due to the pseudo-incestuous motif. She is both pure and tabooed. Wang Lung's young wife serves, subconsciously, yet another purpose: she cares for the Wangs's retarded daughter, who is modeled after Carol Buck, the author's real-life daughter born with disabilities. Shadows of Carol run through Buck's corpus, a working professional mother's guilt expiated by a self-sacrificing mother surrogate and alter ego, Pear Blossom. Whereas the unnamed daughter is in good hands, Wang Lung's other legacy—his land—seems destined to be squandered for profit by his sons upon his death. Thus, the rise of the Wangs falls just like the Hwangs, because both houses have strayed from the soil, a message resonating with the Great Depression readership.

None in this gallery of characters comes with full names; they carry simplified Orientalist names instead. Wang's three sons are called Lao Ta, Lao Er, and Lao San (Old Eldest, Old Second, and Old Third in the order of their births). Wang's trusted friend is Ching; Wang's father is just Father, his uncle Uncle. Females are named after flowers and songbirds: Lotus, Lotus's maid Cuckoo, and Pear Blossom. This naming practice is not conducive to creating individual characters; rather, it signals types. Even Wang Lung and O-lan are not so much proper names as common nouns—Lung or the patriarchal dragon over the mother/land—for Buck's allegory in the name

of China. *Wang Lung* used to be the title of Buck's manuscript, which The
John Day Company editor and her future husband Richard Walsh scrapped
in favor of *The Good Earth* to strike a chord with Americans besieged by
economic woes during the Great Depression. At one point, the illiterate
Wang Lung hesitates over a contract writer's quip as to whether "Lung"
means "dragon" or "deaf," two of many homophones in Chinese. Shame-
facedly, Wang rejoins: "Let it be what you will, for I am too ignorant to
know my own name" (161). While borrowing the iconic symbol dragon to
name the peasant as the lifeblood of traditional China, Buck unwittingly
deconstructs her own novel because she appears "deaf" to the rustic tongue
of an unschooled peasant. Buck assigns a gesture of resignation to Wang
entirely too elegant: "Let it be what you will" may just as well describe the
natives' frustration over their Maker's whims. After all, unlike run-of-the-mill
Orientalists without the Chinese language or in-depth cultural immersion,
Buck had promoted herself as an insider, a missionary's daughter in China
well versed in the local tongue. Yet this good earth plowed and harrowed
by her pen yields scant Chinese voices, other than this one moment over the
mythical creature of Chineseness and/or the dumb beast that hears not and
knows not. The pause over "Lung" remains the only place where she self-
reflexively dwells on linguistic and cultural translation.[2]

In fact, this accidental stroke of genius could have provided a golden
opportunity in characterization. No Chinese parent, however ignorant,
would damn a newborn by naming him or her "deaf." The contract writer
is taunting Wang mean-spiritedly. If so, why not rub it in by tripling "lung":
"dragon," "deaf," or "cage," the last being yet another homonym? *Longzi*
in *pinyin* Romanization without the distinguishing Chinese scripts could
mean the dragon's son, one who is deaf, or the cage. The joke, ultimately,
is on Buck. In the new millennium, with a readership far less insular than
that of the 1930s and more attuned to polyphonic performances, these
homophones come back to haunt Buck, caged and boxed in by the absolute
discursive control over her dragon, her worm. Wang Lung et al. are under
Buck's thumb, doing her bidding of defamiliarizing, depersonalizing, and
dichotomizing themselves. These three principles of Buck's Chinglish
are one and the same in splitting apart in the name of bonding together.
Chinglish defamiliarizes both English, although English is exactly what
it is, and Chinese, although Chinese is what it pretends to be. Chinglish
depersonalizes, hollows out Orientalist stereotypes it purportedly breathes
life into—types devoid of individuality, bodies in search of feelings. Finally,
Chinglish dichotomizes Chinese characters into bipolarized extremes—the
childish patriarchs of Wang Lung's unnamed father and Wang Lung himself;
the battered yet bountiful matriarch of O-lan.

In an ingenious sleight of hand, Buck manages to make Chinglish
defamiliarization work both ways. Buck's contrived style turns English
into an alien tongue maladroitly plied by the Chinese, who somehow speak

Chinese like Remedial English of ESL (English as a Second Language) beginners. Buck's fans, the American publishing industry, and the Nobel and Pulitzer Prizes never pause to ask the obvious question: how is it possible that Chinese characters in their motherland speak their mother tongue in such an absurd manner as to resemble pidgin-spewing "Chinamen" in American popular culture in nineteenth-century Chinatowns, struggling stupidly with their stepmother tongue of English? How does the living word of Chinese mutate into alternative facts in trumped-up Chinglish? Buck scholars share a curious oversight, either owing to the lack of proficiency in Chinese materials from which Buck allegedly drew or to the lack of self-reflection on the means of reflection, namely, the English language. Such oversight plagues biographers (Conn), Americanists (Eble, Harker, Kunnemann), and Asian Americanists (Yoshihara). Almost all of them refer in passing to Buck's stylization but none deigns to analyze the pattern, the motive behind Buck's language.

Peter Conn advances what seems to be the critical consensus of Buck's centrality in mid-twentieth-century Orientalist production. Conn maintains that "over the next two decades [mid-1930s to mid-50s], she would exert more influence over Western opinions about Asia than any other American" (185). Conn also reports that Buck "acknowledged that her childhood immersion in the Chinese language had made her permanently uncomfortable with idiomatic English" (178). Indeed, her prose reads at times like a non-native speaker's. She is most likely caught between English and Chinese, having grown up in the missionary enclave of China with neither a large, organic English-speaking community nor the long years of Chinese schooling to acquire native-level literacy. Linguistically, she may have been trapped between two worlds, writing English like an ESL student, while demonstrating a superficial knowledge of the Chinese language in the only text related to the Chinese tongue: her translation of *All Men Are Brothers*. In view of the smooth prose in her autobiography *My Several Worlds* (1954), however, Buck arguably fakes an awkward Chinese-inflected style in most of her novels. Professionally, she had the best of both worlds. To the twentieth-century America and the West, Buck is a spokesperson for China, garnering the highest honors, despite having been derided and "called her bluff" as to her command of the Chinese language.

Kenneth Eble describes "the style of *The Good Earth*" as "based on the manner of the old Chinese narrative sagas related and written down by storytellers and on the mellifluous prose of the King James version of the Bible. At certain times Buck declared that her style was Chinese rather than biblical," without questioning Buck's self-proclaimed entitlement to Chineseness (33). Jaime Harker praises *The Good Earth* for "strip[ping] away exotic stereotypes in favor of a true image of China ... the overwhelming humanity of Wang Lung," oblivious to his stereotypical speech pattern bastardizing pidgin, Basic English, and the Scriptures (101).

Vanessa Kennemann gives a more judicious assessment: "Buck's missionary style, admired by her audience, also became her 'trap' ... too urgent, old-fashioned, didactic, simple, schematic, dull, or even obtrusive." Kennemann keeps a critical distance from Buck's formulaic self-defense of "resort[ing] to the Chinese story-telling. With this strategy, she referred back to her status as a cultural insider and fashioned herself as a 'stranger' who was unfamiliar with American traditions" (32). Mari Yoshihara diagnoses that "the key to Buck's popularity lay in her discursive strategy, which engaged both the discourse of Orientalism and the discourse of gender ... ethnography and domestic fiction" (152). Likening Buck's style to modern ethnography, Yoshihara characterizes it in terms of "the erasure of the author's subjectivity, annihilation of historical and geographic specificity, and infantilization of characters" (156). However, Yoshihara dispenses only one paragraph to analyze her "unique language style" in formulating character infantilization, missing the point that it not only depersonalizes adult characters but dichotomizes them into child-like simpletons versus wise men and women from a lifetime—from generations, rather—of experiences. Buck's "unique" style merits only a short description: "inversion and the repetition of short, simple sentences ... archaic and austere tone similar to that of the Bible or ... to that of children's literature" (155).

The Good Earth defamiliarizes by way of bad English, which happens to be Chinglish with perfect pitch. Prepositions are added or dropped at will. Wang Lung's ox "thrust[s] it out to feel of the air" with a redundant "of" (1). The ox is housed "next the door" with "to" omitted. Awkward phrases abound: "after a hesitation" ought to be "after some hesitation" or "after a moment of hesitation" (2). Shunning compounds, subordinates, phrasal expressions, Buck favors the biblical sentence structure of addition with multiple "ands": "he caught a flame and thrust it into the straw and there was a blaze" (3). The static sentence contains three static pictures chained together, whereas rhetorical force would have intensified by simply dumping one "and": "he caught a flame and thrust it into the straw to start a fire." The three "ands" on page three multiply to thirteen "ands" in a nine-line paragraph of four sentences on the slaughter of the ox during the famine on page seventy-two.

By definition, defamiliarization is wedded to expressions so nonsensical as to depart from reason and logic: "Twice and twice again in my years" (116). Does this mean four times? Confusing numbering is justified under the context of a disorienting Orient. Buck's highly unstable, restlessly morphing Chinglish switches in no time to perfect English and colloquialism. The mousy, mute-like O-lan returns bemused by her visit to the House of Hwang to show off their newborn son: "I believe, if one should ask me, that they are feeling a pinch this year in that house" (50). Even when she shifts back to her formal, wooden English, O-lan uses "whom" in "I had but a moment for private talk with the cook under whom I worked before" (51). The grammatical "whom" and the colloquial "feeling a [the] pinch" soon revert back to the Orientalist "Ancient One" (16), the Hwang family matriarch, "eating enough opium every day to fill two shoes with gold" (51). There is no equivalent in Chinese for "fill[ing] two shoes with gold," an exotic, not to mention imprecise, measurement of precious metal, a measuring device purely of Buck's making. The back-and-forth of Orientalist Chinglish and perfect English testifies to Buck's failure in creating O-lan with a recognizable, authentic voice. Instead, Buck dubs her creature with no qualms.

For critics and readers alike, to pose the question of Buck's Chinglish requires clear-eyed soul-searching; it posits self-examining of the Anglophone privilege as the global lingua franca, something of a birthright for English speakers. Absent such self-scrutiny, a complicit West acquiesces to Buck's making of fake stereotypes sans living voices. In its broad, sweeping strokes, Chinglish also alienates Chinese characters from their surroundings, their bodies, and themselves—the three things which are supposed to be closest to who they are. Or to rephrase à la Buck's favorite Chinglish: the three things "that which" "it/there is" "of a blood." Such Chinglish metastasizes until it takes over a discourse called China. "That which" is as innumerable as the stars in Buck. "There is" or "it is" are littered in Wang Lung's "if there is not sun and rain in proportion, there is again hunger" (125); in O-lan's confession of what turns out to be a tumor, "There is a fire in my vitals" (239); in Wang Lung's reflection on his third son's soldiering, "for sometimes in wars there are those who die" (298); and many more. "Of a blood" occurs in Wang Lung's exasperation over giving in to his Uncle's blackmail: "It is cutting my flesh out to give to him and for nothing except that we are of a blood" (65). The paradox of the language of the body surfaces in O-lan's "vitals" and Wang Lung's "cutting my flesh." Pain is located apparently within the Oriental body but somehow dissociated from it, given the objective, unspecified description.[3] O-lan's "vitals" most certainly refer to Chinese herbal medicine's internal qi (breath, energy) and organs rather than Western medicine's vital signs of heartbeat, pulse, and breathing. But the intangible, almost inexplicable, qi renders "vitals" vague, near mystical. By the same token, so matter-of-fact is Wang Lung's self-mutilation that he is either immune to physical pain or so great is the hurt that it goes off the (human) chart. "Of a blood" is loaded with the same ambiguity: an absurd non sequitur from an essentialized, ill-defined "blood" or shared bloodline that supposedly captures the very essence of existence.

This method of depersonalization deploys Oriental corporeality, onto which the West projects its nostalgia for the premodern, the West's own repression of the darkness of modernity. In that sense, Buck heralds similar approaches from Westerners of Asian extraction. Chinese American Amy Tan in *The Hundred Secret Senses* (1995) portrays a Chinese Miss Moo feeling "a twist in my stomach, a burning in my chest, an ache in my bones" (174) as well as a sensation that "shriveled my scalp" (63). Such biological reactions range from the metaphorical to the hyperbolical. Tan self-Orientalizes Miss Moo, onomatopoeically named after animal sounds, a bundle of senses loosely structured under one consciousness. Chinese émigré Ha Jin avails himself of similar strategies. The short story "In the Crossfire" in *A Good Fall* (2009) depicts a Flushing, New York, Chinese accountant sensing that his "molars itch" (107). A Chinese tooth is said to itch, not ache. Despite their various degrees of whiteness, Buck's, Tan's, and Ha Jin's Chinese bodies look alike in exhibiting near supernatural, extra-sensory perceptions.

Depersonalization arises whenever Chinese bodies fuel or fissure themselves. Food metaphors invariably distance characters even when eating is a natural biological function. Shocked by Wang Lung's luxury of a bowl of tea in the morning, his father scolds: "Tea is like eating silver," to which Wang Lung counters, "Eat and be comforted" (Buck, *Good Earth* 4). Subjects are shunned in accordance with the Chinese language. Yet the connection of tea and silver is as far-fetched as that of gold and the matriarch Hwang's shoes. It falls far short of filial piety to command one's father to eat and, implicitly, to shut up. In their flight to the south, Wang Lung's father intones, "It must be fed," referring to the belly (93). As they return to the north and prosper, he urges: "Eat, make strong the body of my grandson" (282). By contrast, O-lan's body memory of the abuse in the House of Hwang comes through in a rhetorical inversion that abstracts it from searing pain, elevating it allegorically: "Every day was I beaten" (133). Rather than bursting forth spontaneously with the subject "I" that had experienced beating daily, the inversion removes O-lan from her confession in a third-person voice-over on the past.

Dichotomizing of characters takes off from the leitmotif of food. The father figure behaves with child-like self-centeredness when he demands to be fed ahead of and at the expense of his family (6). This self-absorption contrasts sharply with the wisdom of survival as he advises against marrying a pretty woman (8). As the famine persists, he counsels the slaughter of the ox in a language of choice: "Well, and it is your life or the beast's, and your son's life or the beast's and a man can buy an ox again more easily than his own life" (72). While the necessity for survival is plain, the long repetition with "and" is a stylistic affectation echoing the King James Version. The dissociation of body and mind defines this father figure: "Just as the thought of a grandson had made him forget his meal, so now the thought of food freshly before him made him forget the child" (31). Whereas Wang Lung no longer exhibits the same food fetish, he demonstrates a split when he becomes so besotted with Lotus that he takes her into his house, initiating the incestuous chain of reaction. Bipolarization characterizes O-lan as well: her habitual muteness suddenly erupts into a long tirade of her victorious return to the House of Hwang with her son (33), or when she resolutely declares that the moon cakes are reserved for "the Old Mistress" and not for her own household (47). Even the farmer protagonist swings between the self-abjection of a rustic "hind" and his single-minded tenacity to acquire land (56). The repeated use of Wang Lung the "hind" betrays Buck's own psychic dichotomizing or displacing. From her own birthplace of West Virginia's Appalachian backwoods, the word "hind," an archaic word for the country bumpkin or hick, is grafted onto a Chinese peasant.

That said, Buck knows Chinese psychology first-hand. So euphoric over their triumphant visit with their son to the Hwangs, Wang Lung and O-lan fear God's jealousy and immediately pretend to scoff at their baby, an excellent psychological shift in keeping with Chinese preference for moderation and aversion to self-inflation (51). Buck fully grasps the repression within Chinese psychology. Her insights lurk behind double or even triple negatives, attesting to inhibitions besetting her characters. Secretly pleased by O-lan's housework, the father-in-law "felt it would not do to give out anything but complaints before his new daughter-in-law lest she be set from the first in ways of extravagance" (21–22), with at least three negatives.

Although Metro-Goldwyn-Mayer ignores Buck's proposal that, as Peter Conn notes, "Chinese actors be used" (194) in *The Good Earth*, its leads of Paul Muni and Luis Rainer, as well as other white actors with taped slant eyes, manage a performance that resuscitates Buck's verbal mongrelization of the Scriptural and the Orientalist. Intimated by the House of Hwang's "keeper of the gate," Wang Lung introduces himself as "I am Wang Lung, the farmer," a form of self-identification in English comprising one's full name, albeit in Sinologized order of the surname first, and the article "the" before one's occupation. The article makes it incontrovertibly Anglo as the Chinese language does not have the grammatical category of articles at all. The unique feature is followed by the archaic, biblical sounding "I am come" (13), most ill-fitting for a Chinese peasant scared out of his wits. Yet the actor Muni's ingenious stammering to blurt out the three words cover up any infelicity, enlivening the scene of deliberate shaming.

Beyond this one exchange, the film takes full advantage of its soundtrack. The opening credits run its theme music of *Turandot*'s "Jasmine Flower" (*Moli hua*) in the Orientalist pentatonic scale. The Chopsticks-sounding music accompanies Wang Lung strutting to the House of Hwang in his splayed-footed gait and idiotic grin, topped by a skullcap (Figure 1.2). This clownish skit, the stilted dialogue, and constantly-bowing characters, particularly Ching, add to the Oriental flavor. Authentic Chinese folksong makes its way into the celebration of the one-year birthday of the Wangs's firstborn. Muni sings "Flower Drum Song," with his tongue rolling a bit too expertly over "der-r-r-r-piao, der-r-r-r-piao." This tour de force in Chinese elocution is excessive, overly inflected by Spanish, since the Chinese retroflex "er" never becomes anything close to the trilling R. While the film is chock full of ethnographic details—peasants, their dresses, their food, at

FIGURE 1.2 *Paul Muni as Wang Lung in* The Good Earth *strutting to the House of Hwang.*

the center of each frame is the stereotypical slant eyes of Paul Muni's, often accompanied by the Chopsticks music. Such is the contradiction of Buck's yellowface and Chinglish, so close to the Orient yet so far from China.

Hepburn's yellowface and Chinglish in *Dragon Seed*

The title *Dragon Seed* comes from Buck's dual sources of inspiration: stereotypical China in the image of dragon and the King James Bible. Seed, always singular, is a constant refrain in the King James Version, initiated as God blesses Abraham that "thy seed" will multiply. God's covenant with Abraham, his chosen, transcends grammar and logic. The plurality which will be multiplied sprouts from one single seed, in a direct line back to Abraham and, ultimately, to God. The chosen is both plural and singular. Biblical seed diverges from plant seeds that are literal, devoid of its singular form's abstract, transcendent power. Likewise, the creator Buck multiplies and clones her yellowfaces, her chosen—the many are the one. Characters springing from stereotypes are less independent, organic individuals than automatonic types. As in her use of "blood," seed in Buck never comes in the plural form, hence suggesting duplication of the source. That source should be viewed as an Orientalist simulacrum rather than the original.

Dragon Seed continues *The Good Earth*'s Chinglish in defamiliarizing, depersonalizing, and dichotomizing. As Peter Conn notes, reviewers of *Dragon Seed* "complained about the preachiness and the trademark Buck mannerisms—the quasi-biblical style and the one-dimensional characters" (254–255). As for the film adaptation, a *Chicago Tribune* review remarks on the embarrassing "garbled English" (qtd. in Conn 281). Buck found the movie "wrong in almost every detail: Katherine [*sic*] Hepburn wore a man's jacket instead of a woman's because she found it more stylish; Hepburn's bangs were inappropriate." Luise Rainer playing O-lan in *The Good Earth*, Buck maintains, "had done a better job imitating a Chinese woman than Katharine Hepburn" (Conn 281).[4] Kenneth Eble finds "didactic consideration" excessive in *Dragon Seed* (149). Eble believes that "after 1939, she became more facile at constructing her plots, handling dialogue" because "she followed the old-fashioned Chinese story practice of emphasizing event and characterization" (149). Attributing Buck's style to Chinese influence is no different from Buck's dodgy excuse in her Nobel Prize acceptance speech: "so I have been taught in China." Both the critic and the novelist make allowances for mediocre writing under the pretense of continuing Chinese literary tradition.

Published in 1941, *Dragon Seed* reflects the ongoing Sino-Japanese War that began in 1937, particularly the Rape of Nanking (1937–1938) and the subsequent suicide of the Goddess of Mercy, the missionary Minnie Vautrin, who offered shelter to many Chinese.[5] The unnamed white missionary character is unequivocally based on Vautrin. Japanese perpetration of rapes is a leitmotif, crystallizing the trauma on the Chinese body. Ling Tan is the peasant patriarch and the controlling consciousness. The aging mother of Ling's son-in-law Wu Lien is raped, so are one of Ling's daughters-in-law Orchid, his youngest son Lao San (Old Third or the third son), and more. The lack of graphic depiction of rapes may well be due to Christian demureness and the more conservative time. Ling Tan's youngest son is described as "too beautiful for his own good, and now his beauty was his grief, for they [Japanese soldiers] took this boy and used him as a woman" (164). The film has deleted this homosexual rape of Lao San. Orchid's ravishment is equally veiled: "When one after another of those men took their will on her, and no passer-by dared to come into that public space to save her … then she was like a rabbit fallen upon by wolfish dogs" (179). More generally and ironically, Buck juxtaposes Japanese gesture of good will and violence. Soon after a Japanese soldier delivers the pro-Japanese sign to the traitor Wu Lien to ensure his safety, Wu hears a woman's scream, yet another victim of wartime rape (157).

Despite this realistic framework, *Dragon Seed* turns the collective rape of the Chinese into the conclusion's melodramatic and trite, utterly implausible, romance between Lao San and Mayli, a mixed-race beauty idolized as the Goddess of Mercy Guanyin. Subconsciously, Buck transports the Christian paradigm of redemption to ease the Japanese scourge. During the war, Lao San's young sister Pensiao, like Mayli before her, manages to flee to the unoccupied Great Interior of China and miraculously studies under Mayli. Thousands of miles away, Pensiao proceeds to match-make since Lao San has fallen in love with Mayli long before the war started. For good reason, *Dragon Seed* the film unseats this incredulous plot of a romance, refocusing on Jade, played by Katharine Hepburn in yellowface.

Krystyn Moon in *Yellowface* (2005) expounds that the stage makeup technique for Oriental characters in the early twentieth century entails:

> Noses were to be broadened and flattened by highlighting the nostrils and shading the top, or, thanks to new theatrical technologies, they could be completely reshaped through prosthetics. Drawing a line about three-fourths of an inch beyond the eye and adding a highlighter on the lid were techniques used to slant the eyes. In more elaborate characterizations, systems of tape and putty were implemented to slant the eye, a method used predominantly in the movie industry. (117)

Hepburn's unnatural-looking slant eyes probably involve an elaborate technique of stretching, so much so that it tenses up her smiles and facial expression. Like those of other Caucasian characters, Hepburn's slant eyes, taped and puttied, appear to be in a perpetual squint. Turned sideways, the eyes are half-covered by drooping eyelids in a sinister, duplicitous look. These yellowfaces sport a flagrant racial marker, one as ridiculous as the way they hold (clutch, rather) chopsticks as shovels. The facial stylization marking Orientals appears entirely gratuitous in hindsight but was taken for granted in the 1940s. That wartime and postwar periods, after all, witnessed the popularization of Charlie Chan, the stereotype of the good Oriental to overcompensate for the bad Oriental Dr. Fu-Manchu. In 1944 alone, three Charlie Chan movies—*Black Magic*; *Charlie Chan in the Secret Service*; and *Charlie Chan in the Chinese Cat*—were churned out by Phil Rosen featuring Sidney Toler as the yellowface detective with his blackface, buck-eyed clown sidekick played by Mantan Moreland. Raymond Chandler's *Farewell, My Lovely* was also adapted in 1944 as *Murder, My Sweet* with the "Arab" Jules Amthor and other racial stereotypes. Hepburn's almond-shaped eyes opened onto the Orientalist vein secreted within American popular culture in the 1940s and beyond.

Similar to *The Good Earth*, *Dragon Seed* excels in authentic ethnographic details. The opening scene of rice farmers bending down to insert rice seedlings into the well-irrigated fields covered with muddy water feels almost real, with the Caucasian characters' yellowfaces and slant eyes concealed by their bent torsos. A vivid peasant lifestyle comes through when Ling Tan washes his feet after planting in the sludge of the rice fields and when his wife picks her ears with an ear pick after running it through her hair. Against this traditional, idyllic picture, Hepburn's Jade harbors an indomitable spirit that ventures beyond conventional female roles. Contrary to her family of illiterate peasants, she longs for a book. To tame the shrew, Jade's husband is advised to "wait 500 heartbeats, then go to her" at night, Buck's made-up instruction with the precision of an Oriental erotica manual. This Jade in the first half of the film exhibits a young wife's etiquette and naiveté, which jars against Hepburn's film image as the "new" woman from her title roles in *A Woman Rebels* (1936), *The Philadelphia Story* (1940), *Woman of the Year* (1942), and *Keeper of the Flame* (1943). Hepburn is almost painfully out of character as Jade casts her slant eyes down, with flushed cheeks, albeit indiscernible on the black-and-white screen, or as Jade whispers *sotto voce* in a flat monotone, and a monosyllabic staccato to boot. Jade's elocution contradicts Hepburn's signature rapid-fire delivery in her mid-Atlantic accent. Not until the second half when Jade becomes an underground resistance fighter does the speed of her lines pick up and does she behave with a steely resolve in consonance with Hepburn's career.

This split in Jade justifies her guilty conscience over the death of Wu Lien, who prospers as a collaborator. Originally intending to dispose of Wu before he betrays the Lings of the armed resistance, she opts wisely for the bigger fish of the entire Japanese unit by sneaking into the military kitchen and poisoning the banquet's food. Ironically, Wu Lien is not the family traitor. Instead, Jade the New Woman's opposite, a stereotypically bitter, malicious Third Cousin's wife, informs on her own extended family. Buck fashions an independent Jade just as she reprises the stock image of a witch in the Third Cousin's wife. The second half of the film quickens its pace through the intensity of the war, the hardships in the countryside, the perils of the insurgency, and the espionage by Jade. Jade's conscience and tears come as an antidote to Lao San who has turned increasingly sadistic and blood-thirsty. Buck even puts her brand of humanitarianism in Ling Tan's words of doubt: If Jade's book *All Men Are Brothers* be true, muses her father-in-law, then the Japanese would also be one's brothers. This is once again a Christian spin on the Chinese classic without a supreme monotheistic intelligence. Buck offers through her straw man Ling Tan a moot point, given the historical animosity between China and Japan, one that is certainly at its height during the Sino-Japanese War.

In the wake of her luminous career with prestigious literary awards from the mid-twentieth century, Buck is survived by her dragon seed of yellowface characters and their spectral voices in Chinglish. These crepuscular shadows continue to haunt the new millennium as we the blind—writers from the white majority and from the West's minorities of Asian extraction—are being led by the blind Buck into global literature and cinema.

2

Stereograph-cum-Stereotype: Maugham's and Kingston's Chinas

To draw an object, we add perspective and depth to bring alive that which is flat, paper-thin, two-dimensional. To make a motion picture, we make a series of frames go so fast as to breathe life into discontinuous, static 3-D images. To represent China from afar, without what Pierre Nora calls *milieux de memoire* and lived experiences,[1] artists strive to animate "the intangible" by way of the element of time inherent in literary and visual narratives, which turns any alleged fresh-eyed view into a "vu" in déjà vu, already-seen images, or twice-, thrice-told tales, which teeter on the reiterated and the stereotypical. Such conjuring of the cultural discourse on China supposedly deepens viewers' emotional investment in China, calling forth a repertoire ranging from the exotic in colonialist, Orientalist W. Somerset Maugham's *The Painted Veil* (1925) to the ethnic in Maxine Hong Kingston's *The Woman Warrior: Memoirs of a Girlhood among Ghosts* (1976). Surprisingly, the white male gaze and the ethnic female gaze at China resemble each other in their déjà vu-ness, their revisions of stereotypes.

For readers, this spectatorial richness stems from a sense of revisitation; their first impressions interlace with the memory of, and even nostalgia over the course of, reading this and related texts, rebooting extant constructs of Orientalism-cum-ethnicity. After all, neither is Orientalism dead and gone, nor is ethnicity securely ensconced with an entitled ease. Neither is the former extinct nor the latter enjoying any birthright in an America to be made great and white again. Both extremes define an optical spectrum that evinces the remote, inexplicable Other. Given the apparent differences between an Orientalist and an ethnic pioneer, it appears astounding that their Other, their Chinas, would look alike in the modus operandi, a shared stereograph-cum-stereotype, a sense of déjà vu, all over again. What is shocking at first blush only reveals the deep-seated structure of feeling that informs both texts' identifying with and distancing from China.

Deploying the trope of the technology rage of his day, Maugham in *The Painted Veil* gives us colonial stereographics, two similar yet slightly variant pictures to render the object in a stereoscope three-dimensional, akin to 3-D glasses worn in IMAX movie theaters. The Greek word *stereos* for "solid" derives from the Proto-Indo-European root of "ster" for "stiff, rigid, firm, strong," but it also generates the word "sterile." With its original meaning of solid body, stereo comes to name the sound system comprising at least two speakers to amplify surround sound, to give sound "body." By the same token, stereograph or stereocopy uses double visions to produce the optical illusion of three-dimensionality. The related word of stereotype, nonetheless, indicates the human tendency to pigeonhole the unfamiliar by attributing types or group characteristics to individuals, leading to preconception and bigotry. Prejudice results from an attempt to come to grips with such intangibles as abstract sounds, exotic places, peoples of different races and cultures. To mentally fix something or someone in place turns out to displace the object unjustly. To strengthen and stiffen something is also to deaden it. This venturing out into the external unknown parallels an internal probing into the workings of the mind. Such symmetry of the world and the mind lies at the heart of Freudianism, one that informs both Maugham's and Kingston's Chinas.

Sigmund Freud in *The Interpretation of Dreams* (1900) expounds the interplay of out there versus in here, actual versus virtual, in mental perception:

> Everything that can be an object of our internal perception is *virtual*, like the image produced in a telescope by the passage of light rays. But we are justified in assuming the existence of the systems (which are not in any way psychical entities themselves and can never be accessible to our psychical perception) like the lenses of a telescope, which cast the image. And if we pursue this analogy, we may compare the censorship between two systems to the refraction which takes place when a ray of light passes into a new medium. (vol. 5, 611.)

By "psychical entities themselves," Freud refers to "organic elements of the nervous system," which, of course, are not "accessible to our psychical perception." Freud's concept of the mind with its biological functions can be likened to the eye that fails to see itself except in a mirror or water, apt to be distorted or inversed at least. Freud casts the mind's consciousness and subconsciousness in the metaphor of refracting light. When problematic objects under psychic censorship are called up virtually, they nonetheless manifest themselves by means of psychic lenses, a process of disfiguring just as it materializes simulacra of the "original." Such intricate refraction over expression and repression shapes Maugham's protagonist Kitty Fane in and out of China, a projection of the author's guilt-ridden homosexuality transferred onto an adulteress in a foreign land.

In *The Painted Veil*, a beautiful and vain Kitty marries Walter Fane, an epidemiologist stationed in the crown jewel Hong Kong, to flee from family and social pressure in England. Bored in the colony, Kitty conducts an affair with an equally vacuous Charles Townsend. Partly out of vengeance, the cuckolded Walter takes Kitty into the cholera-infested Chinese interior of Mei-tan-fu, where Walter saves lives but dies of the epidemic. To a death-prone Walter, China embodies death with its deformities and otherworldliness. Albeit an epidemiologist who studies bugs, Walter may as well *be* the bug that hates himself for loving Kitty. Kitty returns sadder and wiser, only to have her old flame rekindled, despite guilt and self-loathing. As the distraught widow Kitty leaves China, "The sights of the wayside served as a background to her thoughts. She saw them as it were in duplicate, rounded as though in a stereoscope, with an added significance because to everything she saw was added the recollection of what she had seen but a few short weeks before she had taken the same journey in the contrary direction" (201). Maugham's plot revolves around the metaphor of one of the key inventions around the turn of the last century—stereographs. In stereographs, minute differences exist in the two angles of the same object like the spacing between two eyes. Stereoscopes become a figure of speech for the duality of prior to versus after China/cholera, thus rendering Kitty and, to some extent, China three-dimensional. The doubling or "rounding" allegedly proffers depth to China as much as time has done to the round character of Kitty, except the stereographic stock images smack of stereotypes. This extends even to Walter, on whom China has rubbed off from the outset. Walter is an epidemiologist who has gone native in China, contracts cholera in part because he has become, for lack of a better word, a white Chinaman. Walter has long been relegated "to the other side" by Kitty's lover Charles, who scoffs that "only a Chinese would turn a handle in that way" (13). That handle is a loaded "white china knob" that would open to Kitty and Charles in bed, and a knowing Walter refrains from making a scene (13). Rather, he plunges into the epidemic in China that is to cost him his life.

In narratives, a set of stereographs is strung together temporally, i.e., how characters change from pre- to post-China. The backdrop to silhouette the protagonist's evolution, China comes through in its stereotypical monstrosity, one populated by corpses, beggars, coolies, and such freaks as a retarded girl with a hydrocephalic head and a Chinese crone with bound feet, a hotbed of cholera to boot. The 3-D plus time binds spatiality and temporality, objective perception and subjective affect; however, Maugham deploys this technique of representation to demarcate bodies or characters, to Orientalize China vis-à-vis Britishness, and, finally, to displace his own homosexuality and religiosity onto female lust and sin embodied by Kitty.

Maugham's stereographic gaze remains a filmic long shot, establishing the scene, framing the story, but simultaneously distancing and controlling China.

Not to belabor the obvious, Maugham's setting of China and Chinese is racist at best. Only one Chinese character gets to articulate intelligibly and even that in mangled pidgin. In one of Kitty's trysts with Charles at a curio shop in Hong Kong, she is advised by the shop owner to wait upstairs:

"Mr Townsend no come yet. You go top-side, yes?"
"She went to the back of the shop and walked up the rickety, dark stairs ... It was stuffy and there was an acrid smell of opium. She sat down on a sandalwood chest." (54)

A seedy assignation is set at the quintessential Chinatown store—curio shop, for Hong Kong, even the turn-of-the-last-century "subcolony" of China, is one gigantic Oriental curio cabinet. In his pidgin without a proper verb, let alone verb conjugation, the owner exhorts like the captain of the proverbial immigrant ship, directing Kitty to "go top-side," a maritime term that connotes Hong Kong and China under colonialism as disenfranchised outsiders adrift in their own land. In ascending the "rickety, dark stairs," Kitty descends into the bowels of a Chinatown opium den, furnished with a sandalwood chest. A curio shop with objects of curiosity like a sandalwood chest doubles as a repulsive opium den. Fragrances of the Orient emanate from the exotic sandalwood furniture and the addictive opiate. Opium served as the mid-nineteenth-century British Empire's weapon of choice to break the trade imbalance with the Qing dynasty and eventually to upend it. An Englishman like Maugham has conveniently suppressed opium's historical role or mission, displacing the corrosive drug onto China's own sin. Such is the duplicity of Maugham's Orient, aesthetic and abominable, two poles that supposedly bring alive China like a pair of stereographic goggles.

This aestheticizing verges on a transcendent flight and an apocalyptic epiphany. Out of sin and bestial desire, Kitty experiences the pure joy of the divine upon witnessing the first sunrise in China: "The tears ran down Kitty's face and she gazed ... it seemed to her as though her body were a shell that lay at her feet and she pure spirit. Here was beauty. She took it as the believer takes in his mouth the wafer which is God" (96). This transport by beauty and Christianity plunges into shadows when Kitty's relapse into sin with Charles is depicted in the exact rhetoric of the obliteration of the flesh: "the pressure of his [Charles's lips] upon them shot through her body like the flame of God. It was an ecstasy and she was burnt to a cinder and she glowed as though she were transfigured. In her dreams, in her dreams she had known this rapture" (218). All the pseudo-religious descriptors of "ecstasy," "transfigured," and "rapture" loop back to the lovers' kisses in the opening: Charles "took her in his and kissed her on the lips. It was such rapture that it was pain" (13). Thinly-veiled religiosity throughout suggests a Maugham struggling with a felt sin of homosexuality, having been attracted to lovers like Charles, seeking redemption through Kitty's fall and eventual rise. The ravishing by God and by Charles unfolds in similar images. Death by China and bliss in China—not just the sunrise but Catholic nuns—coexist in one set of stereographs, which are but stereotypes.

Despite the intended metaphor of *The Painted Veil* for Kitty and the nuns, the title captures nicely the blinders Maugham himself wears in approaching China, one as unintelligible as the nonsensical place name of Mei-tan-fu. Taking the veil and entering a religious order, as French Catholic nuns have done amidst the cholera, are tainted by Kitty's repeated giving in to her lust. China is a veil to insulate Maugham, starting from his own Western subjectivity in the Preface moving from Italy and Dante to China. The Preface relates a young, carefree Maugham on vacation in Italy, taught Italian by Ersilia, a widow "consecrated to virginity" (8). Ersilia in Maugham's biographical Preface morphs into Dante's virtuous woman Pia subjected to Maremma's "noxious vapours" (9), which in turn morphs into Kitty Fane thrust into a cholera-infested China. This murder by a husband is now retold by a homosexual keeping up appearances of a family man. Ultimately, Maugham's own homoeroticism motivates Kitty's carnal desire for an unworthy man, Kitty's sin reflecting Maugham's guilt. Since there are at least two, if not more, Kitty Fanes behind the veil and "outed," Kitty Fanes may well be Kitty feigns and Kitty faints. Kitty feigns, both as the socialite and the adulteress. Kitty also faints, once literally due to her pregnancy and on numerous occasions figuratively as she is spellbound by God's grace and/or Charles's kisses, her rationality receding. The multiplying of Kitty circles back to Maugham's seminal trope of stereographs of slightly varied images of the same object or character.

The best evidence of Maugham's transference of homosexuality to Kitty is Kitty's nose or the Freudian nose behind *The Painted Veil*. Freud sees the nose as a phallic symbol in *The Interpretation of Dreams* (1900):

> But here I may draw attention to the frequent "displacement from below to above" which is at the service of sexual repression, and by means of which all kinds of sensations and intentions occurring in hysteria, which ought to be localised in the genitals, may at all events be realised in other, unobjectionable parts of the body. We have a case of such displacement when the genitals are replaced by the face in the symbolism of unconscious thought … The nose is compared to the penis in numerous allusions, and in each case the presence of hair completes the resemblance. (182)

Given the Freudian identification of the nose and the genitalia, Kitty "shuddered a little, for in their [Chinese orphans'] uniform dress, sallow-skinned, stunted, with their flat noses, they looked to her hardly human.

They were repulsive" (117). By contrast, Kitty flirts by pointing to the one flaw in her otherwise perfect facial features—a nose a bit too long. Chinese "no nose" or asexuality highlights Kitty's too much of a good thing, a nose over-long intimating sexual desire running amok, out of control. Her long nose displaces a vagina to be (ful)filled, which in turn displaces Maugham's penis. When Walter dies of cholera, his face collapses, "fallen" (184), acquiring a flat-nosed Chinese face. The white Chinaman reunites in death with his homeland and his own kind.

In *The Painted Veil*, Dante's Italy of the Preface is relocated to Kitty's Hong Kong and inland Pearl River Delta, which happens to be the setting of Kingston's imaginary flight to China in *The Woman Warrior*. In Maugham, the trope of veil functions ambiguously to both crystalize and cocoon his homosexuality and incumbent guilt. Maugham wears two lenses: the other (Italian chastity and, further afield, Hong Kong lasciviousness) and the hidden self (Britishness). Although Maugham's unadulterated Orientalism appears to be beyond the pale in comparison to Kingston's torturous ethnic consciousness, the latter pairs the visions of China and America as well, using a long, establishing shot of the Orient in order to silhouette the close-up of the ethnic struggle, a psychic Freudian refraction reminiscent of Maugham's self-centeredness. Whereas Maugham is obsessed with his sexuality and Christian guilt, Kingston wrestles with her self-identity marked by ethnicity and gender. Despite their differences, the Orientalist and the ethnic pioneer are both motivated by self-fashioning, transferring onto China the repression of homosexuality or of race and gender.

Their angles on China are eerily similar, albeit the styles of embodying China differ somewhat. Akin to Maugham's pre- and post-cholera stereographs, Kingston adopts the strategy of doubling. Her immigrant mother character Brave Orchid's "talk-story" straitjackets and enables at once the daughter Maxine. Maugham dichotomizes China to bring down and to uplift Christian characters and Christianity itself. Likewise, Kingston weds a misogynist, primitivist Orient with the mystique of China—the bad and the good China, as it were. They see fit to resort to age-old stereotypes in place of thick description of a living China to realize their respective visions of selfhood: Maugham's Englishness and sexuality; Kingston's Chinese Americanness and sexuality. Stylistically, how they grant voice to the Chinese other diverges in terms of an extra's botched solo versus an entire chorus, albeit cacophonous at times. To be precise, Maugham's one-liner for the otherwise mute Orientals segues into Kingston's labyrinthine Chinglish. Maugham's technological trope of the dualistic stereograph-cum-stereotype counterpoints Kingston's style of Chinglish, which linguistically and culturally balances Chineseness with Americanness.

A Chinese American born and raised in Stockton, California, Maxine Hong Kingston contributes to Asian American consciousness with *The Woman Warrior*. The trail-blazing autobiographical, ethnographic fiction opens with "No Name Woman," where the protagonist Maxine imaginatively returns to China by way of her mother's "talk-story." Out of the misery of Maxine's unnamed aunt, narrated by Brave Orchid, is Kingston's ethnic feminist identity forged. At variance with the male voice in Maugham's gay projection, Kingston seeks to found an ethnic matrilineage by reacting against the patriarchal discourse. That female-centered tradition is inaugurated, ironically, by a woman robbed of her name. Kingston's dialectical feminist move comprises detaching from, while allying oneself with, her mother/ land. Kingston's China mixes ancestral/parental memory, ethnic history, American "movies" (6), and pure fantasy commencing with a village raid, or mob violence against No Name Woman. The whole point of opening with No Name Woman is to construct Chinese Americans' hyphenated identity, evidenced by the second-person exhortation immediately after this horrendous tale: "Chinese-Americans, when you try to understand what things in you are Chinese, how do you separate ..." (5). The ellipsis proceeds to catalogue a jumble of factors that interweave Chineseness and Americanness within Chinese American identity.

Pregnant out of wedlock, Maxine's aunt transgresses against the traditional community, which exacts collective vengeance by ransacking the aunt's family "on the night the baby was to be born," a nightmarish homecoming for Kingston's debut (3). Not only does the barbaric practice border on phantasmagoria but the precise timing of child-delivery is incredulous. Rather than the village timing to the very hour of the birth of a child, Kingston has delivered the birth of a nation called the Orient. This village raid comes across as less a literal Chinese custom against illegitimate children than a figurative, allegorical blood rite within America itself to purge ethnic female rage over patriarchy in Maxine's immigrant household and in a White Castle that Harolds and Kumars and Maxines try to breach.[2] Kingston's self-projection onto a bifurcated China, which savages one woman while enabling the eponymous woman warrior, differs from Maugham's only in degree and not in kind. Compared to Maugham's deathland with only one pidgin-spewing curio shop owner, Kingston endows far more voice and agency onto her China. Therein lies part of Kingston's problem, which magnifies a thousandfold Maugham's one-liner. Kingston has developed a de facto Chinglish, with Standard English morphing into unintelligible Chinese words and phrases. In between, a wide spectrum of hetereoglossia reflects the forked-tongue Chinese American hybridity, mongrelization.

Like a bad dream, Kingston's nocturnal raid comes "like a great saw, teeth strung with lights, files of people walked zigzag across our land, tearing the rice. Their lanterns doubled in the disturbed black water, which drained away through the broken bunds ... men and women we knew well, wore white masks" (3–4). The beginning of sensory overstimulation, this village raid reprises stereotypical Western impressions of a chaotic and incomprehensible Orient, thrilling yet repelling, be it Hong Kong's open-air market with caged and slaughtered fowls in Stephen Soderbergh's *Contagion* (2011) shot with a shallow depth of field or San Francisco Chinatown's Beijing Opera with its grating, high-pitched song in Orson Welles's *The Lady from Shanghai* (1947). Physical violence and psychological tension depicted on-screen, no different from Maugham's cholera-infested Mei-tan-fu, further ratchet up sensory assault on the mind, pushing it to the brink of reason. Moreover, both Soderbergh's and Welles's Oriental scenes are shot from eyes already blurred, minds already overdosed, delirious, as if the Oriental virus (Soderbergh and Maugham) and Orientalized femme fatale (Welles) had seeped into and rotted Western consciousness.

Neither white nor male, Kingston manages to open with a young Chinese American Maxine who is even more enthralled by China than the two filmmakers' protagonists. Whereas whites can comfort themselves by way of their difference from nonwhites, Maxine is caught in the quandary of identity, the Chinese other deemed as the ethnic self in the eye of the white majority. Detachment from Chineseness in Kingston must be enforced discursively via a white gaze at the Orient. Thus, Brave Orchid's "talk-story" opens with a self-contradictory counsel on the inscrutable Orient. Although Brave Orchid shares with Maxine the story of her aunt No Name Woman, this story is forbidden to be shared by Maxine, whose narrative voice is now sharing it with her readers. This torturous expression and repression thickens in that this aunt committed suicide by having thrown herself into the family well, a method common in East Asia but almost unheard of in the West. But the drowning deliberately poisons, jinxes the water source. The betraying of the mother's confidence enacts the secret, unspoken matrilineage of passing down female suffering. But the transgression against patriarchy from the No Name Woman's extramarital affair to Brave Orchid's "talk-story" to Maxine's "ghost" memoirs constitutes a feminist streak that endears Kingston to the American public.

Kingston's feminist discourse is built, in part, on Orientalism, a China eerily reminiscent of Maugham's. Maxine's mental bafflement mirrors Maugham's and the two white filmmakers' venturing into the primitive and nightmarish Orient. In fact, Maxine's torment far surpasses her white counterparts as hers is imagined to be an internal journey. Yet this ethnic root-searching is debunked by the author's Western consciousness, amply manifested in her choice of vocabulary and imagery. Although reflecting the Pearl River Delta's rice fields and irrigation, Kingston's "broken bunds" conjure up the turn-of-the-last-century Shanghai Bund in the International Settlement along the Huangpu riverbanks lined with colonial financial institutions and interests. The "Bunds," a colonial loanword and legacy, betray Kingston's Western imaginary and idioms. The villagers' "white masks" and their yellowfaces underneath merely reverse Kingston's yellow mask and whiteface. Just as Kingston visualizes her ancestral land, China, she returns to her birthplace of the West and her birthright in the English language. The dialectical move of entering China while never leaving America comes across most patently via the English language.

But before language, alas, one must mention the "Oriental" body from which language originates, namely, the metonymic, bodily slits of eyes that some Asians try to enlarge and improve. Kingston's Asian eyes evoke Kitty's Freudian nose. Like the genesis of European plastic surgery to correct the "Jewish nose,"[3] the postwar Asian industry of beauty initially specializes in turning "slanting," single-lidded, almond-shaped eyes into the Caucasian prototype of round, double-lidded eyes.[4] This self-mutilation contextualizes Kingston's agonized self-discovery caught between the white and Chinese cultures. The Korean adoptee documentary filmmaker Deann Borshay Liem confesses in *First Person Plural* (2000) that she had such a surgery in her teenage years to look more like her Caucasian older sister; the cover design of the Knopf Doubleday 2010 edition of *The Woman Warrior* features prominently a double-folded Asian eye, presumably the result of surgical intervention. Kingston even touches on that in such statements as "other Asian girls were starting to tape their eyelids" (182). Stereotypical American eyes on stereotypical Asian faces flips Kingston's rhetorical style giving an Asian feel to the King's English.

Kingston resorts to awkward, pidgin-sounding slang and hyphenated, well-nigh un-English expressions to accomplish that. Given that Maugham blithely draws from the racist pidgin of "top-side" to be transported into the Orient, Kingston concocts hyphenated Alienglish to denote aliens speaking English and English that alienates.[5] In the name of "talk-story" from Brave Orchid, Kingston transforms Pierre Nora's *lieux de mémoire* from "sites" to "bodies" and "voices" of the immigrant generation, corporeal carriers of racial memory and its inevitable loss ("Between Memory and History" 19). Such "talk-story" is as much Kingston's artistic license in general as her immigrant license in particular, whereby she attributes to the racial other fallacies so Orientalized that they would have come across as unequivocally racist otherwise. Kingston speaking for the immigrant subaltern dances between two magnetic poles: the positive one of Gayatri Spivak's "strategic essentializing"[6] and the negative one of crowding out the voiceless, reminiscent of white feminism "speaking for women of color."[7]

A bastard phrase neither traceable to English nor to Chinese, "talk-story" encapsulates this paradox of the self and the other, the ethnic American and the immigrant alien. Presumably, "talk-story" transliterates *shuoshu* (spoken book), a classical term for oral performance of folk legends and, by extension, novels. "Talk-story" thus "authenticates" the immigrant mother's tales of a faraway land, exotic and terrifying, yet uncannily close to Maxine's heart. As such, the mother proceeds to narrate the ancestral village's "hurry-up weddings" prior to the laborers' departure for the Gold Mountain of San Francisco (3). Not only are marriages hastened in order to ensure potential heirs in China but the language used in America to describe it is deliberately so ungrammatical and simplistic as to imply the mother's infelicity with English, as if she is hurried, harried by the very medium of her retelling, resorting thus to her own nonstandard Chinglish.

The strange-sounding "talk-story" and "hurry-up weddings" are but the initial salvo of the plethora of Kingston's hyphenated compound words in Alienglish. Each of the list below is followed by Standard English in parenthesis, if need be: "drowned-in-the-well sister" (6); "Chinese-feminine" and "American-feminine" (11); "food-money" (remittance 13); "hero-fire" (courage 16); "scar-words" (tattoos 42); "small-person's voice" (puny, vulnerable voice 48); "were-people" (ghost 83); "once-people" (ghost 84); "not-eat" (fast 92); "Pee-A-Nah" (219). One hastens to add that not all compounds derive from Orientalized speech, though. In the same breath as hyphenated compounds that disorient, certain compounds come straight from English itself. For instance, "Chinese-feminine" is preceded by the adjectival "pigeon-toed," which is a perfectly American expression nowhere to be found in Chinese, hence a testament to Kingston's medium of English. Exceptions aside, the style that characterizes the bulk of such compound words intimates a fragile grasp of English, the simplistic linguistic command of a child's or a foreigner's. Instead of the mot juste—"remittance," "tattoos," and "fast"—"food-money," "scar-words," and "not-eat" are coined, respectively, by conjoining entry-level words. Kingston's Chinglish-sounding compound words suggest a direct translation from immigrant characters' native tongue, except no such expressions exist in Chinese.

In lieu of Kingston's "alternative fact" of the immigrant speech, immigrants would arguably resort to their native tongue for *huikuan* (remittance), *ciqing* (tattoo), and *jinshi/shouzhai* (fast), daily common parlance effortlessly called up. But this genuine immigrant voice, if known to Kingston at all, would only put off English-speaking readers. Lest I be labeled a carping critic for bringing up *huikuan*, *ciqing*, and *jinshi/shouzhai* at all, I hasten to add that Brave Orchid's talk-story of simplistic English and compromised Chinese may well be for the sake of her daughter-protagonist Maxine, whose grasp of Chinese is questionable. Instead of the proper Chinese terms, Brave Orchid has to speak in baby English for Maxine. This rationale is a moot point, though, considering the fact that Brave Orchid's voice is consistently childish, even in her supposedly Chinese dialogue with her own generation in the United States. In the aftermath of the disastrous "reunion" of her dreamy sister Moon Orchid and her Americanized brain surgeon brother-in-law, Brave Orchid the "mastermind" of this transoceanic meddling goes for the consolation prize: "'The least you can do ... is invite us to lunch ... At a good restaurant?' She would not let him off easily" (154). The authorial caricature infuses not only Brave Orchid's words but also the narrator's last words: a meal to pay for the husband's abandonment and Moon Orchid's eventual nervous breakdown. Brave Orchid does not opt for a simplistic English in her "talk-story" to Maxine; she is a simpleton in the eye of Maxine and American readers.

Kingston's popularity hence grows out of a general indifference to the immigrant voice, which is dubbed by the quintessential ethnic writer. That so-called immigrant voice may well be voicelessness, overwritten by the exigencies of ethnic American identity politics. As such, Kingston exploits the fissure between two cultures and languages, writing in effect a grammar of Chinglish without appearing to do so, as though she is merely transcribing the immigrant speech act. Should it be a truthful transcription, publishers would likely turn down Kingston's manuscript for part of the dialogue and narrative voice would be in non-English, Romanized and glossed as in previous examples. The code-switching is wont to be unwieldy, much more of a disruption than, say, Spanglish. While it may simulate faithfully immigrant disorientation in an Anglophone world, it is a tall order to ask English speakers to subject themselves to this linguistic labyrinth in order to get a peek of the true immigrant condition. But this multicultural collusion between Asian American writers and American readers in the name of alien immigrant stories has gone on far too long with impunity[8]; it is time to push back from a truly bilingual, transnational perspective.

Even when hyphens are dropped, the sense of mystique persists. Does "ghost plagues, bandit plagues" (13) refer to ghost, bandit, plagues, and/ or something else altogether? The latter word and the point of reference, "plagues," floats between a figure of speech and literal epidemics. In addition, Kingston sprinkles her novel with Romanized proper nouns, such as Sit Dom Kuei (88), Ho Chi Kuei (204). Only the meaning of the last word Kuei (ghost or *gui* in the *pinyin* system of the People's Republic of China) is clear, leaving the narrator searching in vain in dictionaries for the other words. Proper nouns are names that denote specific persons, things, or events; they point to concrete particulars. Once taken out of context and shared with outsiders, however, proper nouns immediately self-destruct. Without that shared context or further elaboration, they obfuscate rather than elucidate, which is what they are designed to do. These proper nouns have lapsed into common nouns, or even non sequiturs, losing their one-of-a-kind uniqueness. Akin to mood music, they conjure up a general aura of Oriental inscrutability. Proper nouns no longer shed light; they deepen darkness. Beyond compound words and Romanization, Kingston's Chinglish also comes in the form of Standard English but the content is so bizarre, the meaning so meaningless, that this Chinglish may well be an alien in sheep's clothing, not only to English speakers but also to Chinese. Certain alleged American customs are downright outlandish, seemingly of the New World only to immigrants without any understanding of the host culture. "The American custom of stomping of straw hats come fall" professes an element of fancifulness on the part of Kingston (60). Newsboy ghosts are said to deliver papers made from ingredients of boiled children (97).

Such speculativeness, even playfulness, regarding the host culture is no different from the representation of the ancestral culture. "The idioms for *revenge* are 'Report a Crime' and 'report to five families'" (53), thus mis-reports the narrator. *Baochou* (報仇) does mean revenge, but the first word *bao* is used in the context of *baoyin* (karmic retribution) and *baofu* (vengeance). *Bao* in this case has nothing to do with report, which is one of its multiple meanings. If *bao* means "report," then why does Kingston not render the phrase as "newspaper a crime," since "newspaper" is yet another meaning for *bao*? Indeed, report to whom? If a victim does report the grievance to the authorities or the even more fantastical "five families" (*wujia*), then it ceases to be a revenge. Appealing to the official justice system cancels out any private action to even the score. By the same token, *tianji* (field frogs or simply frogs) transforms in Kingston into "heavenly chickens" (65) because of the homophone *tian* for both heaven (the first tone) and field (the second). Finally, Kingston no doubt confuses Chinese history when the Six Kingdoms had purportedly risen up to annihilate the Qin dynasty. It happened the other way around, that is, the First Emperor of Qin defeated all Six Kingdoms and united China for the first time in history (78).

Even though Chineseness is part of the three-legged stool—Orientalism, feminism, and ethnicity—of Kingston's ethnic classic, her Chinese leaves much to be desired. In an intimate moment, the adult Maxine reflects that her mother has always called her the "Biggest" rather than the "Oldest" daughter for fear that it would prematurely age her. While the Chinese word *da* means "biggest" (102), no Chinese would ever imagine calling their firstborn the oldest. Some Chinese practices are inexplicable: as parents embark for the United States, they fling coins to their crying children for them to roll in (103). Such gesture of appeasement is surely futile to even the most "affectless" Oriental automatons, children or otherwise. Kingston apologists are bound to justify these linguistic and cultural miscues in the same way they rationalize Kingston's blending of the historical figures of the Song dynasty general Yue Fei and the cross-dressing woman warrior Hua Mulan. Specifically, Kingston has Hua's back carved with Yue Fei's tattoo. Like the opening, collective exhortation to "Chinese-Americans" (5), such imaginary mixing aims to suggest the depth of pain in ethnic struggles.

Kingston's artistic license hinges on a China susceptible to stereographic-cum-stereotypic molding. Tears and love come to be blended with Orientalist stereotypes. Soon after the "Biggest" daughter episode, Brave Orchid takes leave of Maxine and calls her "Little Dog … She has not called me that endearment for years—a name to fool the gods. I am really a Dragon, as she is a Dragon" (108–109). One is unsure whether "Little Dog" is a Chinese or Cantonese term of endearment. Rather, it doubles back to the repeated claim that rural women give birth in the pigsty, as No Name Woman describes her newborn therein: "lovely as a young calf, a piglet, a little dog" (15). The ridiculous Orientalist touch of pigsty delivery as a common practice embodies Kingston's own split love–hate relationship with her ancestry. China is a trauma, a primal wound, where the affectionate term of "little dog" is wedded with the abject "piglet," despite the euphemistic self-image of dragons, the icons of Chineseness. China is the implied venue of a pigsty, where love and hate cross-breed, where a woman is a cross-dressing warrior and a baby girl drowned in the family well nearby. Kingston's repetition compulsion reprises in female scapegoats of No Name Woman, of the crazy lady stoned to death by villagers (94), of Maxine leading "an American life" of "disappointment" (45), of Maxine with the "small-person's voice" fired by her white boss in a business suit (46).

The nightmarish return of female suffering correlates with the incessant movement of the plot's fall and rise. The fall from grace in the first chapter "No Name Woman" leads to the ensuing chapters' rise of Maxine-Mulan's *wuxia* (swordplay and kung fu) heroics and of the mother Brave Orchid's medical training to become a "bare-foot" doctor in communist China. But the imaginary height is unsustainable once characters are transplanted across the Pacific Ocean throughout these chapters and, more importantly, in the last two chapters. Once Brave Maxine, chapter 3's eponymous "Shaman," decides that she cannot save the crazy lady from mob violence, she resolutely "turned her back ... she never treated those about to die" (96). Yet her unwavering self-agency is summarily drowned, as it were, in the wide spacing, the textual blank, that leads to the following paragraph. That textual gap indicates a change of scene and degeneration in the United States. Her bravery dissipates when she is "terrified" by Ellis Island officials' interrogation, when she fails to remember what year her husband "cut off his pigtail" (96). Given the authorial proliferation of pigsty in peasant women's alleged preference for pigsty delivery, Kingston may not have cut off her own pigtail, which dogs her much like the "double binds" China continues to wrap "around my feet" (48). Foot-binding remains a metaphor for the arduous road toward Kingston's salvation from, and haunting by, the hog pen of Chineseness.

Female trauma, however, comes with its own deconstruction, in keeping with Kingston's subversive style. Just as trauma is destabilized by playfulness, a Chinese-sounding rhetoric is upended by English expressions and Americana. In the midst of "White Tiger," the legendary woman warrior Mulan-Maxine's mythical apprenticeship in the vein of 1950s and 1960s Cantonese *wuxia* movies is suddenly deflated by her private thought that she prefers "chocolate chip cookies" to Chinese fares (21). Upon her return to substitute her aging father in battle, Mulan-Maxine maintains that she had gone away to acquire "science" (34). After a battle, she muses that her *wuxia* masters would "laugh to see a creature winking at them from the bottom of the water gourd" (38). Although the water gourd functions as a crystal ball in Taoism and the *wuxia* film convention, "winking" remains an anachronistic body language distinctly Western, one that is impishly projected onto the mythical and Maoist China. These drips or slippages from Chinglish back to English gradually give way to the flood of Americanism in the last two chapters, as Standard English takes over the narrative as a result of the American setting and the American-born characters' perspective. The language toward the end of the book moves away from the choppy, fragmentary Chinglish of the first three chapters. However, the characterization of pidgin-spewing Brave Orchid falls apart when she casts doubt in idiomatic English on her children's trustworthiness: "I wouldn't put it past them …" (114). Here, Brave Orchid's refined, even sophisticated, phrasing jars against her mangled English earlier. As Kingston herself writes, "Chinese-Americans, when you try to understand what things are Chinese …" Kingston is one such Chinese American and what she has written may not be entirely truthful to the characterization of immigrant voices. An immigrant is likely to have said in the most unvarnished way possible: my children "lie" or "would lie," probably not even the subjunctive past tense "they would have lied." Rather than a round, integral character, Brave Orchid, along with others from and in China, is a mouthpiece for Kingston, self-licensed to speak on their behalf.

Whereas one expects a colonialist Maugham to recycle racist and sexist stereotypes, the ethnic Kingston evinces similar proclivity to the cliché of immigrant schizophrenia, or a split self within Asian characters. Whereas Maugham polarizes China between the stereotypes of the sinophiliac aesthetics and the sinophobic abomination, Kingston splits her Chinese immigrant characters in *The Woman Warrior* (1976) as well. In the heat of ethnic struggle to claim America, Kingston does it on the back of a construct of Chineseness. In the name of Brave Orchid's "talk-story," Kingston exercises poetic license in conjuring up a ghost land called China. The gallery of grotesques ranges from No Name Woman, a rape victim and a suicide, to the woman warrior of vengeance, one with a name—Fa Mulan; from the protagonist Maxine's mother Brave Orchid to her aunt Moon Orchid, two extreme stereotypes of a crone's intransigence and a girlish silliness; from Maxine empowering herself to the weak, hyperfeminine Chinese classmate— her doppelganger—whom she bullies in the school restroom. These alien phantoms serve as familiars to the exorcist Kingston, who calls up and dispels apparitions at will, since ghosts have no subjectivities other than the authorial mental constructs. These ghosts ring around and de-alienate Maxine, the Asian American girl protagonist undergoing an identity crisis in the vise of a racist America and a misogynist Chinese heritage. In the vein of a young girl's toys, Kingston kneads these dough-like, malleable dolls to suit Asian American needs in her ethnic bildungsroman. Hence, the identity of a person of color constitutes itself on the pale shadows of non-persons; the Asian American feminist voice in English dubs immigrant characters, who must be muted in the first place for any dubbing to unfold.

The Woman Warrior has indeed founded an Asian American literary tradition of taking "immigrant license," a forging of the Asian American Self by means of forgery of the Asian Other. This license lies to a large extent in the pidgin or Chinglish of Asian characters. Kingston has not begrudged her Chinese characters English, like Maugham's one-liner, but their spoken English is so off-balance, so un-English as to tap into an Orientalist reservoir of an alien tongue for aliens who are, ironically, dear to the protagonist's heart. In that regard, Kingston's "talk-story" of the 1970s echoes Maugham's 1920s stereograph in doubling, and in lending more "body" to, the Other, except the novelists traffic overtly or covertly in stereotypes. Ethnic struggles repurpose, stylistically, colonial Orientalism; the shared pidgin Chinglish quickens the Orientalist's and the ethnic minority's Chinas.

3

Chink in Our Holmes: Oriental Sesame and Anglo-American Detective

In modern Western culture, our Sherlock Holmes and company are the imaginary armor against evil, keeping our homes safe. The "l" in Holmes etherealizes into a separate "I," the tall slim private eye looming above, watching over our homes. Formulaically and obsessively, however, a barely noticeable chink, both a narrative opening and a stereotypical, negligible Oriental, clues the quintessential Anglo-American detective to solving the crime. This miniscule chink in our Holmes serves as the "Open Sesame" to the Anglo-American detection tradition: it embodies in its abject, demeaning otherness soon to be stricken from memory the magic genesis of Western masculinist hegemony. As if a passing nod to the Orient, this chink character or overture manifests the West's repetition compulsion, its Tourette tic to tick off the Asiatic Other, an itch that has to be scratched until the urge reconstitutes itself. The narrative body of detection emerges from the chink shaped like a vulval sesame; the detective solves the "whodunit" while oblivious to the chink from whence he is sprung. The detective enacts a chronic Orientalism, whereby the chink comes across as predetermined, subliminal. This argument analyzes Anglo-American practices of the detective genre from Holmes to the new millennium's thrillers by Thomas Harris to uncover the xenophobic neurosis. Even in such unlikely, quasi-detective texts as Jonathan Lethem's *Motherless Brooklyn* (1999) and Paul Auster's *Oracle Night* (2003), we continue to find chinks who bedevil and facilitate Lethem's tourettic and Auster's invalid protagonists.

Fusion of East and West in Sherlock Holmes

Rather than biblical light in the Book of Genesis, Arthur Conan Doyle initiates Sherlock Holmes stories with "Let there be Orient!" One of Conan Doyle's earliest stories, "The Sign of the Four" (1890) opens with a scene of cocaine addiction: "Sherlock Holmes took his bottle from the corner of the mantelpiece, and his hypodermic syringe from its neat morocco case," a synecdoche of the Orient, for a dose of the "seven-per-cent solution" of cocaine (3), observes Dr. Watson. Thus, Watson returns in kind Holmes's first impression of himself in the very first Sherlock Holmes story, "A Study in Scarlet" (1887): "you have been in Afghanistan, I perceive." From Conan Doyle's first two Holmes stories in 1887 and 1890, both the British Empire's physician and its quintessential detective are tainted by a touch of yellow or evil. Watson not only served in Afghanistan but he still limped owing to a "Jezail bullet" from the "Afghan campaign" (5). Watson is indeed marked/marred by the Orient, no different from Holmes injecting himself with the content from the "morocco case." Indeed, the mutual Oriental "staining" from the colonies of Afghanistan and Morocco culminates in the detective readying himself to shoot up cocaine from the morocco case.

A mantelpiece anchors the hearth, the heart of any English household, where most treasured memories are displayed in the form of the loved ones' photographs and favorite souvenirs. Yet at the corner of such a "display window" of warmth and domesticity lies Holmes's cocaine in a morocco case and, by implication, Holmes's sleuthing "cases," both equally close to Holmes's heart. This case denotes not only the container for the syringe from the non-English other but also the cases of murder from the dark side of England. The "seven-per-cent solution" from the Morocco leather case inspires Holmes to solve his cases, providing temporary redresses to a never-ending stream of crimes. The syringe releases into Holmes's bloodstream that which he craves, just as the evil other infiltrates the streets of London and breaches the integrity of England. The drug coursing through Holmes's veins parallels the evil other snaking through the River Thames and London's alleyways, both enabling the detective, empowering the West. Such otherness is nearly imperceptible as the story goes on, except when Holmes is stumped in solving any case and must venture into the bowels of the earth such as the Limehouse District's opium den in "The Man with the Twisted Lip" (1891), or when Holmes bids adieu by prophesizing in "The Last Bow" (1917) that "There's an east wind coming, Watson … It will be cold and bitter … and a good many of us may wither before its blast." This "east wind" has never stopped blowing in the West's sails, only forgotten in its voyage toward Western supremacy. After two Sherlock Holmes stories, we will return to see how this east wind continues to fan the BBC's and CBS's contemporary TV remakes of the supreme intelligence of the detective.

In "The Sign of the Four," Sherlock claims that "The only point in the case which deserved mention was the curious analytical reasoning from effects to cause" (Conan Doyle 5). Despite such valorization of the power of reason and the method of scientific deduction, Holmes soon falls back on the morocco case of cocaine and the intuition of the Orient. The story itself also circles back to India's Agra Treasure when the antagonist Small narrates the backstory of betrayal and revenge. Indeed, whereas Sherlock demonstrates the science of deduction by reading the clues on Watson's watch recently inherited from his deceased brother, the deduction relies as much on logic as imagination (7–9). The high or satisfaction Sherlock derives from detection has a definite element of play and control, beyond the dispassionate, objective pursuit of truth. Sherlock confesses as much when he bemoans the lack of detective stimulation: "None [no case]. Hence the cocaine [substance from the morocco case]. I cannot live without brain-work" (9). Cocaine blunts the lack of intellectual stimulation as well as the absence of imaginary flight. To solve "whodunit," Sherlock oftentimes puts himself in the shoes of the criminal, taking on, imaginatively, the role of the villain. Unbeknownst to the University of Edinburgh-trained surgeon Conan Doyle, "brain-work" calls on as much reasoning from the left side of the brain as dreaming from the right side. In the absence of pleasure-inducing dopamine at the satisfying conclusion of a case, Sherlock's body craves chemical substitution from the Morocco case. By the same token, "The Sign" offers an escapist thrill for contemporary readers and viewers, as they experience viscerally dark secrets of the erstwhile British Empire to relieve the doldrums of life or, in the new millennium, to mirror the anxiety over global terrorism and strife.

Thaddeus Sholto, the heir to the traitor Major John Sholto of "The Sign," bears unmistakable signs of the Oriental, long viewed as duplicitous and untrustworthy. Not exactly guilty by association, genetic association, that is, Sholto's Oriental touches, however, contribute to the Gothic milieu. With "a Hindoo servant, clad in a yellow turban" as its gatekeeper, Sholto's drawing room is decorated with an "Oriental vase," where "two great tiger-skins thrown athwart it [the carpet] increased the suggestion of Eastern luxury, as did a huge hookah which stood upon a mat in the corner" (18–19). The carpet is likened to "a bed of moss," evoking a wild rain forest or jungle. Sholto finds his "hookah an invaluable sedative" (20), much like Sherlock's cocaine. Both Sholto and Sherlock seek either the exhilarating euphoria created by the East's evil or they abuse substances from the East to suffer through lulls in life. Both Sherlock the detective and Sholto the criminal's heir live in extremes, either mastering the overstimulation of crime or numbing themselves against ennui. They become most alive when they cheat death; otherwise, they medicate themselves. If they cannot repeatedly wrest life from death, they lapse into a pseudo-inanimate death-in-life.

Avenging the Sholtos's betrayal is Jonathan Small, the sole survivor of
the four soldiers who pilfered Agra treasure, which was in turn stolen by
John Sholto. Small is described as somewhat inhuman: "bearded, hairy face,
with wild cruel eyes and an expression of concentrated malevolence" (24).
One-legged, Small leaves the "impression of a wooden stump" in his tracks
(34). Small's disability arouses repulsion from readers. Furthermore, Small's
"Oriental familiar," an indigenous Tonga, is so diminutive that his "prints
of a naked foot" are "scarce[ly] half the size of those of an ordinary man"
(35), rendering him subhuman and animal-like. The Tonga morphs between
an object and a man:

> The huddled bundle upon the deck ... straightened itself into a little
> black man—the smallest I have ever seen—with a great, misshapen head
> and a shock of tangled, disheveled hair ... Never have I seen features
> so deeply marked with all bestiality and cruelty ... his thick lips were
> writhed back from his teeth, which grinned and chattered at us with half
> animal fury. (73)

The superlative, hyperbolic rhetoric describes a monstrosity closer to a beast,
with apes' long lips that turn almost inside out. Although accompanied by
the "hell-hound, Tonga," Jonathan Small remains strangely gentlemanly
(75) and most English in his self-introduction: "a Worcestershire man
myself, born near Pershore" (81). Conan Doyle subconsciously portrays his
Easternized villains as more English than the English. Small is faithful to the
sign of the four, the pact of trust among one "Worcestershire man" and three
Sikh soldiers. His vengeance against the Sholtos—specifically, Thaddeus's
avaricious twin brother Bartholomew—is undertaken as much for himself
as for his deceased companions. Small is further accompanied by a hound-
like Tonga, who sacrifices himself for his master.

Conan Doyle may well be unconscious of this Orientalist conundrum:
he sets out to depict evil Orientals or a corrupted Englishman who has
gone native, all of whom turn out to be far more English than Britons.
These "tainted" Englishmen may be crippled or disfigured, with a wooden
leg or a twisted lip (as in "The Man with the Twisted Lip"), but they are
surrounded by dependable and steadfast Orientals. Conceivably, the British
Empire represses and projects its sense of guilt over colonial domination
onto a distorted self-image of Englishmen gone native, served by Oriental
subordinates. While the subtext of "The Sign" reflects the repression of the
empire, the story on the surface balances detection with romance, namely,
Mary Morstan soon to wed Watson. Yet even this happy ending doubles
back to the colony India, for Captain Morstan, Mary's father, was also
betrayed by Sholto. As for Agra treasure, it is either buried in India or
sunken in the Thames. Ironically, this wealth lies irretrievable on the bottom

of the Thames, despite the fact that the colony's blood money has been brought back to the heart of the empire. Small realizes that Agra treasure is a treasure but also a curse, seducing him, enslaving him, and bringing him ruination (76). India, Hong Kong, and other crown jewels enrich the empire where the sun never sets, but they haunt like nightmares of a guilty conscience. To stanch the return of the repressed, Sherlock Holmes comes to the rescue, a feigned paragon of reason and intellect, armed with modern science and technology.

In an arguably subconscious turn, Conan Doyle invariably debunks Western stereotypes of the East. Set in an opium den in London's Limehouse District or today's Chinatown, "The Man with the Twisted Lip" purports to portray Englishmen who are depraved drug addicts. Conan Doyle is oblivious to the historical irony that England used to be the international drug lord that planted poppies in its colonies of South Asia, shipped opium through the Malay Archipelago by the East India Company, and prosecuted two opium wars in the mid-nineteenth century to ensure access to the huge market of China. The opium den is supposed to symbolize the evil Orient in the heart of London, yet it unwittingly registers England's checkered past. The story's theme of shifting identities reflects exterior masks and inner truth.

From the outset of the story, such shift opens with Watson's mission to hunt down a friend, Whitney, languishing in a seedy opium den run by a Lascar (a sailor from India or Southeast Asia). Deep in this underworld, Watson chances upon Holmes disguised as an opium addict, investigating the case of a missing Englishman St. Clair, supposedly wasting away there by his crave for a smoke. Notwithstanding his Christian surname, its connotation of clarity and transparency to boot, St. Clair has been masking himself as a panhandler with the twisted lip to appeal to people's pity. This constant shift signifies the imperial method of subconscious deflection: one drug addict Whitney morphing into another, St. Clair, who deploys the opium den as the front; one investigator Watson morphing into his partner.

Against the historical canvas of a hypocritical, drug-pushing England, the Lascar turns out to be the loyal accomplice to St. Clair, keeping the promise to conceal the panhandler's identity, no different from the slavish Tonga to Jonathan Small. Although "a man of the vilest antecedents," the Lascar is St. Clair's most trusted ally, his secret sharer (169, 181). "The vilest antecedents" signal the Lascar's past, even ancestors, which would include his Victorian Maker—the British Empire—that made an entrepreneurial seafarer out of the Lascar, one still in command on land of a "shipshape" drug house. This hidden genealogy boomerangs right back to England itself. What is truly twisted is history and England's conscience, crystallized in the dirty trick played by one of the upright citizens, St. Clair. Even the opium den visited by Watson suggests the empire's implication.

To enter the opium den in Upper Swandam Lane, Watson:

Passed down the steps, worn hollow in the centre by the ceaseless tread of drunken feet, and by the light of a flickering oil lamp above the door I found the latch and made my way into a long, low room, thick and heavy with the brown opium smoke, and terraced with wooden berths, like the forecastle of an emigrant ship. (163)

Watson catches glimpses of an opium den as he descends into the belly of the beast, except this dark Oriental enclave points to the dark lord—the British Empire—that swallows it in the first place. The opium den is likened to "the forecastle of an emigrant ship" run by aliens like the Lascar. A "forecastle" is the crew's quarter at the bow, so the den's wooden berths for its clients constitute the common bed for white and nonwhite drug fiends alike. The common bed destroys the racial hierarchy buttressing colonialism, not to mention the fact that this "emigrant ship" is captained by an Oriental. When opium comes home to roost, Conan Doyle displaces the blame onto the Oriental other.

To solve the mystery, Holmes stays awake throughout the night, smoking "cross-legged" on "a sort of Eastern divan" (177) constructed by cushions. A divan is a long low couch originally imported from the Ottoman Empire. Hence, Holmes nestles in an Eastern shell to hatch a breakthrough in the case of double identity. At the crack of dawn, Holmes awakens to the fact that the crippled beggar Hugh Boon with a twisted lip is one and the same as Neville St. Clair. This deductive leap springs from the nocturnal dreaming whereby the English sleuth and the Eastern smoker are one.

Such an episode of enlightenment recurs throughout the Holmes corpus. Holmes with his iron constitution and mental excitement over a case does not sleep, smoking all night long on an Eastern divan to contemplate his case, while Watson sleeps, only to awake to find a Holmes ready for action since he has already solved the case mentally. In this particular case, Holmes has already seen through the disguise of Neville St. Clair as the beggar Hugh Boon (176–177). Holmes either needs the cocaine inside the Morocco case to dull his nerves or he needs the overstimulation of a murder case. In the former state, he "sleeps"; in the latter, he never does, like a robot. That slumber of reason literally embodied by a napping Watson silhouettes Holmes's nocturnal flight into the other—racially on an Eastern divan consuming "shag tobacco" reminiscent of narcotics (177). Watson's sleep is Holmes's "wake," who remains on watch over the case of a disappearance. Holmes plays the guardian to a slumbering Watson as well as to the West's rationality. Watson's death-like slumber coincides with Holmes's night-dreaming in the image of the racial other, which bestows an intuitive grasp of crime beyond the domain of reason and logic alone. A detective who scoffs at anything other than science and reason during the day turns out to lean heavily on nighttime "daydreaming."

Even in our new millennium, the BBC, Britain's national industry of nostalgia over the empire, continues to grind out Holmes against the backdrop of a mysterious Orient. The 2004 BBC production of *Sherlock Holmes and the Case of the Silk Stocking* returns the audience to an opium den where Holmes played by Rupert Everett sinks into an opiate nirvana while the crosscut takes us to a female victim strangulated by silk stockings and discovered on the banks of the Thames (Figure 3.1). Both opium and silk invoke an Orient that is abhorrent and aesthetic at once. Everett's Holmes then frequents a Chinatown teahouse where he mangles what is supposed to be Cantonese. The sounds he butchers are indecipherable to English speakers, who play along in the suspension of disbelief for a good story. The opening credits of the BBC's *Sherlock Holmes and the Baker Street Irregulars* (2007) with Jonathan Price as the lead prominently feature a green jade spoon in which heroin is being cooked (Figure 3.2). This Oriental prop then branches into one of Holmes's Baker Street Irregulars from Chinatown where crimes are spawned in the image of ancient jade spoons. All such Oriental objects—opium, silk, jade trinket—in the employ of, or associated with, criminals evoke Orientalism of a bipolarized East.[1]

The chic BBC series *Sherlock* (2010–) starring Benedict Cumberbatch also sees fit to "jump species" to the Orient in the second episode of its first season. Coming on the heels of the exciting pilot episode "A Study in Pink," after Conan Doyle's "A Study in Scarlet," the second episode, "The Blind Banker," is of the TV producers' own making, a compulsory reenactment of opium dens and Chinatown tongs, a lackluster episode but an inevitable link to the third episode, "The Great Game," where the mastermind Moriarty

FIGURE 3.1 *Sherlock in an opiate nirvana in* Sherlock Holmes and the Case of the Silk Stocking *(2004).*

FIGURE 3.2 *Jade spoon cooking cocaine in* Sherlock Holmes and the Baker Street Irregulars *(2007).*

materializes. Indeed, the last shot in "The Blind Banker," pun intended, shows the Dragon Lady Shang being eliminated by her online chat pal M— conceivably, for Master as much as Moriarty (Figure 3.3). Full of Orientalist clichés, "The Blind Banker" demonstrates the West's blind spot and fixation on the extravagant, sadistic China, which is compensated by a beautiful Chinese victim and her tea ceremony and antiques, a gesture to political correctness. The bad China witch is being balanced out by a good China girl, so *Sherlock* maintains. The sadistic China manifests itself in Shang's torture instrument that horrifies its victim, who cringes under the threat of an arrow to be released once the sand drains away (Figure 3.4). Shang grins, clearly deriving joy from her victim's horror and pain; Shang embodies the yellow peril from medieval Europe's fear of the marauding Mongolians to contemporary West's fear over the rise of China.

When CBS relocates Sherlock (played by Jonny Lee Miller) from London to New York in *Elementary* (2012–2018), the British detective is a wreck of an addict, devastated by the loss of his one and only true love Irene Adler. The drug addict is shadowed by a "sober companion," Joan Watson played by Lucy Liu, a token minority and an honorary white. The "sober companion" is variously called "addict-sitter," "personal valet," and "helper monkey." CBS's casting of Liu subverts Dr. Watson's gender and ethnicity. Liu's Watson character used to be a surgeon, but she has left the practice

FIGURE 3.3 *The "last shot" of "The Blind Banker" in the BBC series* Sherlock *(2010–), where Moriarty eliminates Shang.*

FIGURE 3.4 *Shang with her torture instrument in the BBC's* Sherlock.

after a failed operation. Despite her role as a sober companion, Watson is also "on the mend" herself, stumbling upon her calling of a NYPD consulting detective under Sherlock's tutelage. Similar to New Age food porn, Liu's Watson brings to mind a fusion fare whereby two stereotypes are reprised as well as transgressed. Watson's loyalty and level-headedness counterbalance Sherlock's eccentric, Asperger-esque genius. Despite this adherence to the traditional Watson, *Elementary* casts against type by repurposing Asian hyperfemininity. Liu enjoys an utterly asexual, most un-Hollywood-style relationship with Sherlock throughout the six-year run. CBS's strategy hinges on having the cake and eating it, too: having the bromance of the original stories while spicing it up with an exotic Oriental, who is to remain safely asexual, never romantically involved. One hesitates to point out that Liu who plays this exotic Oriental happens to sport eyes tilting upward in conformity to the stereotype of slant-eyed Orientals. At any rate, this safe, buddy relationship of Sherlock and Joan Watson is made explicit from season 1's debut episode. As the sober companion assigned to watch over Sherlock, Lucy Liu walks past a prostitute who has just satisfied Sherlock's sexual needs. The prostitute ignores Liu's query of Sherlock's whereabouts (Figure 3.5). Liu's role is briefly teased as Sherlock plays with Joan Watson by parroting a movie love scene (Figure 3.6). Whereas Sherlock heals under Joan Watson's care, Irene re-emerges to devastate him again in episode 22 (Figure 3.7). Figure 3.8 is from episode 23, where Irene Adler's deception is said to have given him "perfect clarity" while the "nursemaid" Watson attends to his shoulder wound inflicted by Irene. One angel of death takes; the other angel of maternity gives. The former is white and hence compatible in the mind of CBS's fans; the latter is not white enough and serves. Jonny Lee Miller's repeated nudity in front of Lucy Liu does not lead to the Hollywood formula of love-making. Symbolically, Miller undresses to dress down Liu by unsexing her. A nude Sherlock puts her in her place, on the side of sobriety, as opposed to prostitutes or even Irene who bestow orgiastic ecstasy and momentary departure from consciousness. Nearly a century after Conan Doyle and contemporaneously with Sherlock Holmes filmic remakes, Thomas Harris's thrillers continue to manifest chinks in the age-old tradition of detection.

FIGURE 3.5 Elementary, *season 1, episode 1, Joan Watson passing by Sherlock's prostitute.*

FIGURE 3.6 Elementary, *season 1, episode 1, Sherlock playing with Joan Watson.*

FIGURE 3.7 Elementary, *season 1, episode 22, a distraught Sherlock finds Irene alive with his trusted companion by his side.*

FIGURE 3.8 Elementary, *season 1, episode 23, Watson attends to Sherlock's shoulder wound.*

The Yin-Yang of *Red Dragon*

Thomas Harris is a Southern writer famous for his tetralogy of thrillers featuring the serial killer Hannibal Lecter. This tetralogy is suspended between the detective genre, on the one hand, and the Gothic and horror, on the other, as Peter Messent maintains.[2] *Red Dragon* (1981) pits Detective Will Graham against serial murderer Francis Dolarhyde, also known as Red Dragon. To hunt down Dolarhyde, Graham seeks advice from Hannibal the cannibal, whom Graham put in prison. *The Silence of the Lambs* (1988) replaces Graham with a young FBI cadet Clarice Starling.[3] On the trail of another serial murderer Jame Gumb, Starling likewise solicits Hannibal's counsel, hence ratcheting up the romantic tension between the protagonists. *Hannibal* (1999) continues the ambiguous relationship between the detective and her "consulting detective," between law and lawlessness. *Hannibal Rising* (2006) is a prequel on a young Hannibal losing his dear sister Mischa to Nazi collaborators and his revenge after the war. A Freudian reading would associate Starling and Mischa, both young and vulnerable like lambs under the knife. Hannibal's attraction to Starling borders on a pseudo-incestuous obsession to resuscitate the lost sister and prewar innocence.

In his thrillers, Harris deploys serial killers, modern Satans, but pairs them with, not to mince words, serial detectives.[4] A serial killer is an addict to the most extreme of blood sports with humans as game, practicing human sacrifice in a repetitive blood ritual. Rather than alcohol, drug, cyberporn, and other forms of addiction, which are bad habits repeated to feel good, serial murderers take lives to relive God's thrill of creation, only in reverse. If serial killers are the new Satan, evil incarnate, of our secular age from which God has receded, perhaps even deceased, then serial detectives—Thomas Harris's Will Graham (played in films and on TV by William Peterson, Edward Norton, Hugh Dancy), Clarice Starling (Jodi Foster, Marianne Moore), and, surprisingly, Hannibal the Cannibal (Brian Cox, Anthony Hopkins, Gaspar Ulliel, Mads Mikkelsen) in the Hannibal genealogy— are the new saviors self-resurrecting for our sake. The seriality of both villains and victors suggests, however, a hidden symbiosis and bonding in that although their life span is limited in each reincarnation, they sire their descendants in perpetuity—always together like parents to each filmic and TV remake, in pairs of good and evil.

This reincarnation crystalizes in the serial killer Francis Dolarhyde's belief in "Becoming" in *Red Dragon*, or his metamorphosing into the Book of Revelation's and William Blake's Red Dragon, not to mention the Old Testament's leviathan. Mythical beings that they are, dragons are known as (super)beings rather than (under)becomings, with the latter undergoing stages of transformation. Instead, Dolarhyde's becoming resembles a snake's shedding of skin; his birth defect of a cleft palate externalizes a snake's forked tongue, resulting in the lisp and the split in psychosis; his oral obsession with biting and figuratively swallowing victims comes from snakes' anatomy and feeding habit.[5] Very much a Christian symbol of the Fall, Dolarhyde the serpent red bestirs Graham, serpent blue, if you will, the prototype of serial detectives who empathize and visualize rituals of blood.[6] Graham's capacity to see and intuit stems from the hidden darkness within himself, which is passed down to Starling. That innate darkness distills but nightmares—metaphorical and/or literal—of fear and repression in all of us, which explains why the public braves Hannibal and Hannibal-slayer as entertainment either in denial of real horror or in hopes of psychic catharsis or both. To apprehend Dolarhyde and Buffalo Bill, both detectives resort to Hannibal's insights, unwittingly rendering the criminal a crime-fighter or a "consulting detective" like Sherlock Holmes. Arguably, Hannibal himself assumes the role of the hound, the long arm of justice, in the prequel *Hannibal Rising*, in which Hannibal avenges his young sister Mischa eaten alive by East European Nazi collaborators during the Second World War. The anti-Christ in defiance of God's order, Hannibal blurs corporeal boundaries of self and other by ingesting human flesh, becoming his victims and ultimately consummating a pseudo-incest with the primal victim Mischa/Clarice. Hannibal, along with his soul mates among officers of the law, fuses serial detectives and serial killers, justice and blood debt, awe-inspiring dragon and serpent of chaos and nihilism.

Yet another fusion involves the notion of seriality and originality, be it serial originality or originary seriality.[7] Serial murders are repetitions of the same crime committed by the same person. That the crimes are serial points to the failure of the law in apprehending the serial killer. Each crime demonstrates "originality" in its shocking execution and its blood-letting, ritualistic dimension. Rituals consist of the same procedure, yet each reprise renews and rejuvenates. As the plot thickens in such ritualized killings, Harris deploys the narrative strategy of increasingly short chapters, alternating between the killer and the police, as if in a simulation of characters and readers breathing hard, gasping as the body tenses up. The pace of narrative equals the pace of breathing, both in a serial nature. Seriality, by definition, is stop-and-go, akin to breathing in and breathing out, with brief intervals in between as we hold our breath. Seriality is also seen in muscular, psychic contraction, followed by relaxing. Breathing is not a non-stop, ongoing movement, nor can physical and mental contraction last forever. Seriality is a pattern of presence and absence, on and off, expression and repression, or fort/da (gone/there) as in Freud's *Beyond the Pleasure Principle* (1920).

The detective tradition in the West is itself marked by seriality amongst a long line of detective characters, from Edgar Allen Poe's Auguste Dupin to Arthur Conan Doyle's Sherlock Holmes to Thomas Harris's Will Graham and Clarice Starling and many more. Each detective engages in an investigative episode, the conclusion of which only leads to the next assignment. The repetition of investigation is often serialized in magazines; moreover, the formulaic plotline of investigation resembles a Möbius strip of crime, detection, crime, detection, and more. Counterpointing detectives, Red Dragon itself is one in a series of monsters: the Old Testament's leviathan or sea monster, the Book of Revelation's Beast with the number 666 on its forehead, Romantic visionary William Blake's drawing, and Thomas Harris. Paradoxically, Dolarhyde sees himself as becoming the one and only Red Dragon, even ingesting Blake's original drawing at Brooklyn Museum to complete the (e)merging. If one can become the one and only Red Dragon, then Red Dragon cannot be unique, inimitable. What is emerging cannot be already in existence; singularity and replicability are mutually exclusive.

Repeatedly, which is also seriality, Harris plays with doubles or doppelgangers of killer and detective. First of all, killers resemble each other in that both Hannibal and Dolarhyde are "carnivores" devouring their victims figuratively by taking their lives and literally by eating them. Hannibal cooks his victims' body parts for some fine French cuisine, "sweetbread" for the thymus or the pancreas, for instance. As Nicholas M. Williams contends, Hannibal yokes the "the taste of the mouth and the taste of the mind" (140).[8] Although not a killer, the abusive grandmother in *Red Dragon*, who made a monster out of Dolarhyde, shares a similar set of dentures with her grandson.

In terms of killers and detectives, they are presented as shadows of one another. "We're *just alike*," Hannibal flings at a retreating Graham in *Red Dragon* (83). Despite the fact that Hannibal is the criminal in prison,

Graham is the one who tries to flee from truth, i.e., "it takes one to catch one" (112). Will Graham resembles Hannibal Lecter in being an eideteker with photographic visual memory. Although the book does not describe Hannibal as such, he seems so refined and so encyclopedic that one almost has to conclude that Hannibal is also a person with an eidetic memory. Indeed, subsequent novels in the tetralogy, *Hannibal Rising* in particular, elaborate on Hannibal's "memory palace." Hannibal further takes on the role of the lecturing Lecter when he taunts Graham in a letter by pointing out the obvious, which Graham represses. The obvious is that killing feels good because of the sense of omnipotence. Graham's detection involves putting himself in the criminal's shoes, to finger and touch the evidence, to feel the criminal's mind. In other words, Graham tries to be the killer imaginatively.

The thin line keeping Graham from becoming Hannibal or Dolarhyde is his fear: "He wondered if old, awful urges are the virus that makes vaccine" (*Red Dragon* 443). Weakened or dead virus is made into vaccine, so Graham who identifies with the killer but fears to become one is the only deterrence against lapsing into a serial murderer. Graham plays the role of the hunter, which is only possible because he becomes the hunted imaginatively, resulting in his feeling haunted and leaving the FBI. The hunter-hunted role reversal inhabits Dolarhyde as well. A mutilated, terrified child grows up to mutilate and terrify. When he finds himself being hunted down by Graham, the prowling Red Dragon turns into the prey. In fact, a shocked Dolarhyde instinctively calls Graham "a monster," which is what the society thinks of him (394).

The shifting roles of the hunter and the hunted evoke a yin-yang dynamic. Yang and yin in Chinese cosmology symbolize complementary opposites of light and dark, sun and moon, man and woman that engender all things and life itself. In Harris's fiction constituted by words, there are only two graphics: the book cover's biblical-Blakean Red Dragon and the Chinese ideogram 中 on the top half of page 108. The former is far better explained than the latter, hence the yang or the prominent over the yin or the recessive. Indeed, Harris does not even bother to Romanize 中 as "zhong"; the Chinese ideogram remains unpronounceable to English-speaking readers, unfathomable until the narrative voice explicates it lamely as "You hit it" or the "Mah-Jongg piece ... mark[ing] the Red Dragon," a duality that further throws the reader (129). The graphic 中 creates an aura of mysterious evil hailing from the stereotype of an inscrutable Orient. The West's prominent gene, as it were, of Red Dragon from biblical leviathan to Blake's apocalyptic vision and to Harris's monstrosity, all in the English language rather than the unsayable, unfathomable Chinese character, threads itself with the East's recessive gene of 中. The double helix of yang and yin, or the Western patriarch and the Eastern maiden, sires Harris's horror. Not to mince words, Red Dragon springs from the yang of biblical Blake and the yin of Orientalized Chinese Mah-Jongg.

This pattern of yang and yin continues in the last installment of the Hannibal tetralogy, or the prequel of *Hannibal Rising*, if not before. The dominant patriarchal villain remains the West, the blue-eyed Nazi collaborator Grutas, who cannibalized Hannibal's young sister Mischa during the last days of the Second World War in the Eastern European Theater. To avenge Mischa, Hannibal is nurtured by the yin of his aunt and almost lover Lady Murasaki. Lady Murasaki focuses the palette of Orientalism that is no longer shadowy and marginalized, such as the one single Chinese ideograph in *Red Dragon*. The frontispiece to *Hannibal Rising* is Japanese painter Miyamoto Musashi's "Ink Drawing of a Shrike on a Twig" on exhibition at a Japanese museum, a water and ink drawing that has absolutely nothing to do with the unfolding plot other than as a portal into *japonisme* symbols of samurai swords, kimonos, flower arranging, lute playing, Hiroshima bombing, and whatnot. Narratively, the mother-lover-samurai master is the fulcrum to set in motion an entire Oriental universe. Not to belabor the obvious, Hannibal's first impression of his "stepmother-mistress" is that "her face" launched "his first step on the bridge of dreams … " (79). "The bridge of dreams" is a literary trope that goes back a long way, from *The Tales of Genji* to Junichino Tanizaki. The concluding ellipses obviously herald more to come. What used to be an Oriental trickle in 中 in the first installment of the tetralogy becomes a flood in the last; what used to be a mere yellow stain bleeds into an ink wash-style mise-en-scène for Harris's last hurrah.

The yang of *Red Dragon* traces back to the prominent gene of English-language Western classics of the Bible and William Blake. Dolarhyde chances upon Blake's drawing "The Great Red Dragon and the Woman Clothed with the Sun," which, he believes, "approached his graphic thought" of his "Becoming" (92, see Figure 3.9). "The Woman Clothed with the Sun" may well be Blake's subconscious Oedipal pun of "The Mother Clutched by the Son."[9] William Blake's drawing happens to be the book cover of Harris's *Red Dragon*, except the book title darkens and occludes the woman lying supine in a golden halo beneath Red Dragon's feet, with a phallic tail wrapped around her groin. The sexual connotation in Blake is downplayed in Harris's book cover. This shift does little to disguise the masculinist, patriarchal quest for power that motivates the serial killer. In lieu of facing up to his childhood trauma and lifelong sense of inadequacy in the hands of his mother, grandmother, and one childhood playmate, Dolarhyde idolizes male predecessors: Hannibal Lecter becomes "John the Baptist" to his own anti-Christ "Becoming." Dolarhyde imagines "sit[ting] on him [Lecter] as the Dragon sat on 666 in Blake's Revelation series" (118). What Dolarhyde represses is his misogynist assaults against women, akin to Blake's monster lording over and incinerating the woman. Here, Harris resorts to the pop psychology of childhood trauma to account for Dolarhyde's crimes.

FIGURE 3.9 *William Blake's "The Great Red Dragon and the Woman Clothed with the Sun."*

Complementary to the yang of Red Dragon, Harris subconsciously features the yin of 中 (zhong). Treating the Orient cavalierly as a minor literary trope, a forgettable tease to pique reader interest, Harris nonetheless returns to it compulsively throughout his tetralogy. Dolarhyde in his lair in *Red Dragon* favors kimonos: "The kimono hung on the wall like the shed skin

FIGURE 3.10 *Dolarhyde receiving his dentures at a dentist's office in NBC's* Hannibal.

of a tree snake" (349). A Japanese kimono in sheer silk or cotton associated with women merges with the biblical symbol of the Fall. Stripped of the kimono-biblical skin, Dolarhyde flashes his dragon tattoo, harking back to the dragon of the Book of Genesis and to William Blake. However, this is body art commissioned in Hong Kong, hence the autograph of the Orient on his torso. NBC TV series *Hannibal* meticulously depicts Dolarhyde's tattoo and denture procured in an Oriental milieu. Whether it is Hong Kong or Chinatown no longer matters, since they all look alike, alas, in the collective mind of Western producers and consumers of pop culture. The opening five minutes of season 3, episode 8, "The Great Red Dragon," shows Dolarhyde receiving the dragon tattoo from an Asian tattooist and, subsequently, the dentures to conceal his snaggletoothed and cleft palate from another Asian (Figure 3.10). Such exotic, Gothic Other infects Dolarhyde through the window display of *yayi* (dentist), red chinoiserie window lattices, and the grotesque tongs stretching open an Asian patient's mouth on the lower left corner. The window's red smiley lips parodies the patient's immobilized mouth. Oriental inscrutability and evil rub off subliminally on the audience's mind.

The kimono motif also runs through Harris's oeuvre. After Dolarhyde sheds the kimono like the shedding of a snake, Jame Gumb in Ted Tally's screenplay for *The Silence of the Lambs* (1991) dances to "Goodbye Horses" in a kimono, striptease-style, "us[ing] the dishmop to tuck his penis and testicles back between his legs" to dissemble femininity (Figure 3.11). Ted Tally's screenplay does depart from Harris, who simply writes "Gumb put on his robe" (136). Kimonos are never associated with Hannibal Lecter, until the Oriental motif culminates in the prequel *Hannibal Rising*'s

FIGURE 3.11 *Jame Gumb in a kimono in* The Silence of the Lambs.

Eastern European trauma, from which a young Hannibal survives, nurtured by Lady Murasaki oftentimes in a kimono. Widow to Hannibal's uncle, Lady Murasaki plays the stereotypical China doll-cum-Dragon Lady, the white man's quintessential erotic fantasy: a pseudo-incestuous stepmother, a samurai's daughter instructing Hannibal in Kendo swordsmanship, and the damsel in distress to be rescued. The French detective Popil describes the young Hannibal as Lady Murasaki's "pet snake," once again collaging snake and Oriental *japonisme* (266). Indeed, Harris is in good company, as countless Western artists have dabbled in things Oriental, from French impressionists enamored with *japonisme* to contemporary film and TV remakes of Harris. Rather than *Hannibal Rising*, it is Orientalism rising, the tetralogy's swan song from an Orientalist unaware, or simply pretending to be unaware, of being one.

Harris's yin or subconscious Orientalist impulse would not have come to fruition without his accomplice: American pop culture. Beyond Ted Tally's screenplay and Jonathan Demme's award-winning film, this collaboration by film industry is evidenced by the fact that Harris's mere nod to China in Dolarhyde's "signature" of 中 constitutes a key scene in contemporary film and TV adaptations. Thomas Harris gives a visual illustration of a Chinese ideogram 中 (*zhong* 108). *Zhong* (中) means, according to Harris, "bull's eye," "you've hit it," or "Red Dragon," a lingo in Westernized Mah-Jongg. The imprimatur of the Orient is so instinctual and so welling up from within that Dolarhyde would sign his first mass killing in Chinese, the alleged Mah-Jongg character 中 (*zhong*), on the bark of the tree. Graffitiing a tree with his "initial" initiates waves of serial murders. In that one ideogram, which will soon be forgotten by the English-speaking author and readers, *zhong* draws a blank, a lacuna in readers' roving eyes, a pause in readers' moving lips. It embodies not so much the presence of a word as the absence that is the unknown. Is it any surprise that *zhong* is in fact the name for China, *zhongguo* (Middle Kingdom)? China is an unfathomable Other to Anglos.

An American serial killer thus hails with evil from afar, and autographs in Chinese his masterpiece of killings, by means of one of his murder weapons. Given that Harris's 中 comprises a moment when the literary and the visual copulate, what do we make of the fact that a Chinese character in the realm of the literary has been turned into a picture, an unknowable carving awaiting CIA Sinologists' decoding? A Chinese word that has its own meaning is carved into the bark but cut off from itself, becoming an empty sign, a placeholder, an X. Such relationships point to one of total asymmetry, one side subject to the other side's whim, the very definition of Edward Said's Orientalism. Ironically, this is the exact trope to which subsequent visualizations of Harris gravitate, not only for the genesis of Red Dragon but also for the very first clues that guide FBI detectives.

This pictorial or secret sign is dutifully repeated in Figure 3.12 (Edward Norton's fingers in Brett Ratner's *Red Dragon*), Figure 3.13 (Hugh Darcy's profile in Bryan Fuller's *Hannibal*), and Figure 3.14 (what William Petersen sees in Michael Mann's *Manhunter*). In all three figures, they reverse the literary and visual relations in that a word, albeit indecipherable Chinese "writing on the wall/tree," accompanies on-screen visuality of the protagonists sleuthing in the woods. Each of subsequent visualizations of Harris would doggedly reproduce this subliminal sign of evil, one that is just as soon forgotten in the plot, until the next round of retelling. This is symptomatic of repetition compulsion by a culture addicted to Orientalism.

FIGURE 3.12 *Edward Norton's fingers in Brett Ratner's* Red Dragon.

FIGURE 3.13 *Hugh Darcy's profile in Bryan Fuller's* Hannibal, *with* 中 *in the backdrop.*

FIGURE 3.14 中 *in Michael Mann's* Manhunter.

Prior to the tree carving, Graham in Thomas Harris happens upon three clues: the "ring-pull tab" for the "soft-drink can" (106–107) that flowed into Red Dragon's body while waiting for nightfall; the core of an apple that sustained him; and the shearing of a twig for surveillance of the victims' family home. The first two items are inedible, spit out after the food and drink have been consumed. The third severs the twig and leaves behind the detritus on the forest floor no different from the victims' remains. These clues culminate in the Chinese ideograph. The carving's sharp angles, particularly the vertical middle stroke with a bluntly tilted top and a pointy tip on the bottom, take on the semblance of daggers. The ideogram is not only carved by a knife but each stroke literalizes a stab of the knife. Whereas the pull ring, the apple core, and the trimmed twig are leftovers from the life of products and plants, the Chinese word has likewise been sucked clean of life, a signifier divorced from its signified, deemed the fingerprint of evil.

The range of meaning attributed by Harris to *zhong* denote piercing, incursion, infiltration, all for the purpose of possession. In archery, Mah-Jongg, and negotiation, *zhong* signifies the bull's eye, a winning hand, and the highest bid. To explicate 中, the FBI forensic scientist Beverly draws ironically from her hobby of Mah-Jongg rather than from her professional expertise. Nor does the exegesis of the Chinese word by FBI Sinologists fare any better beyond a fortune-cookie joke, which would at least Romanize 中 as *zhong*, something Harris does not even bother to pen. In fact, *zhong* in the fourth tone (重) also means heavy, hefty, loaded, and fraught. The irony of 中標 (*zhongbiao*, hit the target, winning the bid) lies in the double entendre of contracting venereal disease. Unbeknownst to its creator Harris, the fraught word choice of *zhong* flashes back to Red Dragon's birth defect of a cleft palate, the primal wound slashed by God, resulting in his oral fixation. *Zhong* foreshadows as well his repetition compulsion of biting and devouring his victims—a disease of the mind that contaminates and takes over the innocent. Harris's gesture to the Orient, a simple loanword 中, opens a can of worms that morph into snakes and dragons eating back at Harris himself. Revealingly, the plot soon moves away from the yin of *zhong* to focus exclusively on the yang of Red Dragon.

Some other Orientalist touches come across in Dolarhyde's flashback of the Hong Kong firework called "The Dragon Sows His Pearls" (331), which instantly destroys his intimacy with the blind Reba, returning him to Red Dragon demanding blood sacrifice. A firework on "The Dragon Sows His Pearls" may well be Harris's own invention, akin to Western Mah-Jongg's neologism on *zhong*. Dragons are indeed routinely painted, sculpted, and performed in Chinese New Year dragon dance with a pearl tantalizingly close to the dragon's open maws. In fact, dragons are believed to play with pearls rather than sowing them like his seed. Likewise, Harris repeatedly describes Dolarhyde's "yellow eyes" (294, 332, 431). That this uncanny eye color is merely mentioned in passing, serving no function in the plotline other than a distant echo of the yellow peril, demonstrates the offhandedness of Orientalism. Intertextually, the serial killer's yellow eyes evoke another serial detective Sam Spade's "yellow-grey eyes" in Dashiell Hammett's *The Maltese Falcon* (1929, 3). Part-time Orientalists like Hammett, with his bit character Joel Cairo of "Levantine" features (42), and Harris, with his kimonos and Lady Murasaki, monopolize the racial other with no fear of backlash from a public sharing their Orientalist fallacy.

Incidental Orientalism serves to silhouette the real story of Red Dragon born of a series of bad mothers. Harris's *Red Dragon* concludes as the serial murderer Francis Dolarhyde is shot dead by Molly, the detective Will Graham's wife and the mother of Willy Foster from her first marriage. In Harris's glib deployment of pop psychology, Graham reverses the fortune of war by distracting Dolarhyde. Despite the handgun pointing at them, Graham turns to verbally abuse Willy, who is so scared that he has wetted his pants: "You filthy little beast." Graham deliberately triggers Dolarhyde's childhood trauma of bed-wetting and his grandmother's threat of scissoring his penis as punishment. This momentary distraction gives Graham the opening to attack Dolarhyde. Dolarhyde's lifelong castration anxiety has driven him to avenge himself by raping mother-like victims and then killing them to ward off the incest taboo. Right before Dolarhyde's death in Harris, the action is interspersed with two lines: Graham crying out to his stepson to "run!" and Dolarhyde's, literally, last word "Muhner."

Dolarhyde utters his last word "Muhner!" instinctively when Molly blows "a rat hole through his thigh," before she repeatedly pumps bullets into his face, turning him into a literal "Cunt-Face" (432–433). Here is another unseemly, figurative and literal, tie between the serial killer and the serial detective. Nicknamed "cunt-face" for his birth defect, Dolarhyde dies with bullet holes in his face. Graham may have survived Dolarhyde's knife attack in the cheek, yet Molly calls out Graham's employer, the FBI, in anger to give him "a face transplant," evidently to mask the deformity similar to that of "cunt-face."

Dolarhyde's last word to a world he has terrorized reverts back to the very first sound "m" infants and toddlers babble. "M" is a well-nigh universal sound that "mellows" into "mom" in English, "maman" in French, "mutter" in German, "mor" in Danish, "ma" in Mandarin, "umma" in Korean, and more. "M" is itself a reaching back, part of a serial return, to the source of life. This origin takes Dolarhyde by surprise and turns into the source of his demise. The primordial "m" that initiates "Muhner!" dangles ambiguously between Dolarhyde's birth mother Marian who abandoned him, repulsed by his birth defect, and Dolarhyde's executioner "mother" Molly, his intended victim who kills to protect her own son Willy.

Dolarhyde's last cry to "Muhner!," a perversion of "mother," culminates a lifelong obsession with and vengeance against mother figures. His rape and murder victims, Mrs. Leeds and Jacobi, are chosen not only for beauty but for their maternal role. Psychiatrist Alan Bloom speculates: "The savage attacks aimed primarily at the women in the presence of their families were clearly strikes at a maternal figure" (197). The sexual assaults realize his incestuous drive, followed by the incest taboo that leads him to "disappear" substitute mothers to make possible psychological denial.

Femininity comes in the three faces of Granny, Mummy, and Baby. Granny points to Dolarhyde's controlling and abusive grandmother with snaggleteeth and with, "in the cast of her features and her hairstyle," an amazing likeness to George Washington (259). Dolarhyde loves and hates his grandmother to the extent that he keeps her dentures by the bed and puts on a duplicate set "with dark [blood] stains" to sign his letters and bite his victims (119). That hate stems from his castration anxiety caused by Granny. To compare the matriarchal grandmother to the nation's patriarch, George Washington, signals either that she has usurped manhood or that any civilization embodied by a founding father hides a shadow self. Mummy refers to Dolarhyde's beautiful yet hard-hearted mother Marian, who was so repulsed by Dolarhyde at birth that she deserted him. The term Baby includes his victims and the blind almost-victim Reba from the workplace.

The likeness of the grandmother and Washington dawns on Dolarhyde, intriguingly, minutes before he tears up and consumes Blake's watercolor *The Great Red Dragon* at the Brooklyn Museum in hopes of absorbing the monster into himself. The doubling of masculinity coincides with the realization that the Founding Father is but the dead ringer to his grandmother. As he freezes before the "Gilbert Stuart portrait of George Washington," the curator kindly suggests that "you see a similar one on the dollar bill" (371). Dolarhyde hence is a portmanteau of dollar-hide: if the monster maker grandmother is visible on the nation's dollar bill, then the serial killer resides in the American psyche and capitalism as well.

In its very sound, "muhner" mutilates "mother." Despite its strange look, the first syllable "muh" regresses to a baby's simple cooing, whereas the second syllable "ner" eschews the fricative, air-blowing "ther." Compared to "ther," "ner" keeps in the sound more than lets it out. The tongue moves minimally from the first consonant "m" to the second "n" as opposed to the plosive "th" that requires a sudden thrust of the tip of the tongue between the front teeth in order to force the air out. The close-lipped "m" flares outward to produce "th," much like a newborn's growth into an adult, the natural course of life denied to Dolarhyde stunted in his mental development, arrested in an oral fixation of sucking, biting, and devouring. Instead, Dolarhyde's "Muhner" comes across almost as a murmur before he dies akin to a baby's purr falling asleep. The inward, backward movement of both syllables in Dolarhyde's farewell is brought about by the shock of Molly the mother's shot. Mothers like Mrs. Leeds and Mrs. Jacobi used to be the victims whom he penetrated, only to have another mother penetrate him in the face, creating literally a "Cunt-Face" in death.

The first gunshot wound in his loins invokes Dolarhyde's childhood trauma when his abusive Grandmother threatened to scissor his penis for bed-wetting. This castration anxiety epitomizes Dolarhyde's sense of lack, from his birth defect of a cleft palate to his abandonment by his beautiful mother Marian to a felt inadequacy in manhood. Dolarhyde's serial murders subconsciously avenge maternal cruelty, cancelling out in his perverse mind the inferiority of his masculinity. By the hands of the "good" mother Molly, punishment is exacted for his serial transgression against "bad" mothers. In the face of this monster, Molly's only thought is of her son, her only line being "Run baby, run baby, run baby! Don't look back!" (432). Neither abandoning nor abusing Willy, Molly shields him by letting him go. Because of Molly's versus Marian's motherhoods, Willy the boy's future manhood is bound to be the opposite to Dolarhyde the man-child's infantilization. Harris's motherhood and manhood bring us to Jonathan Lethem's *Motherless Brooklyn*, a semi-detective story with a predictable touch of the Orient.

Neuro-tic in *Motherless Brooklyn*

Like his tourettic protagonist Lionel Essrog, Jonathan Lethem suffers from Euro-American Orientalist Compulsive Disorder in *Motherless Brooklyn* (1999). Lethem's oeuvre has been punctuated by the detective genre and film noir, a key influence of which appears to be "a touch of yellow" embodied by Joel Cairo in Dashiell Hammett's *The Maltese Falcon* (1929), the Asian opium den in Raymond Chandler's *The Big Sleep* (1939), not to mention Sherlock Holmes's Limehouse District, Dr. Fu-Manchu, and Charlie Chan. The Orientalist pattern resembles that of Conan Doyle and Thomas Harris: a mysterious Orient initiates the crime story and proves to be the source of evil. In his early novel *Gun, with Occasional Music* (1994), the dystopia of genetically engineered mutants and humanoid pets is governed by "karmic points" like bank accounts. When "karmically defunct," one is "iced"—frozen and put away in the manner of sperms and eggs—for years. A futuristic vision irrelevant to the East, Lethem feels compelled somehow to shroud it with the New Age Buddhist concept of karma.

In *Motherless Brooklyn*, Essrog takes it upon himself to track down the killer of his father figure Frank Minna. His first full-blown tourettic outburst, all in italics to underline the foreignness of his utterance, is triggered by "Yorkville Zendo," which he is instructed to stake out: "*Don't know from Zendo, Ken-like Zung Fu, Feng Shui master, Fungo bastard, Zen masturbation, Eat me!*" (4). Inspired by the signage's wordplay of Zendo out of Kendo, Lethem interweaves, in the name of the Tourette syndrome's echolalia, Orientalist pop culture of quiescent martial arts with active sexual fantasies, including a suggestive gesture to Lewis Carroll in the last exclamation. The stakeout fails, leading to Minna's murder. Minna's last words to Essrog is a long-winded Irving joke on the said Irving who has become the Tibetan High Lama, prompting Irving's East European mother to insist: "I vant to go to Tibet" (88). Essrog eventually figures out that the Zendo's master, Roshi Gerry, is in fact Frank Minna's double-crossing brother Gerard whose meditation center is a mere front for yakuza bosses-cum-Fujisaki Corporation businessmen, all disguised as Japanese monks, in the trafficking of uni, sea urchin's eggs, back to the lucrative Japanese market. Coming at the height of Japanese economic power and the resultant Japan-bashing, Lethem embroils his deeply flawed private eye Essrog with the Orientalist ethos of the 1990s.

In the final showdown, the mastermind Gerard sheds his Oriental mask and strikes at the heart of Essrog's emotional attachment to Frank Minna, like a good Zen master would: "Surely you've got my brother's money in your pocket even as we speak, Lionel. Do you really believe that it came from detective work ... Or perhaps you imagine he *crapped* money" (231). Both brothers—and Essrog indirectly—have profited from the Japanese connection, one ascending to the smuggle ring's "High Lama," the other tagging along as a small-time errand boy. Nonetheless, Essrog muses: "Was *crapped* a chink in Gerard's Zen façade, a bit of Brooklyn showing through?" (232). To crap in the sense of defecating evokes Freudian psychology of "filthy lucre" out of fecal "gold." Just as Essrog wonders if the vulgarity reveals a chink in the Zen master front, Lethem's deployment of metaphors from Zen to yakuza is symptomatic of Orientalism, a chink or crack in Lethem's craft.

Paul Auster's Book of Chang(ee)

Paul Auster's *Oracle Night* (2003) is a pseudo-detective, truth-seeking metafiction, a story-within-a-story-within-a-story, while each one circles back to the others like a Möbius strip, thoroughly porous between real historical facts and the imaginary. The novel opens in media res with the novelist protagonist Sidney Orr convalescing from a near-death illness. Debilitated and uncertain whether he could ever write again, Orr chances upon Paper Palace in his daily stroll across Brooklyn, a store run by a Chinese man M. R. Chang, or Mr. Chang.[10] Orr discovers on Chang's shelf a bluebook from Portugal that has since miraculously enabled the novelist to practice his trade by reimagining the Flitcraft episode in *The Maltese Falcon*, an intertextual metafiction that ultimately returns to Orr's here and now. Entering Paper Palace, Orr recalls that:

> The stillness was so pronounced that I could hear the scratching of the [Chinese] man's pencil behind me ... To the extent that the story I am about to tell makes any sense, I believe this was where it began—in the

space of those few seconds, when the sound of that pencil was the only sound left in the world. (4–5)

Chang's moving pencil, like Escher's drawing of a hand drawing a hand, extends into Orr's writing in his bluebook, the Book of Chang(ee), so named after the proprietor and the classic *Yijing, The Book of Changes*. Purchased from Chang, Orr's Book of Chang(ee) à la the long "e" sound of "No Tickee, No Washee" fame in pidgin English indeed keeps morphing, despite being dropped from the plot summarily a few times. Insofar as the pivotal role Chang has played, it is telling that he remains a marginal extra.

In their brief encounter, Orr is too embarrassed to ask if M. R. are initials or a honorific, thus accentuating the hologram of an enigmatic Orient. In keeping with the Other's inherent indeterminacy, Chang's stationery store materializes out of nowhere and vanishes into thin air. Orr revisits the store to pick up more bluebooks, only to find that Paper Palace is gone, in the words of an adjacent shopkeeper, "just like some magician dude waves his wand, and poof, the Chinaman is gone" (111). When Orr bumps into Chang again, Chang drives him to a shady sex club secreted behind a sweatshop in the Flushing Chinatown. Despite his moral qualms, Orr avails himself of a quick service, a treat from Chang who is in the process of "iron[ing] out the kinks, but I see large potential here. They ask if I want to invest as minority partner" (149). The proprietor of Portuguese bluebooks is about to become a co-owner of a brothel, trading in his variety of pens and notebooks for women of various races and types. In comparison to their initial meeting, Chang's broken English has improved remarkably. "Iron out the kinks," "large potential," and "minority partner" are idiomatic phrases and business terminologies beyond the scope of Chang. Like his fellow artists dabbling in Orientalism, Auster may have relaxed the stringent representation of his character's pidgin halfway through the story, forgetting to do the accent except the dropping of "a" before "minority partner."

The last chapter of Orr's Book of Chang(ee) witnesses the purveyor of bluebooks and "broads" degenerating into a murkier riddle, a cross between physical brutality and verbal clownishness. Stricken by shame and unable to locate Chang, Orr leaves the Chinatown sex club by himself. Subsequently, a born-again Paper Palace greets him like a mirage in Manhattan's Upper East Side, quite a ways from Brooklyn. This time around, however, Orr is roughed up by Chang, now full of rage over having been abandoned. "You give big hurt to my soul" (205), screams Chang while karate-ing Orr out of his store: "I cut out your heart and feed it to the pigs!" (208). This is the Chang who graces the first of many footnotes to form a parallel text to the novel, who in footnote #11 narrates his trauma during the Cultural Revolution. The level of irrational violence inflicted on Orr typifies the inscrutable Orient, even the yellow peril, violence-prone because of personal trauma. Yet the horror is undercut by his baby English, as if a child rants and raves incoherently in a temper tantrum. The Book of Chang(ee) shifts from a bowing, sycophantic Chinaman to a Mephistophelean corruptor to a feral animal, all courtesy of Paul Auster's three faces of the Orient.

What Western detective tradition has done to Oriental characters, Chinese detective novels are paying back in kind, made possible by global distribution of Chinese-language materials translated into English, financed in part by Beijing's campaign to assert its soft power. Zhou Haohui's *Death Notice* (2014) depicts a serial killer by the name of Eumenides, a word repeated in English in the Chinese-language trilogy. Like the namesake from Greek Goddesses of vengeance, or Furies, this serial murderer terrifies Chengdu, Sichuan, leaving a trail of blood while ingeniously eluding the police throughout. Evil incarnate, Eumenides signals the doppelganger to "Chink in Our Holmes," the Occidental sesame to commence Chinese detection for "the China Century." What Beijing tries to achieve by means of Zhou's translation and distribution diverges from the English-language Chinese émigré detective writers of Qiu Xiaolong and Diane Wei Liang of, respectively, Inspector Chen Cao and private eye Mei Wang mystery series.

4

Dr. Fu-Judge Dee: Serial Yellowface of, for, by the White People

That hyphen in the title evokes the veiled connectedness of apparent opposites of Sax Rohmer's evil versus Robert van Gulik's righteous protagonists, the Orient's serial killer versus its serial detective in the authors' respective mystery series. That hyphen also recalls Rohmer's misnomer of "Fu-Manchu," while Chinese last and first names come without any hyphen between them. One white writer's erroneous, whimsical Romanization of an arch villain is stylized as the white people's stereotype of the East, which another white writer redresses with the positive stereotype of Judge Dee, whose name, nonetheless, anglicizes "Di," the long "e" bearing an odious ring of pidgin: "savee," "No tickee, no washee." Despite their divergent images, Rohmer's Satan incarnate misspelled and Van Gulik's God of Chinese vengeance pidginized are both narrative strategies to ingest/secrete, serially, foreign bodies/subjects by the King's English.

That hyphen is the balancing pole held in the hands of a West hallucinating, "high" on the tightrope stretched taut between, at one end, the bad Orient dissociated from the territorial and psychic integrity of the West and, at the other, the good Orient with which the West associates for said integrity. A short, choppy horizontal line comes to suggest the ambiguity of both splitting from and sticking to the Orient, severing the Orient as well as sewing oneself back onto it. That "It" is the West's Id, repressed yet returning perennially. A cross-dissolve between Jekyll and Hyde, the hyphen represses Orientalism as much as flaunts it. The Orient is "hyding" in plain sight as the Anglo-American detection tradition is partially born from Rohmer's frenzy to kill Dr. Fu in order to resurrect him, and from Van Gulik's kneading of the good Judge Dee in the West's own image. The "y" in lieu of "i" in "hyde" harks back to Middle English yet to be standardized in its spelling. Its root in Middle English betrays what Modern English is hyding—the "I"—in plain sight. The West plays hyde-and-seek with itself via Dr. Fu-Judge Dee.

As such, Dr. Fu readies himself to pounce at one end of the spectrum, the paranoia relieved somewhat by the counterpoint of the beautiful Kâramanèh, Dr. Fu's slave in love with Dr. Petrie, the Watson to Holmesian Nayland Smith in Sax Rohmer's mystery series. Intertextually within the West's collective unconscious, Judge Dee overcompensates for his fellow countryman Dr. Fu. Both Dr. Fu and Judge Dee lurk in either corner of the tightrope walker's eyes, as the walker role-plays the daredevil in a mind game. Balancing Rohmer's and Van Gulik's inaugural text of their mystery series, *The Insidious Dr. Fu-Manchu* (1913) and *Celebrated Cases of Judge Dee* (1949), the following argument listens to the garbled evil and good out of both sides of the West's mouth.

Sax Rohmer's Dr. Fu-Manchu

Unabashedly emulating Arthur Conan Doyle's Sherlock Holmes and Dr. Watson, Sax Rohmer gives the detective stories an Orientalist spin in not only enlarging Conan Doyle "touches" of yellow in select stories but also in racializing Professor Moriarty as Dr. Fu-Manchu. Sax Rohmer's plot involves multiple episodes of Nayland Smith and his sidekick Dr. Petrie pitted against Dr. Fu-Manchu bent upon taking over the world. The fictional invasion of the West displaces the actual invasion of the East. To defend English territorial and cultural integrity is to erect a smoke screen for colonialism that mixes, hydridizes: Dr. Fu's female slave Kâramanèh is apparently mixed-race ("With the skin of a perfect blonde, she had eyes and lashes as black as a Creole's," Rohmer 21); Dr. Fu's targets of assassination are all great white men who have made their names in Asia and elsewhere; even Oriental pidgin betrays, not to mince words, traces of the British accent. Manifesting a Western obsession compulsion over the yellow peril, Rohmer's plot lends itself to being repeated, reshuffled, with the Oriental mastermind contemplating, sadistically, the infinite tableaux of death: "O God of Cathay! ... by what death shall these die" (129). It matters little whether the Zayat Kiss takes Sir Crichton Davey's life or the Call of Siva that of another victim. This textual "interchangeability" reflects Rohmer's series of Fu-Manchu over four decades, a series of thrillers that can also be reshuffled. To wreak havoc, Fu-Manchu is a pioneer of techno-Orientalism, straddling primitivism and technology. Hence, he deploys primitive, premodern methods of murder such as poisonous ant as well as high-tech science in the vein of the proverbial mad scientist.

Since Western detective tradition has given birth to itself out of darkness and chaos, wet through, as it were, in the dewy half-light from the East, Sax Rohmer's turn-of-the-last-century Dr. Fu-Manchu mystery crystallizes the "half-naming" that veils and occludes as much as it reveals and enlightens. Despite the purpose of identification and illumination implicit in any act of naming, his very name, Dr. Fu-Manchu, disorients. It is not only foreign-sounding, defamiliarizing, but it begs the question: which is his surname, before or after the hyphen? Why a hyphen at all? Given the publication of *The Insidious Dr. Fu-Manchu* in 1913, two short years after the overthrow of China's last dynasty of Qing, otherwise known as the Manchus from China's northeastern corner of Manchuria, part of Sax Rohmer's inspiration may have come from contemporary history. Fu (傅) is a legitimate family name, but it suggests the homonym of recovery (復), even the phrase "imperial restoration" (fubi 復辟) with the implication of the return of the Old Orient. Out of a plethora of possibilities, fu may simply mean "rich" (富), a shared wish amongst turn-of-the-last-century Chinese immigrants in London's Limehouse District where Rohmer professes his one and only contact with the subject-matter of the Orient. Rohmer practically prides himself on his not knowing anything about China other than experiences from Chinatown excursions.[1]

In terms of Fu's backstory, Nayland Smith evokes the nebulous semi-underground crime syndicate, or what he calls the "Third Party" amidst the "Young China," fashioned in the image of Chinatown triad and tong (67, 224). The capitalizations and quotation marks of the two terms elevate common nouns into proper nouns, albeit devoid of any semblance of specificity. A fictitious boogeyman, Dr. Fu is symptomatic of the West's recurring paranoia over the yellow peril. Such revenant of Orientalist stereotypes stems from the Freudian concept of the uncanny, or *unheimlich*, "unhomely" for what used to be familiar or homely, only repressed by "the negative prefix *un-*" and projected out ("The Uncanny" 151). This half-naming by Rohmer with neither the language nor any in-depth knowledge of the East constitutes the narrative strategy of deepening the uncanny, embedded within the West's own psyche and history, in the name of naming it. Half-naming is worse than not naming at all, for it teases with what lies beyond one's ken, which is nothing but a recurring nightmare dreamed up by oneself.

Like a newborn, Dr. Fu-Manchu is named, allegedly given an individual identity by Nayland Smith, as if Smith were the biblical (white) father pointing an accusing finger at a Cain figure (26). Smith acts as the Master who names his creatures, from the mastermind Dr. Fu to his "agents of death" (139), those series of murdering devices/tropes and torture chambers—the Zayat Kiss, the dacoit assassins, Lascar, Kâramanèh, the Call of Siva, the mark of Káli, *phansigar*, the Golden Elixir, and more. Rather than dispelling uncertainty over the unknown, Sax Rohmer's conceit of half-naming thickens it by means of partial revealing that, akin to low-key lighting in film noir's chiaroscuro, accentuates the shadow in which the object in question lurks. Whereas language aims to communicate by shedding light on its subject, Rohmer's language confuses, the darkness enveloping his subject as a result. Language clarifies, yet Rohmer's obfuscates. Language elucidates, yet Rohmer's eludes. Language specifies things, yet Rohmer's suggests un-things.

Thus, "Dr. Fu-Manchu, the yellow peril incarnate," serves as the antagonist. He is described as "with a brow like Shakespeare and a face like Satan" (25). Apropos half-naming, these similes of physical attributes hardly illuminate Fu's features. Instead, they disorient because neither Shakespeare's brow nor Satan's face presents a clear, photographic image. The quintessential English bard and the distillation of pure evil are collaged to suggest a Burkean sense of the sublime, by which the reader is awe-struck and terrified at once.[2] The fact that both are body parts from Western—not Chinese—consciousness, Christian to boot, signals Rohmer's projection onto the racial other of an enigmatic, hyphenated sinophilia-cum-sinophobia. The West's serial detectives from Holmes to Smith spit out the names of the serial murderers, who are spitting images of themselves.

Despite being the series' namesake, Dr. Fu-Manchu is largely absent and silent. Even in his rare cameo appearances, he remains occluded behind opium smoke, otherworldly in his physique, particularly his green eyes veiled by the nictitating membranes of a snake or amphibian. "The *membrana nictitans* in a bird" is how Rohmer describes Dr. Fu's third eyelids, estranging in part owing to the Latinate spelling (58). Yet the Latin words, like Shakespeare's or Satan's facial features, betray Rohmer's own Orientalized freakishness on account of the fact that Latin forms the very foundation of the Western Indo-European linguistic family. Self-implication aside, this yoking of subhuman bestiality and superhuman intellect renders Dr. Fu more of a repugnant phantom than a person, whose invisibility and silence ratchet up horror. His "reptilian gaze" horrifies with its "greenness ... of the iris; the pupil was oddly contracted—a pin-point" (127), or the pin-point pupils of a drug addict.

What comes out of that alien body alienates as well: "His English is perfect, though at times his words were oddly chosen; his delivery alternately was guttural and sibilant" (127). If so perfect, then the flaws of diction and elocution must be few and easily identified. Without any specifics, the narrative voice leaves a feeling of utter unpleasantness, a bad taste in the reader's mouth, so to speak, as both guttural and sibilant sounds associated with foreign tongues and snakes grate on the nerves of English speakers. This is immediately contradicted by Fu's graceful, literary diction: "In any event I shall not be privileged to enjoy your advice in the future" (128), a statement of upper-class, even Oxbridge, circumlocution that seals the detectives' fate. In plain English, it says they are to be killed. The roundabout way of announcing their death sentence sharpens Fu's deviousness and duplicity, a connoisseur of high culture thirsty for blood, reminiscent of Hannibal the Cannibal.

As Dr. Fu's henchmen are all brawn and no brains, they hardly speak or even grunt at all, except one "front man" in charge of the opium den. Approached by Nayland Smith and Dr. Petrie under the guise of sailors, the den's manager denies them entry: "Allee lightee [all right] ... Full up—no loom. You come see see" (53). The British expression "full up" is juxtaposed, incongruously, with pidgin transposition of "l" and "r," and the obligatory suffix of the long "e." In such skimpy representation of foreign speech pattern, Rohmer unconsciously deconstructs his own style, the Britishness of "full up" poking out like a white cock, figuratively speaking, out of a yellow coolie's uncouth, uncool high-water pants. This is Anglo-America's bad habit of impersonating, with its own voice squeaking through. From W. Somerset Maugham's maritime parlance in "Mr Townsend no come yet. You go top-side" to Paul Auster's business lingo in "They ask if I want to invest as minority partner," these Freudian slips expose the white lies of fiction. Laughing at these ethnic clowns who babble and stumble, authors and readers partake an inside joke, exchanging a wink or two over their shared heritage of yellowface and Chinglish.

The manager's refusal notwithstanding, Smith and Petrie strong-arm their way into the opium den, greeted by a scene mirroring what Watson witnesses in "The Man with the Twisted Lip":

> Here an extended hand, brown or yellow [not white], there a sketchy, corpse-like face; whilst from all those rose obscene sighings and murmurings in faraway voices—an uncanny, animal chorus. It was like a glimpse of the Inferno seen by some Chinese Dante. But so close to us stood the newcomer that I was able to make out a ghastly parchment face, with small, oblique eyes, and a misshapen head crowned with a coiled pigtail, surmounting a slight, hunched body. (55)

"Brown or yellow" hands are expressly nonwhite; racial markers like "a coiled pigtail" set apart the hellish realm from the Anglo-American self. Yet consistent with the analogy of Shakespeare and Satan for Dr. Fu, the opium den is cast in a Western frame of reference, an "Inferno seen by some Chinese Dante," Rohmer's yellowface Dante, rather. Dr. Petrie soon catches his first chilling glimpse of Dr. Fu: "an archangel of evil [with] ... the most uncanny eyes ... narrow and long, very slightly oblique, and of a brilliant green. But the unique horror lay in a certain filminess" (58). Windows to the soul, Dr. Fu's eyes are half-human, half-animal. This pair of uncanny eyes, "narrow and long, very slightly oblique" inherits as well as sires the stereotype of slant-eyed Orientals, resonating with the opium den manager's eyes a moment ago. In a master stroke of synaesthesia, Rohmer conjoins sight and sound. The accent of "oblique" falls on the second rather than the first syllable, thus emulating the rising slope of the eye. Both pairs of "oblique" Oriental eyes pun on a physical tilt upward and a psychological deviousness downward, a racial marker deprecating the Other's body and mind in one fell swoop.

The names of Dr. Fu's henchmen and their methods of execution fare no better. These names are doubly removed—by means of spelling and pronunciation—from Anglo-America and from the English language. The signifiers all purport to be proper nouns on concrete, specific things, yet they invariably lapse into common nouns without individuality, even into non sequiturs. The so-called "Call of Siva" that has done away with quite a few prominent Western men, for instance, comes across as a puzzle, not to be explicated until much later: "the mark of Káli" by a "*phansigar*—a religious strangler" (146, 148). While strangulation hints at the nature of the crime, the exact offense is clouded by "Káli" and "*phansigar*," foreign words in italics and with diacritics denoting pronunciation, utterly lost to English speakers. The forward slash above "a" in "Káli" eludes the reader. Diacritics dislodge italics further afield spatially and auditorily. Spatially, Rohmer's London is strewn with "a sort of combined *Wekâleh* and place of entertainment" (177), Oriental (pleasure) quarters that captivate outsiders who are held captive by the word and by the world it alludes to. The befuddling word with a caret above "a" gestures toward a black hole that is neither sayable nor definable. For that matter, how does one negotiate the caret and backward slash above Dr. Fu's second-in-command and Dr. Petrie's soul mate "Kâramanèh"? A pivotal conduit between good and evil, the name "Kâramanèh" is at least glossed by Smith as "a slave" (163). This annotation does not so much endow roundness or individuality as flatness or type, setting up Oriental schizophrenia between repulsion against Dr. Fu the male mastermind and attraction to Kâramanèh the mixed-race female serf.

Kâramanèh in fact implores Dr. Petrie to take her away from Dr. Fu, the height of Oriental male fantasy of being irresistible to the fairer sex. To illustrate her devotion to Dr. Petrie, Kâramanèh enumerates modern slavery in London as well as her own saga in foreign words and locales: "the *razzia* [raid], the desert journey, the whips of the drivers, the house of the dealer, the shame. Bah!" (115). Note the fragments and their cumulative effect, closing with her scorn and an exclamation, as if all the pain would vanish in Dr. Petrie's arms. No attempt is made to order the experiences into a statement or complete sentence, leaving it as vignettes that shock, which is one side of the Orient, the half that Dr. Fu personifies, the other being the Orient that pleases. Her suffering accentuates her sensuality under the cloak—the "gossamer silk" which she "flashes" for Dr. Petrie's and, of course, the reader's eye (115).

To embolden Petrie to take Kâramanèh by force in the most sexist, Neanderthal manner, Smith the Oriental erotica guru counsels: "Love in the East … is like the conjurer's mango-tree" (41). A mango is a fruit associated with tropical lushness, juicy and sweet, decidedly messy if peeled and eaten by hand. The dripping juice and stringy fibers intimate a "wet" female sexual organ. A "mango-tree," with the defamiliarizing hyphen in between, has a distinctly Orientalized flavor of the West's own making. The hyphenation evokes the "rose-tree" in the palace courtyard to be touched by the suitor of the princess in *The Thief of Bagdad* (1924). The hyphenation goes back a long way to the fairy tale "The Rose-Tree" collected by Joseph Jacobs in *English Fairy Tales* (1890). The revenge story against the evil stepmother is then transplanted by Douglas Fairbanks to the Middle East as a symbol of romantic love. In other words, the exotic fruit of mango is grafted via a hyphen to English folklore and Hollywood silent film's formulation of the rose-tree for a sniff and a taste of Eastern exotica. Inadvertently yet predictably, Rohmer in 1913 bridges Jacobs and Fairbanks in the long representational relay of off-white characters and their parole.[3]

Gender rests at the heart of Rohmer's appeal in the Dr. Fu series. Western masculinity fears a loss of power encapsulated in Dr. Fu's first victim, a distinguished gentleman Sir Crichton Davey. Sir Crichton lies dead in the customary "evening dress … an old smoking jacket … on the back of the hand was a faint red mark, not unlike the imprint of painted lips" (14). The Western male body is written over and written off by the Orient. The mysterious Zayat Kiss—the kiss of death by the Orient—castrates and in effect decapitates the best of the West. The effeminizing surfaces not only in the fact that Sir Crichton is kissed on the hand *like* a woman, but he is, at first blush, kissed *by* a woman with painted lips, which turns out to be the bite mark of "a great ant" or "a giant centipede" (33). White men regain control in Rohmer through fighting yellow men and through, in a manner of speaking, being fought over by yellow women like Kâramanèh.

Because of her devotion to Dr. Petrie, Kâramanèh is the weakest link in Dr. Fu's arsenal of foreign assassins and methods: bestial savages (dacoit, *phansigar*), animals (marmoset), insects (red ant), and poison (green mist, biological warfare). These agents of death are equipped with primitive tools of bamboo rods, silken cords, and knives. The Oriental art of killing manifests a well-nigh erotic game of death, a strange blending of Freudian eros and thanatos. Props of bamboo and silk are deceivingly fragile and invisible, yet deadly, living up to Dr. Fu's "insidious" reputation. Against the solid mass of Redmoat, once a priory and now inhabited by Parson Dan, one of the targets of assassination, "a narrow ladder of bamboo joints and silken cord hanging by two hooks" enable the assassins to scale the wall (90). Oriental chicanery turns the property of fragility and flexibility in bamboo and silk, ostensibly Asian matériel of war, into means of conquest. It piles on a sense of Oriental treachery when a site with "Roman *castrum*" for fortress or encampment is invaded by "a yellow man" via such flimsy gear (69–70, italics in the original). An ancient military and political installation evolves into a priory, a religious institution. Rohmer illustrates, unintentionally, the two arms of imperialism—military and religion; the sword and the cross— in synch in its defense against the yellow peril, quite an about-face of the nineteenth- and twentieth-century encroachment by the British Empire across the world.

Indeterminacy in naming continues in the (mis)identifying of crimes and criminals. In the wake of a murder, the detective "could have sworn that there was something crawling up behind a party" (143). This policeman-witness testimony in effect forswears itself due to the uncertainty over subhuman crawlers, hidden behind other guests. Rather than physical presence, "a breath of astral incense" announces "the presence of the priests of death" (145). One potential victim Sir Lionel has a pet, "a young puma, or civet-cat, or something," remaining a mystery even when it is identified (101). Attended by a "Chinese body-servant," a manservant further castrated and neutered on account of being Chinese, Sir Lionel is a Western man who has gone native and brought on the calamity. His residence is practically tropical, "damp as a swamp; smells like a jungle" where the "steam smell [is] almost malarious" (97, 98). An Egyptologist, Sir Lionel spews out a string of Arabic names regarding the sarcophagus of Mekara in "the valley of Bibân-el-Molûk," Mekara being the high priest who "contested in magic arts with Moses" (110). However far-flung from Western consciousness and however tongue-twisting to English speakers, all things Oriental are rounded off with a Judeo-Greco-Christian closure. Moses, after all, brings Judaism out of the tyranny of the East, back to the homeland for its next life with the coming of the Messiah, so claim Christians.

Sir Lionel is nearly murdered by the "*green mist*" seeping from the sarcophagus. Good old English words italicized, Rohmer estranges traces of death. Green mist creeps along the floor and kills like one of Dr. Fu's poisonous insects. The inanimate is animated, the color of nature and youth turned deadly. Such green mist foreshadows the fungi poison that drives insane Scotland Yard's Inspector Weymouth, a modern-day nerve agent experimented by Dr. Fu, "the greatest fungologist the world has ever known" (239). Dr. Fu is indeed associated with drugs and narcotics: opium to which he himself is addicted; the drug Hashish, variously called "*Cannabis indica*" or "Indian hemp" (191), which succumbs American inventor Norris West; the biological spores that dispatch police officers and drives mad Inspector Weymouth. Dr. Fu even lays a trap by feigning intoxication, "a figure from the realms of delirium" with "faint smell of opium … upon a divan" (165). Consciousness-altering drugs like opium work in cahoots with mental derangement and the slumber of rationality on an Eastern divan to bring about the entrapment of the West, whereas, in world history, they lead to the demise of the Qing dynasty and beyond. History writ small and turned upside down informs Fu's repeated trick of "an opium sleep," Fu's "hand, which held a little pipe. A sickly perfume assailed my nostrils" (231). Rather than the history of two Opium Wars prosecuted by the British Empire to breach the Qing dynasty's close-door policy, opium is attributed to "the Chinaman" in Limehouse Reach. Instead of the British enslavement of China, Fu enslaves Westerners. Fu feigns an opiate euphoria and triggers the trap door to capture Holmes and his entourage.

In the subsequent herculean struggle with Dr. Fu, Inspector Weymouth sacrifices himself to save Smith and Dr. Petrie. Weymouth's sanity gives way to the delirium caused by Fu's poison, as the Inspector falls into the Thames. Fu's yellow peril never fails to spread through fluids and even air, despite the solidity of London's infrastructures and institutions.[4] The crazed Weymouth is left to wander the banks of the Thames, returning to knock on his home's front door at night. Smith senses it as Weymouth's lifelong routine of homecoming in the wee hours after a long day's work at Scotland Yard. Knocking on the front door of one's own home equates hailing, beckoning oneself: "His [Inspector Weymouth's] trick of knocking upon his own door at half-past two each morning (a sort of dawning of sanity mysteriously linked with old custom) will be a familiar class of symptom to all students of alienation" (271). Structurally, the Weymouth episode can be deemed an extraneous tag-on celebrating the West not leaving behind one of its own, a wounded comrade in the limbo between humanity and madness. Such camaraderie has been consistent even before this structural tag-on. For example, on the doorstep of death in one of the rapid-fire action sequences, Smith pauses to apologize to Petrie, "Sorry, old man ... My fault, I shouldn't have let you come" (172). This amounts to such an incredulous bromance that it resembles a frozen moment of cinematic emoting like the clichéd teardrop in slow-motion amidst quick cuts of gun fights and explosions. However, Weymouth's resurrection at the expense of Dr. Fu's escape is not so much a tale of heroic feats as symptomatic of the West's deep neurosis. Rohmer gestures toward this trade-off: to restore the integrity of the West, it must let go of the East, again and again in the mystery series.

Alienation is the Victorian term for psychiatry: an alienist is a psychiatrist who studies patients with split selves, or aliens within their psyches. The sane and the mad Weymouth epitomize the West and its Orientalized shadow, flipped within the West itself in the name of foreign contamination. "The dawning of sanity" of the diseased West coincides with the imminent rising of the sun from the East. The knocking on the door is a neurotic symptom of repetition compulsion, an involuntary reprise of old habits of individuals and communities. Here, it suggests that the residual of Weymouth's old self comes home, subconsciously accessing his previous life—to no avail. Arguably, however, the delirious Weymouth infected by Fu's poison from "Chinese swamps" (251) symbolizes the West's own paranoia. Paranoia, by definition, is nightmarish repetitions for no cause other than one's own.

Weymouth evinces the divided self of, on the one hand, embodiment of law and order, power and righteousness, and, on the other, haunting fear and guilt over the British Empire's cannibalistic imperialism. Inspector Weymouth is Walter Benjamin's "document of civilization"; madman Weymouth is the verso of "document of barbarism."[5] To echo the Weymouth doppelgangers, Fu is arrested in his disguise as "the celebrated Orientalist" Professor Jenner Monde in a Sherlock Holmes-style "black Inverness coat" (257, 258). The yellow peril Fu assumes the alterity of a white Orientalist in the costume of the quintessential hound of evil, quite a contortion that only underlines the (con)fusion of us and them. Rohmer's inaugural story concludes with the crazed Inspector Weymouth finally restored to sanity by Fu, who nonetheless flees in the conflagration. Fu not only brings about Weymouth's delirium, but Fu *is* the West's delirium, the antithesis of the supposedly rational West. Once Fu effects his escape, Weymouth returns to the fold.

Sax Rohmer continues to tell his Dr. Fu stories for nearly half a century with a slant. This slant puns on the italics that slant from upper right to lower left; on offensive, racist slant against Asians; and on rhetorical and filmic visualization of slant-eyed Orientals. Such deployment of slant exists within the context of Rohmer's stylistic trademarks of hyperboles by means of the proliferation of uppercase letters, exclamation points, and the superlative degree. In effect, Sax Rohmer's use of slanting italics betrays a bipolar syndrome. Nowadays, to italicize in Microsoft Word, the author needs to either select "*I[talic]*" after right clicking the mouse or to highlight the word already typed and select "*I.*" Even in Sax Rohmer's time before the advent of computers, the mechanics of writing would compel Rohmer to either underline in longhand or to backspace on a typewriter and then underscore. Be it a computer, a typewriter, or in handwriting, italics requires a twice over, to go over the already made a second time. Not only in its mechanical formation, which is always a re-formation, but italics also serves a dual function: to emphasize and/or to indicate foreign words. To stress is to elevate the importance, raising the word to a higher plane of visibility and distinction. Foreign words, on the other hand, suggest unfamiliarity, something below the reader's radar, the tip of a submerged world under the reader's cognition. Lifted up or sunken below in relation to the reader's here and now, italicized foreignness uplifts the mind to sky high or plunges it into an abyss or both. A typically smooth reading experience is instantly disrupted by italics, which soar as well as dive from the reader's mental horizon. The eyes tarry a while over italics. The lips move imperceptibly, as if touching and caressing italics. The mind tries to anatomize the syntax, to puzzle out the meaning, and to connect with one's existing frame of reference. Italics invites sensory identification yet denies it by an act of self-splitting into the otherworldly, both up above and down below. Sax Rohmer thus favors italics to titillate and to defamiliarize, to exoticize and to terrorize, hence making Fu-Manchu into transcendent horror, apocalyptic abomination. The inherent fissure within Sax Rohmer's bipolar italics sets the stage for the schizophrenic split of Western sinophobia, the yellow peril that is in our midst but unseen, unpronounceable, un-remembered, unknowable.

Filmic visualization of slant-eyed Fu-Manchus played by Boris Karloff and other yellowface actors stem in part from Rohmer's racist description of Dr. Fu's eyes as "narrow and long, very slightly oblique." Even his dacoit assassins run like slouching backslashes: "more like dreadful animals they looked than human beings, running bent forward, with their faces curiously uptilted" (170). These racial markers are universalized on-screen. Inverse to what George Lipsitz views as the privilege, the boon, of whiteness in remaining the invisible norm, rarely subject to question, slant eyes are the bane of Asianness, so taken for granted that it comes across as the first and last impression, unthinkingly borrowed by filmmakers and acquiesced to by viewers. The mind reads between the lines, so to speak, and fixates on Asianness with a slant, with an age-old bias.

Robert van Gulik's Judge Dee, closing with a bang from Tsui Hark

Van Gulik's text derives from the legend of Magistrate Di Renjie of the Tang dynasty in the seventh century. The title's plural *Celebrated Cases* comes from the fact that Van Gulik formulaically entwines three cases in each mystery in accordance with Chinese detection tradition, "a new literary device that," Van Gulik posits in "Translator's Preface," "has not yet been utilized in our [Western] popular crime literature" (v). Instead of Western linear thinking of "one thing at a time," the Chinese appear to countenance a more looped, cyclical narrative. Whereas the US national motto is "In God We Trust," printed on every currency bill, the Chinese uphold their "One Just Man" in Di Renjie, the incorruptible official memorialized in literature, plays, and oral performances. Along with his "brother-in-justice," the eleventh-century Song dynasty Bao Gong, they form a majority of two against the misuse of power in the long history of authoritarian dynastic China. Van Gulik bases his translation on the Chinese novel, *Wu Zetian sida qi'an (Four Strange Cases of Wu Zetian)*, written in the Ming dynasty of the eighteenth century and featuring Empress Wu Zetian who "usurped" the Tang "bloodline" by establishing her short-lived Zhou dynasty. Van Gulik purportedly translated the novel while repackaging it in the genre of Western detective mysteries, paving the way for his Judge Dee mystery series from 1957 to his death in 1967, currently published by the eminent University of Chicago Press. In "Translator's Preface," Van Gulik decries "misrepresent[ing]" the Chinese as "Super-criminals like Sax Rohmer's Dr. Fu Manchu, or super-detectives like Earl D. Biggers' Charlie Chan." Van Gulik believes his translation allows the Chinese "to have their own say for once in the field" (i). Van Gulik's self-promotion as an antidote against Orientalist stereotypes is challenged by his excising of the last thirty-four of the sixty-four chapters on grounds of an educated guess that the latter half grafts Empress Wu onto a coherent, self-sufficient narrative on Judge Dee investigating three murder cases in the opening thirty chapters.

Van Gulik was a Dutch diplomat, scholar, writer, and a polyglot fluent in multiple languages. Van Gulik found time to write Sinological monographs on a wide variety of subjects that caught his fancy, as he was clearly not subject to academic pressure. These subjects include Chinese lute (*ch'in*); the gibbon (*yuan*), China's most famous primate; and Chinese sexuality and erotica. In addition, he published in 1956 the translation of *T'ang-yin pi-shih* (*Parallel Cases from under the Pear Tree*), a thirteenth-century legal manual. Of course, Van Gulik wrote Judge Dee murder mysteries. He belonged to the rare breed of amateur Sinologists and Orientalists who are gifted in languages but also given to stereotypes and shallow, cursory narratives of the Other.[6]

This westernizing of Judge Dee familiarizes, even endears, the protagonist hailing from afar. However, such drawing close to the West never merges the foreign Orient with the West. Indeed, or in Dee, the white and modern gaze launched from the West is captivated by the strangeness of a magisterial trickster and a divine swordsman. Van Gulik features a judge who doubles, ironically, as a trickster in the prosecution of the law, not to mention having the professional trickster Tao Gan in his employ. Hong Konger Tsui Hark's martial arts films on Detective Dee (2010, 2013) not only borrow from the Western detective tradition, Van Gulik included, but also recast Dee as a God-like swordsman, the hand of divine justice, for global cinema.

Mainland Chinese TV series on Di from 2004 to 2018 have largely restored Empress Wu as a leading character, contrary to Van Gulik's total omission of her. Moreover, these TV series frequently relocated from the original setting of Shandong and the central part of China to the exotic Muslim region in the northwestern Xinjiang province bordering Central Asia. This change of scene can be attributed to two causes. First of all, the Wild West legend befitting the *wuxia* (swordplay) genre had been established by Ang Lee's *Crouching Tiger, Hidden Dragon* (2000) based on Wang Dulu's pentalogy *Hetie Wubu Qu* (*The Crane and the Steel* 1938–1944) set in the Xinjiang region. The remote site magnifies the genre's otherworldly fantasy and martial feats. Secondly, the rise of China around the turn of the century led to Beijing's policy of "stepping out" onto the world stage, which necessitated negotiating with non-Han, non-Chinese cultures that may impinge on Chineseness. To avoid the charge of anachronism, the TV series displace the Western Other onto non-Han ethnic minorities and foreigners in Western China and Central Asia.

In most Chinese TV productions, Magistrate Di does not carry a sword, and his safety depends on the subordinates. To draw a sword is not only beneath the dignity of the high-ranking magistrate but also Di is a *wenguan* (literary official) rather than a *wuguan* (military general). The Chinese Di is statesman-like, a magistrate, a Confucian gentleman (*junzi*). So dignified is he that he would not deign to pick up a sword and fight. Western(ized) Dee in Van Gulik and Tsui Hark, by contrast, is far more martialized and "weaponized," prone to kung fu fighting. Deviating from the Chinese separation of *wenwu* (literary/martial), no different from the division of male and female, yin and yang, Van Gulik militarizes his Judge Dee. Tsui Hark's Detective Dee films further endow him with the brawn of a supreme martial artist, in addition to his investigative brains. Such appeal to English-speaking audiences in Van Gulik's mystery series and in Tsui's global cinema lies in the fact that aesthetic violence through choreographed kung fu sequences constitutes a "universal" language, a cinematic lingua franca that transcends language barriers. Tsui's martial artists speak with their body, whose body language crosses with ease linguistic and even cultural barriers. By the same token, Tsui Hark resorts to computer-generated images (CGI) to visualize technology's antithesis: supernatural powers. Both literary and filmic conceits and strategies aim to imagine their opposite: the military Dee. If Van Gulik Orientalizes Di Renjie, Tsui Hark the Hong Konger is presenting an Orientalist vision that borders on self-Orientalizing.

The Chinese scholar-official and local magistrate is "reassigned" and westernized by Van Gulik as the "judge" in the vein of biblical King Solomon sitting in judgment, or even God in the Last Judgment, the symbol of supreme intelligence and probity. Van Gulik willfully remakes Magistrate Di as Judge Dee with the association of the law. The overarching importance of the law in Van Gulik is wrong-headed: Judge Dee is Van Gulik's, pardon the expression, "flying Dutchman," pirateering, cross-culturally, multiple personages of Sherlock Holmes, King Solomon, Di Renjie, and more. In the Chinese original, Di Renjie is never referred to as a mere judge, let alone demoted, as in Tsui Hark, to a detective. Rather, he is a *xianguan*, or district magistrate. The second word *guan* (官 government official, magistrate) could only mean a "judge" if it is prefixed by *fa* (law, or "law official" for judge). *Qingguan* (clean, incorruptible official) covers far beyond the Western notion of judges restricted to the law of human society. *Qingguan* acts as the absolute authority figure yoking Confucian parents and Freudian imago as well as political and cultural icons. The definition of community is not limited to human interactions and conflicts, but the living and the dead, heaven and hell.

The concept of law in the West entails a collection of abstract principles and concrete precedents governing human conduct. Even when capitalized, the Law represents the law of nature or the divine law. Yet Chinese law is intertwined with *qinglifa*, emotion-reason-law, oftentimes in that order of importance. Human relationships appear to take precedence over laws. Even when applied to the divine, the law is not necessarily tied to a supreme being, a divine god. Instead, the polytheistic, pragmatic Chinese favor the notion of Tao, the Way, a force like the mythical *qi* (breath) that enlivens all, even the dead.

Van Gulik indulges in revising and embellishing throughout the first thirty chapters, culminating in its happy ending: Van Gulik "forges" an imperial edict which promotes Dee to the imperial court, a forgery because it is not in the Chinese original. The full-page edict resides within an oblong box along the four edges of page 221. This box frame characterizes all nine of Van Gulik's illustrations, three of which are "reproductions of Chinese pictures, and six plates drawn by van Gulik after ancient Chinese model" (front matter). This hair-splitting distinction no longer exists in Van Gulik's subsequent Judge Dee series as each illustration bears his initials RHVG, vertically stacked into a square Chinese colophon in the corner à la the Chinese literati painting and calligraphy convention. This imperial edict that concludes *Celebrated Cases* makes, in fact, the tenth illustration, although the Dutch writer-illustrator does not include it in the "list of illustrations" in the front matter. The graphics of borders literalizes a scroll of various fonts Judge Dee "slowly unrolled" to "read aloud in a reverent voice" (220). The edict on the following page hence gives not only voice but a full-page body to the edict: the emperor's words are made flesh, so to speak.

Yet an ironic discrepancy arises. The first nine illustrations are on unnumbered pages inserted into a continuous pagination of the verbal narrative, as though the graphics are a part of, or contained within, the translation. Pictorial representations that stamp the reader's imagination far more than words do are not even counted amongst the consecutive pages of the translation. This unwittingly reveals the airiness, the fakeness of Van Gulik's male, Orientalist fantasies over female nudes on the cover design and on page 62, with such nudes proliferating in his mysteries in subsequent decades. The cover renders in "technicolor" the torture of the naked Mrs. Djou on page 62 in black-and-white, further eroticizing the abhorrent practice of courtroom torture, now turned into a salacious sales pitch on the book cover. The verbal description of the torture on page 62 on the left mentions nothing about stripping Mrs. Djou naked, yet the illustration on the right lays bare her upper body and breasts. At most, at the end of the previous chapter on page 60, Judge Dee orders "forty lashes with the whip" and the constables "bared her back"—no frontal nudity even if one relies solely on Van Gulik's translation. The Chinese text refers to this torture at the opening of chapter 8 as *sishi bianbei* (forty lashes on the back), thus shielding Mrs. Djou's breasts from the public eye, preserving a semblance of female decency. That both the words and the illustration exist on facing pages gives the false impression that they are one and the same, while, in fact, they diverge considerably. Van Gulik appends his male, Orientalist fantasies of female nudity and slant-eyed Orientals onto an allegedly authentic translation. Illustrations in the Chinese style are supposed to be visual facsimiles closer to the subject-matter than the English alphabet. What purports to be the most genuine depiction of China turns out to be the most forged, giving a whole new meaning to the proverbial "white lie." Indeed, the torture of the naked Mrs. Djou is the height of a yellowface character amidst an Orientalist fictitious universe. While the overall milieu emulates chinoiserie, her nakedness is blatantly un-Chinese, childish, and phantasmagoric.

The backdrop of the illustration stands out as a bastardization of Eastern and Western drawings as well. Mrs. Djou lies on her back on the formulaic diamond- or rhombus-shaped floor in accordance with checkerboard floors in Western architecture and visual tradition. This Western floor design does not recede to a vanishing point as the principle of perspective entails. Instead, the chessboard backdrop is laid out on a flattened surface, creating a sense of two-dimensionality of classical Chinese painting. This Western floorboard without depth, or, as contemporary Beijing propaganda has it, "with Chinese characteristics," was to become a familiar setting in many of Van Gulik's illustrations in subsequent Judge Dee mysteries.

Likewise, page 220 on the right shows Judge Dee unrolling a horizontal scroll, which is literally represented on page 221 as a vertical page. That literal depiction may well be figurative. The imperial scroll ought to be unrolled like a side scroll to the left, with the words written from top to bottom and right to left. This classical Chinese side scroll is turned ninety degrees into a vertical scroll, as it were, with modern English going from left to right. The imperial edict even contains a typo: "meretorious" (221). Is Van Gulik's "creative" translation a merit or a demerit in Sino-Anglo relationships?

Major rewriting takes place in the expurgation of the last thirty-four chapters of *Four Strange Cases of Wu Zetian*, in the forging of the imperial edict, and in characterization. A case in point: Di is made to recruit his seconds Ma Joong and Chiao Tai, highwaymen from the Green Woods, in a progressively martialized manner. In the Chinese original, Di simply tells the highwaymen waylaying him to desist and lectures them roundly. His words and courage awe them so much that they faithfully serve him henceforth. In Mainland Chinese TV, as a matter of principle, Di does the talking and his second in command does the fighting. Van Gulik's "translation" of the encounter with the highwaymen verges on a gratuitous fight: "the passes they [Ma Joong and Chiao Tai] made at him showed him convincingly that they were well versed in the arts of fencing and boxing ... Thus Judge Dee, not deigning to draw his sword, just ordered them sternly to desist" (9). Any discerning reader would call Van Gulik's bluff since "fencing and boxing" are terms for Western martial arts, now transposed onto Chinese fighters. This scene grows into a full-fledged fight in words and in illustration in one of Van Gulik's mysteries, *The Chinese Gold Murder* (1959): the highwayman, who turns out to be Ma Joong, "attacked with a quick thrust at the magistrate's breast. He easily parried it, then followed up with a few swift feints that made the ruffian fall back with a gasp. The man now attacked with greater caution, and the sword duel began in earnest" (10). Tsui Hark's global cinema further elevates Dee into a kung fu master by way of special effects and CGI. Classical Chinese mythology of *qi* that enables swordsmen to fly and leap over rooftops is the result of technological sleight of hand.

Even the debut of Judge Dee's support staff is reshuffled. Van Gulik moves Sgt. Hoong first for he is closest to Dee, followed by the two martial artists Ma Joong and Chiao Tai, concluding with the one-time swindler Tao Gan, as if in descending order of importance to Dee himself, from his valet to his instruments of investigation. Van Gulik embellishes these characters substantially, intending to launch his own mystery series based on them (8–9). In the Chinese original, the order of appearance for Dee's assistants in the first chapter is Chiao Tai, Ma Joong, Sgt. Hoong, and Tao Gan.

Chinese proclivity for balance and harmony extends to detection and justice in the Western symbol of the scales of justice. The living and the dead are balanced as Di or Bao Gong traverse the opposing realms. The dead brings injustice and crimes to the attention of the righteous judges. Van Gulik's Dee presides over all cases, merging in one person the role of the investigator, the father figure, and the manifestation of imperial authority. In his pursuit of justice, Dee has no qualms in resorting to unorthodox, potentially unjustifiable, means, such as deception and disguise. For instance, made up as an herbal medicine doctor, Dee uncovers a case involving three women: the stupid mother-in-law, the evil adulteress-murderess Mrs. Djou, and her girl abruptly gone dumb after the suspicious death of her father Bee Hsun. Bee Hsun turns out to have been murdered by his spouse Mrs. Djou. Their daughter had witnessed her liaison with the lover and had been silenced through a dumbness-inducing drug (33).

The masculinist tradition rears its ugly head in the unflattering representation of women. Only the righteous male embodied by Judge Dee can bring justice to the innocent girl and to overwrite the grandmother's stupidity akin to blindness. As for Mrs. Djou, her ingenious camouflage of the crime through a nail driven into the top of Bee Hsun's head—the method of murder copied from a classical Chinese text—is finally exposed when Judge Dee puts on a "masque" from hell, the horror of which is so unbearable that Mrs. Djou finally confesses. Remaining obdurate despite torture, Mrs. Djou ultimately cracks when she is led to believe that she is on trial in hell after death. Her confession to the method of murder closes the case. Dee later pretends to be a fellow silk merchant from Peking to investigate the twin murders of the first case (100). Repeatedly, Judge Dee behaves like a trickster in folklore in the prosecution of the law. Mrs. Djou also relies on the trapdoor, tunnel, and multiple deceptions for her liaison with her lover Hsu (176). To outwit a trickster like Mrs. Djou or the inveterate thug Shao, Dee relies on treachery and falsehood.

To all intents and purposes, the Chinese legal process in Van Gulik is, not to mince words, extra-judicial, even supernatural. The grievance is brought to Dee's attention by a ghost by way of air currents, an ephemeral and random natural phenomenon which comes across as preordained: "Suddenly the light of the sun darkened, and a violent gust of wind blew over the graveyard, making sand and stones whirl in the air for more than a fathom. Then there appeared a dark shape of indistinct outline, floating towards them in midair" (45). If a ghost seeks justice, then the supernatural is taken for granted, consistent with the Chinese ideology of a yin-yang, dead-living, symbiosis. This acceptance of the otherworldly leads to the sanctioning of courtroom torture for confession, specifically of Mrs. Djou (61–62, 197); of Shao (136–138); and of Hsu (194–195). The democratic ideal of individual rights on one's innocence until proven guilty is upended in ancient China's authoritarian and centralized control. The criminal is guilty until proven innocent. Torture of the body is permitted to elicit confession. Yet unwarranted torture and official abuse of power bear consequences. Dee risks losing his "black cap" (symbol of his official status) and even suffering the same torture (60). After the unsuccessful exhumation of Bee Hsun's body, Judge Dee reports to "the higher authorities" of his own "crime of desecrating a grave, and recommended himself for appropriate punishment" (79).

The fact that Bee Hsun's exhumed corpse closes its eyes upon Dee's promise of justice is not evidence enough. The fact that her accomplice Hsu has already confessed under torture is not enough (197). Mrs. Djou has to confess to close the case. When even physical torture fails, Dee has no other recourse than psych-op and wins. The confession routinely concludes with the criminal signing and imprinting the document with his or her thumb. This final act of signing in the Chinese script and in the thumbprint legitimizes the key step of confession. This leads to execution, or the authority's final writing on the body of the offending parties (213). The heads severed from the bodies are marked on the forehead by Dee with a vermilion brush before being displayed on the city wall for three days (216–217). State violence is doubly sanctioned, "signed off," by the criminals affixing their thumbprints to the confessions and by Dee dotting the decapitated head. The marks left by the thumb or the brush are the periods, the full stops, to conclude the protracted legal process of evidence, torture, confession, and execution.

Confession is out of the question, however, in the last case, let alone providing a thumbprint, as the culprit is a snake. Instead, pieces of evidence of material objects are gathered: tainted water from the red adder's ashes; the dead dog poisoned by the tainted water; and the teapot. In fact, even confessions with thumbprints can be categorized as evidential material objects. While the phrase "This he [Judge Dee] sealed" is indeed used with respect to the evidence of "the tainted water" as well as "the dead dog and the teapot" in the original, the notion of courtroom or "tribunal" exhibits is Van Gulik's addition to his "creative" translation in hopes of an alignment with the Western legal system and the detective genre (170). The original simply says that the poisoned dog is collected to prevent people from eating it by mistake. Di's concern is the health and safety of the community; Dee's the collection of evidence in a murder inquiry. To that purpose, the stray dog is given the poison in the first place to prove Judge Dee's theory.

Whereas naturalistic events are accepted in a court of law, supernatural ones are not. The supernatural proof of Bee Hsun's corpse closing its eyes does not count as forensic clues. Even the coroner's autopsy yields no evidence of foul play. The coroner reads the corpse, or the corpus of the murderer's handwritings, in a manner of speaking. Metonymically, this textual, corporeal reading mirrors Van Gulik's corpus of Judge Dee mysteries. The Dutchman exhumes and cuts open the corpse of age-old Orientalism in the name of pitting his good, "positive" Oriental Dee against the bad, negative Oriental of Fu-Manchu.

It is true that the element of surprise and suspense in Western detection novels is utterly deemphasized in Chinese detection. "Whodunit" is no longer the page-turner as the couplets of chapter titles summarize in advance, giving away the plot. Villains are identified as such in their debut in the narrative. Characterization is done according to types or roles in the tradition of Beijing Opera's *sheng dan jing chou* (young man, young woman, warrior, and clown). Chinese detection is less a mystery than a reconfirmation of the existing system. Given the literary convention of types over individuals, the Chinese novel is not exactly an abstract play of crime and punishment. On the contrary, it countenances unparalleled insights into human psychology. Dee commands that Mrs. Djou offer a prayer in front of her husband's tomb before exhumation to observe her reaction (70). Her defiance and lack of grief further confirm her guilt. Fearing reprisal if Mrs. Djou is tortured to death before a confession is extracted, Dee's subordinates even sabotage Dee's instruction, feigning to tighten the screws on Mrs. Djou's hands while loosening them (61, 161), one of many touches of the little people's mental calculation throughout the novel.

As if paving the way for Tsui Hark's millennial martialization of Dee, Van Gulik faithfully translates the Chinese novel's kung fu sequences, whereby any action is split, fissured. For example, Ma Joong fights a suspect Djao with each of their kung fu moves identified soon after. Djao "sprang towards Ma," "using the stance called 'a tiger clawing at a sheep.' But Ma Joong dodges the blow by withdrawing one step to the left, a trick called 'enticing the tiger out of his forest'" (104). The name of the move comes on the heels of the physical move just described in words. Each kung fu step is a sign split into the signifier (the name of the move) and the signified (the move itself).[7] Truth be told, each move is a receding sign, lamely suggested in words such as "sprang towards," or "withdrawing one step to the left." Readers must imagine the moves; the imagination is somehow sanctioned when it comes with the imprimatur of a proper name. This proper noun can be traced back to the Confucian insistence of *biye zhengminghu* (必也正名乎 "One must seek the proper name"). Any kung fu sequence, assumed to be an integral whole of action, masks myriad holes, all folded into a seamless reading experience. Splitting is of course inherent in the detective genre. The clues (signifiers) of the crime are put to use in the hunt for their signified (murderer). The signifiers are often written on the body of the murdered and the site of the crime scene, while the detectives, with the help of forensics, read the writing and pursue the "writer."

As the mid-twentieth-century Judge Dee penned by a Dutchman evolves into millennial Hong Kong martial arts films by Tsui Hark, China as a trope turns into quite a tease to pique the interest of global cinema. China as a literary and filmic tease has real teeth, so to speak, capable of taking a bite out of the market. China as tease in Tsui Hark's swordplay film *Young Detective Dee and Rise of the Sea Dragon* (2013) is done through the conceit of Chinese tea and Chinese script. In Van Gulik's *Celebrated Cases of Judge Dee* (1949), on the other hand, China as tease also relies on the twin tropes of tea and written character, except with a far more elaborate scheme on the latter. After all, Van Gulik is supposedly translating an eighteenth-century Chinese text, which thrives on wordplay, pun, poetic allusion, and intellectual riddling integral to Chinese literati culture.

Chinese tease puns on, of course, Chinese teas, a shared motif in Van Gulik and Tsui Hark. Chinese tea is a national drink that stimulates and invigorates, as does coffee in the West. Figuratively, Chinese tease comprises cultural characteristics and symbols that mystify and titillate. Textually, Van Gulik and Tsui deploy teas as the tease in their respective plots. While young Detective Dee is a martial arts master, leaning toward *wu* or military, he operates with a great deal of brains or *wen* (literary, mental strategizing). This comes through at the moment when Dee puzzles out, with some outside help, that Sparrow (or Magpie) Tongue (雀舌 *queshe*) Tea is laced with *gu* (venom, parasite) by Dongdaoren (erroneously subtitled as Dondoers), or Eastern Islanders speaking Japanese, a heavy-handed swipe against China's neighbor to the East. These foreign-looking and foreign-sounding villains poison the Tang court with the tribute of, as the subtitles translate it, "Bird's Tongue" Tea. Such tea originates from China's southwestern border province of Guizhou. In this one Hitchcockian MacGuffin-style trope, Tsui fuses at least three alienating non-Han, non-Chinese images—from the east and the southwest, both layered over by the Muslim culture from the northwest. The Han majority's xenophobia over racial others is compounded by Anthropocene abhorrence over insects, pests—not only bugs but also bees that Eastern Islanders deploy as a secret weapon. *Gu* (蠱) is written with three, suggesting multiplicity in Chinese, *chong* (虫 bug), stacked on top of a *min* (皿 bowl or utensil in general). Visually and conceptually, nonhuman insects are primed for attack in a poisoned cup, in coordination with their master, the subhuman racial other, ranged along China's borders.

Spatially, Japanese-speaking Eastern Islanders from the east of China have infiltrated the Tang capital. In computer-generated aerial shots, the capital is lined with rows of traditional Chinese architecture of upturned tile roof ridges and eaves. Yet one particular computer-generated aerial tracking shot captures what appear to be Islamic quarters of mosques, domes, and minarets—Eastern Islanders' hideouts—soaring above and amidst Chinese architecture (Figure 4.1). These Islamic buildings are typical of the northwestern, Uighur-majority corner of Xinjiang, China. Not only spatial invasions from the east and the northwest are afoot, but Eastern Islanders have breached the body of Tang royalties and their very bodies, from the emperor to boy eunuchs, with teas from the southwestern frontier of China. China is alleged to be under siege from all sides. Not to be outdone, *Detective Dee* (Tsui Hark 2010) features the villainous one-armed Shatou aided by his Central Asian-looking, dark-skinned lieutenant, a consummate kung fu master.

The heating properties of Bird's Tongue Tea is said to initially invigorate the victims, yet it ultimately leads to delirium and bestiality. To combat its heating and feverish effect, young Detective Dee prescribes a cooling antidote of virgin boys' (eunuchs') urine, surely a comic counterpoint to dizzying fights and mysterious assassins wearing Noh drama masks of demons. This comic relief befits the principle of harmony and balance inherent in the Chinese way of thinking, including herbal medicine.

FIGURE 4.1 *Islamic quarters of mosques, domes, and minarets in the Tang capital from Tsui Hark's* Young Detective Dee.

The "index patient" or "patient zero" of the pandemic afflicted by Dongdaoren is a Mr. Yuan, the maker and distributor of Bird's Tongue Tea in the capital. The poison transforms Yuan into a monstrosity, who manages to leave behind some nonsensical doodles on his beloved's silk scarf. Dee in his infinite wisdom is able to piece together from the scribbling the Chinese scripts of Bird's Tongue (雀舌, see Figure 4.2). This close-up of the two ideograms is repeated when Dee arranges slices of ginger on the fish plate to alert the Investigative Bureau (translated as "the Supreme Court") Chief (Figure 4.3). The Chief probes with his chopsticks and finds a note rolled up in the fish belly, requesting a secret rendezvous. Dee resorts to this covert measure for fear of the Dongdao mole inside the Bureau itself. Beyond the indecipherable Chinese ideograms to the global audience, there is another hidden message. This scene alludes to the Spring Autumn era (770–476 BCE) legend of *yuc(h)angjian* (魚藏劍 or 魚腸劍 fish secreting/intestinal sword). Legend has it that an assassin brings an offering of a fish dish to the king, with a dagger hidden inside the fish intestine. *Cang* or *chang* pun on the near-homonyms of hiding and intestine.

These two rounds of secret transmission, first in doodles from the monster Yuan to Dee, followed by ginger slices from Dee to the Chief, are readily intelligible to Chinese. The form of the two Chinese characters and the content of "Bird's Tongue" that the form signifies are one. The script is the tea and vice versa. To the non-Chinese-speaking global audience, however, the two close-ups of "雀舌" come across as tantalizing non sequiturs, a perplexing tease, to be enlightened by the subtitles of Bird's Tongue. They resemble silent films' intertitles more than foreign films' subtitles, though, since actors never read out loud Bird's Tongue as *queshe*. Rather, the ideograms flow

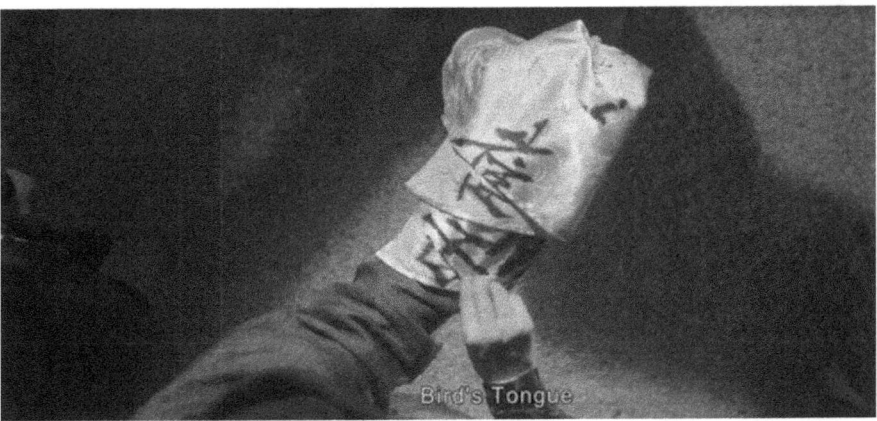

FIGURE 4.2 *Young Detective Dee piecing together the Chinese scripts of Bird's Tongue.*

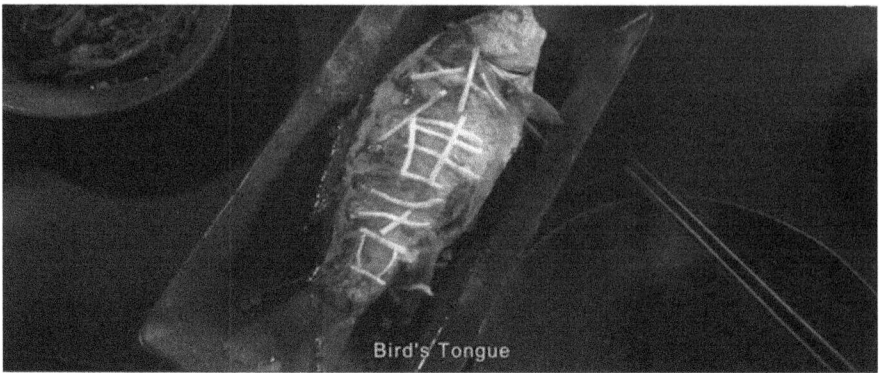

FIGURE 4.3 *Slices of ginger on a fish to warn against Bird's Tongue Tea.*

soundlessly like Chinese fluids from Yuan's ink brush and Dee's fish with ginger garnish into the Chinese viewer's eyes. Intuiting the cause of evil in the tea, yet another Chinese fluid, is a filmic tease beyond dialogue that leads to surprise and joy, emulating the quintessential Zen enlightenment beyond words from the master to the disciple. The most famous case is of course the Buddha passing the flower in his hand to the Chosen, Mahakasyapa, the only disciple who smiles back at the Buddha, a mirroring despite or because of the Buddha's puzzling sermon of a long, silent smile at the flower. This mirroring epitomizes the heart of secret transmission without words. What comes with teeth or great affective power to the Chinese who recognize and intuit *queshe* is utterly toothless, ineffectual to the non-Chinese. The irony remains, however, that the Buddha's story touting no-word has to be told in words.

Although predating Tsui Hark by over two centuries, the Chinese text from which Van Gulik draws his "creative" translation plays with teas and scripts as well. The unreadable, unknowable *queshe* is a tantalizing plot device, which resonates with the unnameable in Van Gulik involving the twin tropes. With two of his three cases pending, two murders unsolved, one exhumation gone terribly awry, the widow of the exhumed accusing the judge of incompetence and corruption, and yet another "murder" filed at the court, a desperate Judge Dee seeks divine guidance at a temple. Praying through the night, Dee dozes off to find "an old gentleman with a flowing white beard," the symbol of elderly wisdom and even celestial being, inviting him to the teahouse to sip "the fragrant brew, listen for a while to the talk of the people there." Conceivably, this old gentleman is either an eighteenth-century spiritual guide sent from the divine or a twentieth-century epiphany welling up from Dee's subconsciousness à la Freud's theory. This either-or may well be both-and since the brew imbibed is to couple with the talk of the town. The West's individual psychology melds with China's communal public opinions. What is within joins hands with what is without to induce dream visions of poems on the teahouse wall. These poems contain poetic allusions, some more opaque than others, which hold the key to the murderers' surnames and identities. The two allusions—"the Child" for the historical figure of "Hsu" and "Yao Foo" whose surname is "Shao"—pinpoint the names of the criminals in two of the three cases (88). Note that both surnames of Hsu and Shao are not in the poem; they are allusions to be inferred or intuited. These allusions are the presence that is absent—absent presence, or present absence.

Taking tea leads to biochemical and mental alterations, parallel to the etherealization from the supplicant's temple incense to smoke and ashes, and from Dee's reality of a temple to his morphing dreamscapes of the teahouse, the theater, and "a lonely plot of land." The riddle of a poem on the teahouse wall in chapter 11 is first enacted, performed on stage, concluding with the clue of "a red adder" for the third and last of Dee's celebrated cases (84), yet to be reported to Dee in chapter 19 and yet to materialize in the narrative. So the dream vision not only flashes back to the murders in the past but also flashes forward to what is to come. The venomous snake in his dream subsequently leaves its writing, as it were, in Judge Dee's tea: "While he was slowly raising the cup to his lips, Judge Dee noticed some particles of white dust floating on the surface" (158–159). Upon closer interrogation of the offending servant who brings him "this dirty tea" (159), Dee "jumps" to the conclusion of a snake on the roof beam disturbed by the steam of boiling water, opening its maws and dripping its venom into the water, hence poisoning the third victim, a bride. Whereas the smoke of an incense transubstantiates hope up to heaven, the vapor brings down a curse on the innocent. Random chance turns into fate, as if predetermined by karma. Originally, the bride's father-in-law suspects a guest on grounds of having been "motivated by Heaven knows what old grudge" (144). This charge almost justifies the death by way of karmic debt and divine retribution. All initiated by tea, subsequent metamorphoses unfold in terms of the puzzling writing on the wall or powder from the roof beam in his teacup for Judge Dee to parse. Brush strokes and the snake's flaky footprints become the act or cause to effect changes. Put another way, scripts from an ink brush or from a brush of the tail are magical and prophetic in enlightening past crimes and foreshadowing future actions.

In addition to Dee the wise man who pieces together answers to the conundrums, an elderly "greybeard" constable is equally responsible in shedding light on the first case of murders of two silk merchants. "The man in Szuchuan Province" in the fourth line of the poem on the wall in the dream is misconstrued by Dee as a perpetrator from that province, until a constable advanced in years and "half deaf" muses "pulling at his beard" on the Turn-up Pass founded by someone from Szechuan (Sichuan). The original's wordplay on *Sichuanzhai* (四川寨 or Sichuan Stronghold) and *Sichuancai* (四川菜 or Sichuan vegetable) hinges on the dialectical variants which turn the retroflex of *zhai* in Mandarin into a flat-tongued plosive *cai*, a most common "error" for non-Beijingers and southern Chinese speakers unaccustomed to retroflexes. Northerners deem such southern pronunciation as substandard, stiff-tongued, and comical. Even if the greybeard is a northern dialect speaker well-versed in retroflex sounds, the fact that he is hard of hearing may have led to a conflation of the two sounds. A traditional *chou* (clown) character, the greybeard unwittingly cracks open a cold case, not to mention his pivotal contributions to the investigation based on his in-depth understanding of bureaucracy, particularly the corrupt kind that has jurisdiction over the Sichuan Stronghold. The wordplay, dismissed as too difficult for non-Chinese speakers to grapple by Van Gulik, is simplified to the place and the vegetable: "Turnip Pass" versus "Turn-up Pass." Van Gulik forgoes not only the playfulness of the original but also the connotation of the treacherous *zhai*, which means a stronghold or bandits' lair.

The West's sinophobia crystalizes in Dr. Fu-Manchu by Sax Rohmer around the turn of the last century. Dr. Fu infects and murders Western men with his army of insects, snakes, assassins, opium, and poisonous viruses in *The Insidious Dr. Fu-Manchu*, so much so that a viral China, or China as the virus, courses through the Thames, the artery of the British Empire. Colonialist exploitation of peoples of color thus justifies itself in the name of self-defense against the viral China. In our new millennium, an ascending China turns the tables while taking a page out of the English playbook, including Van Gulik's English-language Orientalist fantasy. China's expansion comes across as a reaction against foreign incursions. Hong Kong filmmaker Tsui Hark in his Detective Dee films of the twenty-first century pits the quintessential, righteous Chinese official Di Renjie against foreign, non-Han invaders and symbols contaminating China's body politic. While both Rohmer and Tsui deploy the trope of a viral China, the English detectives battle against the construct of the yellow peril. By contrast, the Hong Konger invents China's own Orient in non-Han, darker-complexioned, and Islamic-inflected Eastern Islanders and Muslims from the Silk Road, along with their venomous fire beetles, parasites, and bees, infiltrating and corroding China proper. The West's xenophobia over the "yellow" race mirrors China's own over, alas, the "off-yellow" race.

5

Ghost in the White Shell

The 1990s Japanese manga *Ghost in the Shell* has been adapted as two anime in 1995 and 2004 by Mamoru Oshii, and as the 2017 live action sci-fi film by Rupert Sanders starring Scarlett Johansson. Despite the three-decade-long evolution, the plot continues to revolve around the Haraway-esque cyborg Major Motoko Kusanagi at the heart of a futuristic posthuman struggle between the human soul ("ghost") imprisoned yet also enabled by a robotic body ("shell") as well as by the entire mechanical, technological world.[1] Although the soul appears to soar above the body, the title opts for "ghost," an intangible, elusive revenant, to undercut any thought of transcendence. Without even an article "the" to make a common, even a proper, noun out of the abstraction of haunting, ghost invokes a Freudian melancholia over loss, over an empty shell. Contrary to the color-blind postmodernist approach encouraged by decades of retelling on both sides of the Pacific, I contend that race—or its suppression under the default of universal whiteness—is the pivot to move this sci-fi fallacy. With whiteness as the Unmoved Mover, the off-white or yellow-ish ghost is actually entombed in the white shell, given Oshii's Caucasian-looking Motoko with blue-gray eyes and her partner Batou's Schwarzenegger physique. Oshii's Occidentalism of whiteface protagonists is coupled with exotic Orientalism. Specifically, Oshii the Orientalist is othering the other Orient—China and Korea—in the Chinatown parade and the Korean-sounding hacker Kim in *Ghost in the Shell 2*. In the street lingo of *Blade Runner* (1982), Oshii has performed "skin-jobs" to materialize white and non-Japanese "replicants." Despite the backlash of #OscarsSoWhite, including Johansson's role as Major Mira Killian, aka, Motoko, whitewashing has occurred long ago with the soft porn over fair-complexioned, Caucasian-looking objects of desire in Japanese manga and anime. Johansson is but the wish fulfillment of the East's wet dream, rudely interrupted like coitus interruptus by the West's political correctness.

Explicit eroticism catering to male fantasy has already reared its turtle head (*guitou* in Chinese, the glans or head of the penis) in Masamure Shirow's 1989 manga *Ghost in the Shell*. Shirow's manga cover design opens with a scantily-clad voluptuous female nude, presumably the Major, with hypodermic wiring jutting out of her "exoskeletal" skin and plugged into machines. The nude has a pubescent girlish face, as do all of Shirow's female characters, except witches and crones. The cover's high tech cyborg soon finds herself kneeling in a Buddhist temple receiving commands from old men, mostly bald-pated monks. Techno-Orientalism, one identified by David S. Roh and colleagues in their eponymous collection as a cultural force since the 1960s, is hereby practiced by Shirow the Oriental. "Hypo- or hypertechnology" are wedded in Shirow's opening in terms of what Roh and others describe as a technologically advanced yet intellectually primitive union (2). The latter leans toward a traditional, nativist, even instinctual belief system like Buddhism. Shirow's techno-Orientalist lead is followed by Oshii's anime, where a female choral chant, semi-Buddhist, semi-electronic, so shrill and nasal as to be in falsetto, accompanied by temple bells, constitutes the theme music, creating an aura of time-honored religiosity over an otherwise futuristic fantasy.

Roh and his co-editors trace techno-Orientalism to Sax Rohmer's Dr. Fu-Manchu since the 1910s, "one of the earliest and most potent instances of techno-Orientalism expression ... at once brilliant and technologically challenged," embodying the "premodern-hypermodern dynamic" (1). The co-editors argue that "Whereas Orientalism ... arrests Asia in traditional, and often premodern imagery, techno-Orientalism presents a broader, dynamic, and often contradictory spectrum of images, constructed by the East and West alike, of an 'Orient' undergoing rapid economic and cultural transformations" (3). In particular, they pinpoint the florescence of techno-Orientalism in the 1960s:

> Orientalism in SF [speculative fiction] during the pre-cyberpunk era may have suffered critical neglect because of the perception that the "yellow peril" has been kept in check by the mechanisms of immigration and exclusion acts that were in place for much of the midcentury. It took the repeal of the immigration acts in 1965, coupled with the entrance of Japanese capital and imports into the U.S. economy in the late seventies, to precipitate a renewed wariness toward all things Asian. (6)

An inherent schism of old and new, exotic and evil, lies within the conceptualization of techno-Orientalism. This tendency to halve the Other, to mark it as less than a coherent whole such as the Self, is symptomatic of Freudian transference. The Self projects fear and paranoia onto the Other, which is a subconscious mirror of one's own neurosis. Shirow's Japanese title with a smattering of Chinese and English reflects a postmodernist

Japan's schizophrenia. *Kōkaku Kidōtai Gōsuto In Za Sheru*, literally *Mobile Armored Riot Police: Ghost in the Shell* (攻殻機動隊: Ghost in the Shell), contains the first two Chinese-sounding words and the last four that are transliteration of English. The first word *Kōkaku* consists of *ko* (attack or *gong* in Chinese) and *kaku* (shell). *Kidōtai* for riot police transliterates the Chinese words for Mobile team, as do the last three words of "in the shell" in English. As such, the Japaneseness of the title is encrusted inside the double-layered shells in Chinese and English; the Japanese Self is supposedly secreted in this shell game of three.

Better half

Whereas Shirow's, Oshii's, and even Sanders's techno-Orientalism share the schizophrenic trope, they comprise but part of the millennial complex over exponential technological gain and deepening melancholic loss, which Eric G. Wilson's dubs *The Melancholy Android* (2006).[2] This complex is best described as the "Better Half" syndrome, where cyborgs, fembots, and aspergirls in a millennial wave of fiction and film set out in search of human feeling, besides serial killers. Global popular culture has indeed witnessed the rise of heroines in the image of half-human, half-alien. The exotic alienness originates from the robotic nonhuman and/or the racial/neural non-self, empowering heroines with superhuman capabilities. The awe inspired by such heroines renders them as both objects of desire beyond reach and as fetishized playthings to consummate desires, embodied by fembots verging on sexbots or even sexpots. This paradox veils the male gaze's answer to our feminist ethos, while retaining its will to power over matters of gender. Given that we have consistently created Gods in our varying images—almighty yet vulnerable, these godlike female detectives and hounds are endowed, internally, with the force of ratiocination like the archetype Sherlock Holmes, yet something alien stirs in them, as does cocaine from Holmes's "morocco case" and his last prophecy of "an east wind coming, Watson."[3] This something alien provides the spark of genius. Despite having effected phallic penetration via hacking, bullets, and arrows, these heroines remain, externally, as curvaceous and sexy as any iconic bombshell, perhaps even more so for their muscular athleticism. Truth be told, even these paragons of "girl power" continue to be penetrated: anally raped (*The Girl with the Dragon Tattoo*) or a prosthesis ripped apart (*Ghost in the Shell*).

In addition to fembots, another type of half-human aliens also plays the role of humanity's "better half," as it were. The affective turn amongst detectives turns to female affectlessness, specifically, high-functioning obsessive compulsive Asperger Syndrome detectives, who all fail in social interactions, principally in matters of the heart, like puerile teens. Whereas these "aspergirls" are certainly not cyborg cops, their alienating words and deeds may well be from outer space, often the source of comic relief in unrelenting crime sprees with multiple corpses. Manifesting scarcely any of the robotic half of science fiction's cyborgs, aspergirls continue to be halved to the extent that their lower body with sexual needs seems truncated from their upper body of thinking and detective work, evidenced in the "split" protagonist Saga Noren in the Swedish-Danish production of *The Bridge.* Collectively, these cyborg cops and aspergirls are in search of emotions and memories of being human, in addition to tracking serial killers, of course. If criminals betrayed humanity's repressed worse half, these heroines enact the better angels of our nature. If angels were melancholic, it points to ourselves who have lost the very thing that makes us human.

Aspergirls in the detective genre are led by Lisbeth Salander with her vaguely Eastern dragon tattoo and her conspicuous machinic affinity in *The Millennium Trilogy* as well as Saga the "broken bridge." In sci-fi, cyborg cops include Major Motoko Kusanagi from the anime *Ghost in the Shell* and the Hollywood remake, the fembots in *Ex Machina*, performance-enhanced Alice in *Resident Evil*, vampiric Selene in *Underworld*, and even Katniss in *The Hunger Games*. Audiences project their longings onto the imagined better half of humanity. Cyborgs, fembots, and aspergirls lead our quest for human feeling and memory in a world increasingly atomized and disconnected, even as technology claims to bring us together. Our better half saves us from the monstrosities of serial killers with their weapons of mass destruction, be it firearm, explosive, surveillance and mind control, computer virus, or infectious virus. This argument turns away from the Nordic twin aspergirls, Lisbeth and Saga, to focus on the twin Occidentalist/Orientalist cyborg Majors. Ultimately, it is far better to be half than whole, far better to be mixed than pure.

Oshii

While retaining Shirow's male fantasy, Oshii mellows it somewhat, sprinkling the anime with philosophical ruminations over the human-machine divide in prolonged, still shots of the protagonists. Oshii further rids his anime of the graphic artist's voyeuristic addiction to soft porn mise-en-scène capturing female genitalia framed by mini-skirts or covered in panties in low-angle shots. Yet Oshii's opening credits testify to the unabashedly phallocentric mindset: as the predominantly male production crew's names roll, accompanied by the female choral chant, the Major's nude body is being formed from a vat of viscous liquid reminiscent of the womb's amniotic fluid. The Major is born out of a male crew's fantasy for other males, perverting human birth from the female inner sea. Even when the Major's nemesis, the Puppet Master, proclaims that "I was a life-form born in the sea of information," he does so in a thunderous male voice, which usurps gynecological prerogatives.

Typical of East Asian lyrical style with a distinct predilection for melodramatic atmospherics over plot, Oshii loosely, even messily, spins a yarn around a government espionage artificial intelligence program, Project 2501, which achieves sentience on its own and has gone rogue. Nicknamed the Puppet Master yet without a cybernetic body, it downloads itself into a blonde sexaroid to infiltrate the Major's anti-terrorism Section 9 in hopes of uniting with her, a union of mind and body to sire their seed in perpetuity on- and off-line. In Section 9, Major Motoko partners with Batou, whose cybernetic body parts include his goggled eyes and robotic bulk. Motoko and Batou come closest to a conventional romantic couple, yet their confiding in each other evinces more melancholic loss than amorous sharing. After her deep dive, a flirting with death given her heavy metallic torso and limbs, the Major shares her self-doubt as a human-robot interface. Cinematically, the split intensifies as the Major on the boat, soaking wet, recedes into the cityscape, while the skyscrapers grow over her shoulders. This optical illusion yokes the Major in the foreground getting smaller with the buildings in the background getting larger, when both should increase or decrease together on the screen. The eerie visual spectacle, a split screen in effect, resonates with the heard yet never spoken dialogue, which may as well be the voice-over since the two engage in the conversation through telepathic mind communication without moving their lips, not even opening their mouths. The dialogue-cum-voice-over is punctuated by temple and church bells, elevating it to a near-transcendent tenor. Her existential reverie is vehemently rejected by Batou, as if he were in denial of their cyborg identity. However, Section 9 comprises the apparently human Chief Aramaki and the junior team member Togusa, who shuns all things cybernetic. Like its most valuable asset, the Major, Section 9 balances itself between the human ghost and the machinic shell. The intangible core is the human touch that animates the shell and wins over the global audience's sympathy.

In her debut atop the skyscraper prior to the first of her multiple dives, both physical and through the internet, both actual and virtual, the Major quips that the disruptive static on her mind-com with Batou stems from "that time of the month."[4] She alludes, ironically, to the menstrual period, which a female cyborg does not countenance, nor its implication of childbirth. The self-mocking tone resembles black humor over her fake female body. The veiled sense of bereavement, nonetheless, serves to accentuate her next move: disrobing for the dive down the building to disrupt a crime; what she does not have, namely, menstruation, underscores what she does have, namely, musculature and, pardon the expression, boobs, which are thrust out for maximum effect. Her loss of monthly bleeding contrasts with her idealized, perfectly toned figure flashed for the male gaze, within a series of close-ups of her feet, thighs, and bare back from a roaming, groping camera. A self-exhibition of breasts with protruding nipples straight out of any strip joint or pole dancing, the Major is made to yoke stereotypically masculine daredevil stunts with feminine nudity and vulnerability. Whereas Tarzan in a loin cloth denotes self-flaunting aggressiveness, a scantily clad Jane only invites male protection. This is yet another of the motif of "better half": her masculine power is undercut by her feminine powerlessness, which crystalizes in the refrain of gasps and sighs, gestures of shock and resignation.

Described by Togusa as an "Amazon" with no need for police backup, the Major nevertheless utters a high-pitched, almost girlish gasp when she realizes she must confront the spider tank on her own in the anime's finale (Figure 5.1). Hiding behind a crumbling pillar, the Major steals a quick glance at her rival just emerging from an invisible cloak. The Major shrinks back, gasping involuntarily, quite out of character given her cool, if melancholic, composure throughout. This catching of the breath in shock exposes the vulnerable female half to her otherwise male warrior sovereignty, a moment that captures this cyborg in a dominating, high-angle shot. Such a human touch endows cyborgs with human frailty that invites empathy from the audience.[5] Outgunned, the Major darts in and out of her hideouts, shedding her spent weapons and tight clothing. The latter is ripped off as she lies supine on the ground, gasping, an echo of the flashing in the anime's overture. The ponderously tragic music crescendos as the Major, practically nude, dashes toward and leaps on top of the tank to open its hatch by brute force, to the extent that her exoskeletal skin tears, interior wiring, metals, and microchips bursting out. Her trunk and limbs breaking up, the Major

FIGURE 5.1 *The Major gasps in* Ghost in the Shell.

FIGURE 5.2 *The Major broken up in* Ghost in the Shell.

turns her head up in slow-motion, her sensuous lips slightly open in a silent sigh to the sky (Figure 5.2).[6] Her nipples hard on peach-like breasts on a mutilated body, Oshii reprises Yoshitoshi's nineteenth-century prints on the aesthetics of violence, specifically, the torturing and killing of females.[7] Such gasps and pleas for help constitute a touch of human in cyborg protagonists from Oshii to Sanders and to a TV cyborg Anita/Mia in the BBC's and AMC's *Humans* (2015–2018). To those averse to the hypothesis that our better half, cyborg or aspergirl heroines, is the millennial compromise of feminist political correctness and the good old male gaze, one needs only to point to the Major's savior, Batou with his big gun, pun intended, commandeered from the headquarters to blow the tank to smithereens.

The Major's persistent doubt regarding her humanity, her ghost, culminates in gasps and sighs. Her cool façade reaching breaking point, such reflexive or instinctive body language crystalizes the anime's and its sequel's leitmotif of doubles and reflections. Oshii's filmic refrain denotes an obsessive repetition compulsion à la Freud's "Mourning and Melancholia" (1917). Freud's seminal essay opens with symptoms of mourning over the bereavement of a loved one. Paralleling mourning with melancholia without an obvious loss, Freud theorizes that melancholia stems from "a loss in regard to his ego" (246). A cyborg bereft of a human body is plagued by the reflection that one is a mere ghost, will-o'-the-wisp. That self-reflection proliferates in pale shadows and doppelgangers. The Major repeatedly executes the tableau of stopping in her tracks to, after a considerable pause, turn her gaze at a blonde sexaroid chopped at the waist and hacked by the Puppet Master, at her look-alike sitting for a meal above a Hong Kong-

Venice-fusion canal ferryboat, or at department store mannequins which take after the cyborg. The blonde torso transmits the Puppet Master's male voice without even opening her mouth. She or it manifests a double bifurcation of a broken female nude ventriloquized by a telepathic male voice. In the finale, Batou hooks up the Major to the Puppet Master within the blonde torso reluctantly, for he fears a double suicide.[8] As the Major and the blonde engage, their roles reverse, the Major speaking in the male voice and the blonde in the Major's. Earlier in the anime, the Major even turns to stare at the suspect of a garbage man, whose implanted memories of family and past bode ill for herself, who fears tampering of her sole human body part, her brain or her soul. Even her partner Batou's basset hound, an unlikely canine candidate to doppelgang, evokes cyborg melancholia over lost humanity.

Given Oshii's favorite trope of water, reflections are literal in a cityscape in rain, by the sea, pockmarked by small puddles and large bodies of water, and crisscrossed with canals. Pursued by the Major and Batou in *Ghost in the Shell*, a hacker flees through narrow alleyways, flanked by decrepit tenements similar to Western metropolitan housing projects. Yet the cage-like metal bars on balconies and windows with their tails of rust stain, interspersed with window air conditioners, instantly identify them as low-income residents' *gezilong* (pigeon cage or public housing) of Hong Kong fame. Oshii's cinematic style of juxtaposing dynamic action and stasis reprises as the hacker pauses halfway through the alleyway, an open-air sewage, as it were, to fix his eyes at the sky, triggered by the perfectly mirrored image caught in the standing water near his feet (Figure 5.3). Urban filth and decay below weds through his longing with the cleansed air after the rain. This stunning shot resonates with that of drops of water on the Major's diving goggles, as she floats up from the depth of the harbor (Figure 5.4). Both the hacker and the Major send soaring their "ghosts," as shapeless and ephemeral as water. Oshii's lyrical style transfers cyborgs' repressed tears on to the earth's natural cycle of water. To effect human affects, Oshii's cyborgs affect affectlessness. The tautological flips between presence and absence, expression and repression, Self and Other lie at the heart of this Japanese anime, a cross-breed between postmodernist, sci-fi techno-Orientalism and the century-old tradition of Japanese puppetry of bunraku and Noh drama with masks.

This Other at play in Oshii expands from the nonhuman to the non-Self, or non-Japanese. Precisely, this Other points to Japan's Orient. In keeping with Roh and colleagues' techno-Orientalism as an imaginary shared by both East and West, Japan that has led in Asia's modernization and Westernization silhouettes its rise against surrounding Asian countries. Japan sees itself subconsciously as the West with its own Orient to be colonized circa. the Second World War and to be utilized imagistically in the new millennium. To turn this hypothesis on its head, it is conceivable

FIGURE 5.3 *The hacker and the reflection in* Ghost in the Shell.

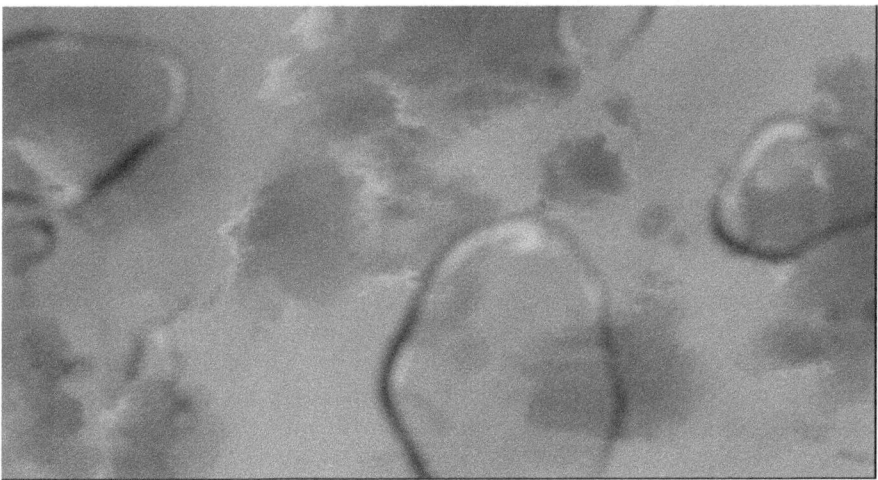

FIGURE 5.4 *Water drops on the Major's goggles in* Ghost in the Shell.

that Japan's Orient doubles as the old ways that the postmodern Japan has forfeited.[9] Hence, the hacker sports a Cantonese-sounding name, Tsuan Gen Fang, and two coils of sideburns from his temple inserts after the fashion of Hasidic males. He also has pale gray eyes and decidedly non-Chinese facial features.

This brew of Cantonese and Jewish spices boils down to a Hong Kong–Venice–Taiwan–Korean fare. Visual spectacles fuse these locales' specific features. As the Major drifts on a ferry across Venetian-style canals, store signs are exclusively in traditional Chinese scripts typical of Hong Kong and Taiwan. Pasted on the walls are rows of identical flyers advertising rental apartments, a common sight or eyesore on those islands. The foreign signage remains illegible to most audiences to fashion an otherworldly dreamscape. Occasionally, department store window displays are in English, including one "Walter Ma designer clothes," a well-known Hong Kong fashion designer. The Major witnesses a flotilla of Hong Kong and Oriental images, to be continued by the Hong Kong–Taiwan festival parade in *Ghost in the Shell 2*. With the Major having secreted herself in the internet, the Puppet Master's domain, at the end of *Ghost in the Shell*, Batou with Togusa in the sequel investigate cybercrimes committed by Kim, a Korean-sounding surname implicating *zainichi* (ethnic Korean residents in Japan). Kim's whereabouts is betrayed by a riff-raff Lin, yet another Chinese-sounding name. Section 9's bird-like chopper lands on a skyscraper-cathedral with flying buttresses and gargoyles in the shape of the Chinese God of War (*Guan Gong*) wielding his trademark crescent-shaped green-dragon halberd. This parade consists of Indian elephants, Chinese temples with upturned roof ridges and eaves, Chinese ideograms, and a full array of Taiwanese Boy-God Nezha and hellish demons with baboon-like lower canines.[10] On each float, these exotic wights strike various tableaux and freeze in sync with the end beats from flourishes of gongs, drums, and clappers. The Chinese opera technique of *liangxiang* (striking a tableau) is in full display, all accompanied by the theme music of female choral incantation allegedly in Japanese. Visual extravaganza pairs with auditory unintelligibility.

When Batou enters Kim's castle to track down Kim, Japan's Orient takes on a distinct Chinese-Korean feel. Around Kim's talking skeleton remotely controlled by the hacker, couplets in *hanji* or Chinese ideograms are incessantly projected into the air. Vanquishing Kim only leads Batou to follow the Major's lead for his own perilous deep dive into Locus Solus ("Site Alone" in Latin) company ship, the belly of the cybercrime beast. The ship's firewalls are guarded by robots, whose helmets are numbered in classical Chinese scripts of One, Two, Six, and so forth, and which communicate in Cantonese. Turning the tables on Locus Solus which hacks into and enslaves sexaroids, Batou becomes the virus that breaches Locus Solus' firewalls.

Oshii's Orientalism, nonetheless, is coupled with Occidentalism in that Batou's savior, the Major, downloads her ghost into one of the horde of turquoise-eyed, blue-eyelinered, cherry-lipped, fair-complexioned, and stereotypically Western sexaroids on the assault. The army of gangly nudes suggest adolescent awkwardness, while exuding a perverse, pedophiliac allure precisely because of their maladroitness and defenselessness. These sexaroids turn on Batou, who is there to rescue them in the first place. Batou teams up with the Major, who looks exactly like any other sexaroid, save Batou's combat vest draped around her shoulders. This act of his demureness acknowledges the Major's humanity, a fleeting gesture from one animate cyborg to the other trying to incapacitate the swarm of cyborgs just like her. Long before her physical intervention on *Locus Solus*, the Major has been Batou's guardian angel, the biblical allusion rather consistent with Oshii's citations from the Bible, Milton, Blake, and other Western classics of heaven and hell. Batou's repeat forays into Kim's Castle are greeted by the hologram of a basset hound and a young girl in the Major's distinct short bob, bangs angled so her hair is the longest by the cheeks, progressively shorter on the side and the back. Both the pet and the girl stare down at a word puzzle. The puzzle constitutes a dire warning, as it changes from Aemaeth (truth), just as the one on Golem's brow, to maeth (death), a decapitating of the prefix "ae" or Golem's figurative head. Not only is the message biblical and Occidentalist, but the soundtrack crescendos out of a potpourri of church bells, Western cylinder phonograph, and the music box. Ironically, this breathing into clay and taking the spirit away foreshadows the Major weaponizing one particular sexaroid, only to have it revert back to a pile of lifeless metal and synthetic body parts.

Not all sexaroids go so quietly into the night. Batou opens *Ghost in the Shell* 2 with his shooting of a homicidal sexaroid identical to the ones he and the Major have disposed of in the first installment. Before the girl sexaroid implodes, however, she implores, *sotto voce*: "Help me!" (Figure 5.5). The SOS under her breath notwithstanding, her face and breast suddenly burst to expose skeletal ribs and a skull head, symbols of mortality that almost invite Batou to pump bullets into her. Her faint, pitiable plea lingers in the air, though, an echo of the Major's gasp and sigh. In the live action remake, Rupert Sanders transposes Batou's execution of the killer-cum-victim to Major Mira Killian shooting a spider geisha, who reaches out her hand in a high-angle shot to say "Help Me!," déjà vu all over again (Figure 5.6).

FIGURE 5.5 *"Help Me!" in* Ghost in the Shell 2.

FIGURE 5.6 *The geisha's plea in Sanders's* Ghost in the Shell.

Sanders

Whereas Sanders repeats myriad anime sequences, this initial dive from the rooftop suggests the live action remake's plot-driven, action-packed, downright Orientalist style. Oshii features a conventional shootout where a wall-sized aquarium with koi is shattered dramatically. Sanders deploys *japonisme* in Johansson's jump to save Hanka Robotics' experts. In a glossy, shimmering set with the dazzling colors of Japanese prints, not to mention the CGI spectacle of mammoth, holographic koi slow-swimming in and outside the skyscraper, an unwitting Hanka host and his guests sit at a low table with their legs crossed drinking sake, served by geisha robots in silk kimonos. The festivity is cut short by assassins, all Asiatic monstrosities with blackened teeth and jawline scars. One geisha crouches into a spider woman to hack into the Hanka expert through the sockets in the nape of his neck. The cables from her neck to his resemble a spider spinning a web over her prey. Countermanding her superior Aramaki, Johansson decides to take the plunge because her virtual reality goggles penetrate the building to reveal imminent danger. These computer-generated interior shots within a building are formulaically in lit pixels, oftentimes flashing against murky backdrop, similar to CGI visualization of the pumping heart, blood flow, and whatnot within the human body, both accomplished by fast moving perspectives and quick cuts as well as crescendos of electronic music. Virtual reality in CGI turns into a metaphor, as cinematography morphs hyperactively between actual and virtual. This shift between the real and the holographic, the live action and the schematic on a screen, pales somewhat in the genre of anime, where the contrast of animation of actual humans and animation of virtual ones is not as sharp.

Immediately after the shootout, the Major turns her gaze from the geisha with bullet holes to her own injured wrist betraying similar cybernetic parts. Killing the geisha cyborg is like slitting her own wrist. Yet rather than Oshii's refrains of Major Motoko Kusanagi's static stares in long takes, Sanders opts for the Major's swift action, in fighting as well as in mental identification. Sanders's preference for lucidity in plot over Oshii's atmospheric lyricism is indisputable given that Sanders opens with the "definition" of the film's title. Emerging from her anesthesia, Mira Killian is instantly fed by Dr. Ouelet (Juliette Binoche whose name conjures up medieval oubliette or dungeon where prisoners are dumped and forgotten, like the dropped letters from "oubliette") with the fake story of Mira's refugee boat sunken by terrorists. Dr. Ouelet laments that she could only salvage Mira's brain to insert into a "synthetic body" or "shell," while "your mind, your soul, your 'ghost'" remains intact and is to serve Section 9 as "a weapon" against terrorism. Not only is the medical assurance slow in coming, if ever, in Oshii, but the facile equation of mind, soul, and ghost is nowhere to be found in the animes. Dr. Ouelet's words are confirmed by Section 9 Chief Aramaki (Takeshi Kitano): "You're more than a weapon. You have a soul ... a ghost. Only when we see our uniqueness as a virtue can we find peace." Slightly pontificating, as is wont of Asian elders and Zen masters in accordance with Sanders's Orientalism, Aramaki does differ from Ouelet in that he is not in on the experiments regarding anti-technology dissidents, of whom Mira used to be one. These young dissidents, including Mira and her hacktivist rival, Kuze, are secretly cut up and "recommissioned" by Mr. Cutter, Hanka Robotics CEO, to silence opposition and to advance technology at once; they are his guinea pigs. Mira and Kuze turn out to be young lovers, Motoko and Hideo, abducted in their Shinto shrine hideout, a traumatic incident repressed medically but one that haunts them in the form of computer signal glitches. Sanders fixates on clarity, contrary to Oshii's indulgence in obscurity. Western scientific definition and organization meet Eastern "negative capability" and ambiguity, to the extent that the animes' melancholic self-reflection is remade as program glitches.

Once upon a time, the Y2K (Year 2000) bug was believed to be the glitch that would have incapacitated telecommunications at midnight on December 31, 1999, wreaking global havoc. That Armageddon, fortunately, did not come to pass. Yet this millennial paranoia over technology is symptomatic of the fear that modernity has outpaced individual cognition, with glitches and bugs plaguing not only technology but also human psyche. However, to rephrase Alec Baldwin and Kurt Andersen's catchy book title on his TV parody of Donald Trump, *You Can't Spell America Without Me* (2017), you can't spell Glitch without Itch, you can't spell Itch without It (Id), and, finally, you can't spell It without I. Syllogistically, this answers

FIGURE 5.7 *"Glitch or me?" in Sanders's* Ghost in the Shell.

Major Mira Killian's quip to Dr. Ouelet trying to delete her cyber-brain's scrambled codes: "How do you know what's a glitch and what's me?," once again a shot from above Mira, or from Dr. Ouelet's perspective (Figure 5.7). Unbeknownst to the Major, the glitch is her, or her residual self, suppressed thus far. The glitch is the side effect to being a cyborg, both an omnipotent goddess of vengeance and a slave who knows not herself.

Originally, a glitch means a temporary malfunction resulting from a sudden spike or alteration in voltage in the electrical circuit. Either scenario disrupts the natural, controlled flow in the system: a glitch is a system out of control. In Mira's case, a spike is akin to a drop. The return of the repressed in terms of fragments of her traumatic arrest and dismemberment constitutes a sensory overload that completely throws Mira. Mira's disorientation stems, paradoxically, from a sensory deprivation, when the present condition of the crime-fighter is erased, voided by a nightmarish return. The phantoms in her mind's eye replace the clear and present danger around her. The recurrence of disjointed images suggests the presence of absence, Mira's presentiment of her possible loss. Melancholia arises when she comes into possession of the suspicion of her dispossession, made all the more poignant by an utter lack of certainty.

This symbiosis of lost and found renders inane Sanders's harping on action. Dr. Ouelet counsels early on that "We cling to our memories as if they define us ... But what we do defines us," a punchline that practically closes the film in Mira's voice after she has annihilated Mr. Cutter and reunited with her Japanese mother. Kuze, on the other hand, has merged into the infinite web, as does Oshii's Motoko vanishing with the Puppet

Master. The self-contradiction lies in the fact that had Mira not had glitches from the past, she would not have ferreted out Mr. Cutter's brutality against her and other dissidents. Actions hinge on memories, the first glimpse of which is of a cat (Motoko's pet Pumpkin) leaping in a short-circuited image with horizontal, scrambled lines and grating static associated with poor reception. To the uninitiated, that glimpse appears to be a mere glitch in her cyber-brain. The glitch in computer lingo becomes in effect an analogue for repression in subconsciousness. Indeed an exemplar of the whole greater than the sum of its parts, the truncated, chaotic visuals of a glitch, tangled with shrill, staticky noise, intimate the Great Beyond, out of the range of understanding either for science and technology or for the human imagination. The genre of Japanese horror has routinely deployed this visual and auditory pair to suggest supernormal beings, such as the ghost Sadako and her video that kills the viewer seven days hence in *Ringu* (1989).

Mira's pet cat parallels Batou's basset hound, both companions for alienated souls. Mira's second glitch is of a Shinto shrine on fire, which recurs with disturbing frequency, so much so that Mira requests Dr. Ouelet scan and delete from her cyber memories this series of errant codes. As much a cliché as Shirow's opening temple scene in his manga, Sanders's Shinto shrine returns unbidden, culminating in an exact image on Kuze's breast plate over where his heart used to be, before his whole body was dissected and cast off. That pictorial of the Shinto shrine clicks; it dawns on the young lovers that the shrine was where they were forcibly separated, their brains surgically removed, their bodies rent, cloven, "shredded" from the physical world. That nightmarish trauma of losing all but their brains sediments into the repetition compulsion for both: Mira sees the shrine, despite Hanka Robotics' eyes; Kuze has it engraved on his chest. Sanders's compromise of an exotic-sounding yet pronounceable name, Kuze is one of the prototypes of "cerebral salvage" that failed. Unlike Hanka's magnum opus, the beautiful and lethal Major, Kuze is ugly, his robotic body parts exposed, lumbering, limping, stuttering. Kuze's jerky, involuntarily arrested body and vocal movement come from the fact that he *is* the system's static of weak signal, its cyber-borne bug, that seeks revenge against Hanka Robotics which has "operated on" him and discarded his "body parts like garbage" while Kuze was still conscious.

Indeed, *Ghost in the Shell* can be renamed *Whiteface from Asian Garbage* or *The Revenge of Garbage*, Sanders's remake even more so than Oshii's. Kuze's gait and speech already hark back to Frankenstein's monster formed out of inanimate scraps. Not only body parts but Kuze's memories are in shambles. Hence, Kuze stages a revolt of garbage like himself against their oppressors. His underground lair lies beneath a seedy strip club run by, who else, Asian gangsters. As Mira infiltrates into the basement, it resembles a drug bust, with white powder covering near-naked Asian operatives. The heart of Kuze's hacking activities appears to be a circle of men with monk-

like shaved heads, cables looping out of the jacks on their necks to Kuze at
the epicenter in a collective transcendent meditation or opiate euphoric high.
Kuze the mastermind of junk or junkies concentrates all these castaways'
sweet dreams of vengeance in the bowels of a high-tech world.

In addition, a garbage collector graces both Oshii and Sanders. The
messy plot involving Oshii's garbage man is symptomatic of Asian pop
culture favoring affective flow, which may be drifting a bit too much to
Western sensibility. Oshii's garbage man, who is manipulated by the Puppet
Master's implanted memories of his estranged wife and teenage daughter,
hurries to warn yet another brainwashed hacker with his Cantonese name
and Hasidic-looking sidelocks. Oshii's hacker in a camouflage cloak then
plunges through an open-air Hong Kong market, overturning a cartload of
watermelons, exotic fruits of the tropics and subtropics, and various other
food stands, splashing bullets indiscriminately, all part of a "carnivalesque"
wreckage that is the trademark of Japan's Orient, the chaotic and abject
doppelganger to Japanese order and superiority. The plot twist results in
the reflection of clouds amid an alleyway's standing water. In keeping with
the plot-driven Hollywood style, Sanders streamlines the chain reaction and
multiple sequences, reducing the cast to one garbage man, cutting the market
scene and the pause in the alleyway, culminating in his fistfight with Mira.

Both Kuze and the garbage man are computer hackers, undesirable,
marginalized, targeted for elimination. This brings out the ultimate fallacy
in Sanders: individual sovereignty that befits American exceptionalism,
ready to vanquish whoever threatens that sacrosanct covenant. Whereas
Oshii permeates his animes with self-doubt, Sanders highlights refrains of
individual consent prior to any action. "My name is Major Mira Killian
and I give my consent," so states the protagonist, a ratification of personal
inviolability. Even when Dr. Ouelet denies that, she does so as a ruse to
save Mira from Mr. Cutter. Chief Aramaki actually requests such permission
from her, as if a subordinate's imprimatur legitimizes the execution of
the archvillain Cutter. What better way to valorize the individual than a
sanction issued from the bottom up! Notwithstanding such valorization of
individuals, the melancholia of trash unites Kuze, the garbage man, and
Mira whenever they look at themselves: their reflections, or their severed
bodies and lost selves which they struggle to recall. Even the strongman
Batou (Pilou Asbæk of *Borgen* fame) asks Mira to feed his stray dog, a
basset hound Gabriel in the dark alley, for fear of "scaring the dogs" after
his human eyes are damaged by a blast in Kuze's den and replaced by a
pair of freakish goggles. The meat Batou collects for Gabriel, by the way,
comes from a typical Hong Kong butcher's stand with hooks of raw meat
on a techno-Orientalist street and cityscape worthy of the udon stands
and neon billboard geishas in *Blade Runner*. Set in this urban dystopia of
Tokyo–Hong Kong–Taiwan, the junk(ie) that is Kuze has deprived Batou of

his eyes, thus opening them to the truth of their shared humanity, i.e., the common denominator of dehumanization under Hanka's digital thumb.

To acknowledge his anime inspiration and, perhaps, Asian and Chinese financing from RELIANCE (India), Shanghai Film Group, and Huahua Media, Sanders retains Motoko and Hideo as the backstory to whiteface protagonists of Scarlett Johansson and Michael Pitt. Supported by Asian extras (along with Asian American Chin Han) and token Japanese of Takeshi Kitano (six-shooter-toting, Japanese-speaking Aramaki) and Kaori Momoi (Motoko's tea-boiling and tea-serving mother), Sanders inlays Johansson, crown jewel of American action fantasies, within a largely white European Union constellation: French Juliette Binoche; British Peter Ferdinando and Danusia Samal; Danish Pilou Asbæk; Romanian Anamaria Marinca who plays the forensic scientist Dr. Dahlin, the equivalent to the anime's Dr. Haraway; and others. This Hollywood whitewashing has long been prepared by Japanese manga and anime's idolizing and fetishizing of the "master race" of whites. Sanders's nominally Asian ghost thus arrives ensconced in the white shell. What happens if one were to flip it inside out: an Asian shell or cyborg body stowing a white soul, or a white man's dream nanny/mummy/baby Anita/Mia (played by Anglo-Chinese Gemma Chan) in the BBC's and AMC's sci-fi TV series *Humans* (2015–2018)?[11] This cross-generic, transnational series of ghost and shell, race and gender, human and nonhuman, "color-blind" future and racist past continues apace.

6

What's UP, Sam Wah?: Whitewashing Chinese Laundrymen

One photograph haunts me, one on "Downtown Houghton" in Michigan Technological University Library's J. W. Nara Photograph Collection (Figure 6.1).[1] Desolate dirt roads intersect at a two-story corner store, a typical frontier scene from Michigan's Upper Peninsula (UP) Copper Country around the turn of the last century. This image is accompanied by a blown-up detail of its left edge, which shows part of the next building with a "Sam Wah Laundry" shop front and two men of vaguely Asian features in Western suits standing in front, one of whom is leaning on a bicycle (Figure 6.2). During the Chinese Exclusion Act (1882–1943), Chinese laundrymen had clearly managed to eke out a living away from Chinatowns on the coastal and metropolitan areas, wherever menial labor was required. At least one Sam Wah landed in the farthest reaches of the Midwest, which comedian Margaret Cho satirizes as the "Midwaste" (98). Name-calling the white-dominated Midwest, Cho in her coastal elite mentality may in fact be displacing minority anxiety over their identity as unseemly, not-to-be-seen "waste matter" expelled by America's body politic. Nonetheless, just as one anonymous viewer comments off-handedly on this particular image in the Nara Collection, "Seems like every town in the Copper Country had a Chinese laundry," the collection's photographs of Calumet and other towns appear to confirm such "sightings" of Chinese laundrymen.

Arthur W. Thurner documents a number of these Chinese laundrymen in *Strangers and Sojourners: A History of Michigan's Keweenaw Peninsula* (1994). One interviewee Annie Aldrich recalls:

FIGURE 6.1 *"Downtown Houghton" showing Sam Wah Laundry, photo courtesy of Michigan Technological University Archives.*

> In the 1930s, Ngan Lee's shop, filled with packages of laundered shirts, seemed a house of horror to some small boys whose parents had threatened to sell them to the Chinese proprietor to be butchered for chop suey. One lad remembered being sent there for his father's shirt collar and discovering Ngan Lee to be a jolly, friendly, enthusiastic man. (153)

Aldrich's testimony reveals the lore instilled in the next generation by the parents, who unthinkingly merge the two survival skills of Chinese immigrants: restaurant and laundry, essential businesses feeding and clothing Americans. Given that Chinese immigrants did not enjoy much avenue for career advancement beyond these two traditionally female roles, it is telling that the local lore would be eating the Chinese Other—their food as well as their cheap labor—while having them around as the exhibit of the ultimate Other: "a house of horror." Not to mince words, the Upper Peninsula small towns eat the "chink" and have him, too. That this is a popular lore is confirmed by the plot of Lon Chaney's silent film *Shadows* (1922), where a boy comes to befriend the "monstrosity" of a Chinese laundryman. In Alma W. Swinton's *I Married a Doctor: Life in Ontonagon, Michigan from 1900*

FIGURE 6.2 *Sam Wah Laundry close-up, photo courtesy of Michigan Technological University Archives.*

to 1919 (1964), an Ontonagon newspaper on April 13, 1907 noted that the town had "only one chink and like most of his ilk he has an inquiring mind and a thirst for the coin of the realm ... He is not averse to turning a few cartwheels in other lines, although washee washee is his regular vocation" (qtd. 335 n. 66). The newspaper article's usage of derogatory terms is the rule, not the exception, of the day; it also brings out the duality attributed to the Orient: source of unknown mystery and horror, but always stupid and comical.[2]

Why did Sam Wah, Ngan Lee, Ontonagon's "one chink," and fellow compatriots of yesteryear choose a life in the midst of what Margaret

Cho and her cohort see today as the flyover wasteland? Was it to ensure plenty of washing? Who was Sam Wah? His familiar Anglicized first name is undercut by a strange foreign surname, an ominous homophone of "what." So, what exactly was UP, or Upper Peninsula, to Sam Wah and vice versa? Symbolically, though, UP implies going up, an ascent from the earth, dirt, and sweat. Cleanliness restores the purity of white and other unblemished true color; it signals the desire to be unto oneself, which ironically points to a levitation above the self. This psychic sleight of hand vests in whiteness, particularly the white skin, an almost airy, ethereal, out-of-body transcendence. Whitewashing turns into a double entendre: by flushing nonwhites out of historical memory and spatial existence, whites make themselves cleaner, higher, more upward-bound.

Given the passage of time and the scarcity of local documents on Chinese "sojourners," any historical question is well-nigh impossible to answer. "Chinamen," after all, only stand "a Chinaman's chance" of ever leaving behind any trace; their role in early twentieth-century US history had been to service white clientele, while being whitewashed into oblivion. In the photograph in question, for example, Sam Wah Laundry is so close to the frame that only a blowup shines light on a Chinese laundry. A positivistic, sociological approach may thus prove futile beyond heavy concentrations of ethnic minorities, such as Chinatowns in Paul C. P. Siu's *The Chinese Laundryman: A Study in Social Isolation* (1984) or in H. T. Tsiang's novel *And China Has Hands* (1937). From a literary and cultural studies perspective, however, much can be gleaned. Tsiang's ironic title on Chinese cheap labor or "Hands," for instance, undergoes a makeover in the Chinese title *Chufanji* (出番記 *Going Out Amongst the Barbarians*). Tsiang's Chinese title inflects an immigrant story of hardships and humiliation with a traditional Sino-centric superiority complex, muting from the outset the novel's bleak self-abjection. To contextualize Sam Wah with Siu and Tsiang: if Tsiang's New York laundrymen evince isolation, Sam Wah in Houghton, Michigan, is surely an extraterrestrial alien. Although few in number, these aliens come to populate, even crowd, American pop culture during the span of the Chinese Exclusion Act and beyond. Such ephemeral, all-but-forgotten sightings of the Chinese laundryman include comics, newspaper editorial cartoons, and Lon Chaney's yellowface laundryman in *Shadows*.

The St. Louis Republic published a revealing comic in 1901, "The Chink Family Robinson at Work" (Figure 6.3). The Missouri newspaper cartoon gives a racist spin to Johann David Wyss's German-language *The Swiss Family Robinson* (1812), which is itself a spin-off from Daniel Defoe's *Robinson Crusoe* (1719). Defoe's lone Englishman pioneers the British Empire's colonialism in far-flung corners of the globe. Wyss domesticates individual heroism, now a family enterprise as the Robinsons are stranded on a tropical island, besieged by a motley crew of pirates played by actors of color in the 1960 Disney family film, including Sessue Hayakawa as

FIGURE 6.3 The St. Louis Republic *comic in 1901.*

the pirate leader.[3] *The St. Louis Republic* perpetrates not only bigotry but misappropriation when the so-called Chink Family Robinson is anything but a normal family. It consists of three males apparently from three generations, possibly a grandfather, father, and son. Unbeknownst to the newspaper, its comic has captured the reality of Chinese bachelor communities across the land, since the Chinese Exclusion Act had prevented family reunion, especially the entry of Chinese women. The trio are related imagistically, if not genetically, most conspicuous in their wooden legs. This shared physical disability silhouettes American perception of the Chinese as a biological deviation to the point of being subhuman.

In stereotypical garbs, slant eyes, long hair queues, goatees, they appear quite content with their lot in life, with idiotic grins on two of the three faces. The grandfather and father figures have their queues tied into a clothesline to dry the washing, with the shortest male, perhaps also the youngest yet to grow his goatee, standing on a stool to hang up articles of clothing. So natural is this bizarre practice of drying that they even read books and smoke! The frame is chock-full of stereotypes other than the freakish, one-legged Chinese bodies: it contains the grooved wooden washboard in the tub, a steam iron on the table, an Oriental screen in the back, and two staggered vertical doodles on the wall right by the screen. The last item supposedly duplicates the Chinese Spring Festival couplet, i.e., Chinese calligraphy in black ink on red paper pasted on either side of the doorframe, usually flush with the top of the door, invariably parallel to each other. Not only are the comic's random scribblings on the couplet self-defeating but the different heights of the couplet give itself away as fake. The caption hanging from the bamboo frame of the comic almost validates all the distortions: "NO TICKET, NO SHIRTEE." The long "e" suffix Anglicizes and estranges supposedly alien sounds for English speakers. Rather than an auditory reproduction of the Other's pidgin, the Anglophone culture betrays its own neurotic fixation, its own neural Tourette tics in dubbing any Oriental from its pen or camera with the long "e" sound. Semantic and cinematic Orientalism remains largely undiagnosed, untreated.

The fabricated togetherness of a Chink Family Robinson can be easily ripped apart in American pop culture. Literally, a 1920s cut-out toy invites "boys and girls" to dismember and reassemble "Lee Ling Chinese laundryman," who becomes a reified object for child's play (Figure 6.4). The education of whites begins early in life with the minority as the plaything, reminiscent of the parents' warning to any truant lad about to be dispatched as chop suey materials. Assembled, one blogger testifies, "as [Lee Ling] scrubs laundry [and] the broom sways back and forth, his head bobs forward as he taps his foot. The action is spectacular" (Figure 6.5).[4]

From the still picture in a St. Louis newspaper to the moving picture of *Shadows*, the Chinese laundryman is a reliable prop in American imaginary of the Other. Man of a thousand faces, Lon Chaney plays Yen Sin the Chinese laundryman with all the turn-of-the-last-century stereotypical trappings of a rice-bowl haircut, slant eyes, buckteeth, a tunic with frog buttons, a skullcap, and platform shoes. Chaney stoops with his arms comically bent behind his torso, shuffling along. A severe case of osteoporosis, the hump-like posture heralds Chaney's magnum opus, *The Hunchback of Notre Dame*, of the following year. A "Chinaman" running a laundry service out of a scow comes as a dress rehearsal for the hunchback on the cathedral's belfry. Both monsters are liminal shadows on the edges of community and consciousness. That *Shadows* sets Yen Sin washing and ironing on a flat-bottom boat at the dock, like a piece of flotsam on the waves, suggests that he remains on the notorious emigrant ship. His debut may be the shivering, pitiable wretch rescued from a shipwreck, but he has never landed in America proper (Figure 6.6). In Figure 6.6, the mise-en-scène has all the townspeople directing their gaze to the right where one survivor is laid down, away from the other survivor Yen Sin shivering on the left. The townspeople will soon gather for a group prayer for the dead, from which the heathen is banished.

Running his laundry service from a scow, Yen Sin maintains an ambiguous relationship with the community. So "outlandish" is his appearance that he clearly does not belong, nor does he draw any closer to Christianity since his banishment on the beach. In Paul Siu's words, "Socially he is a stranger.

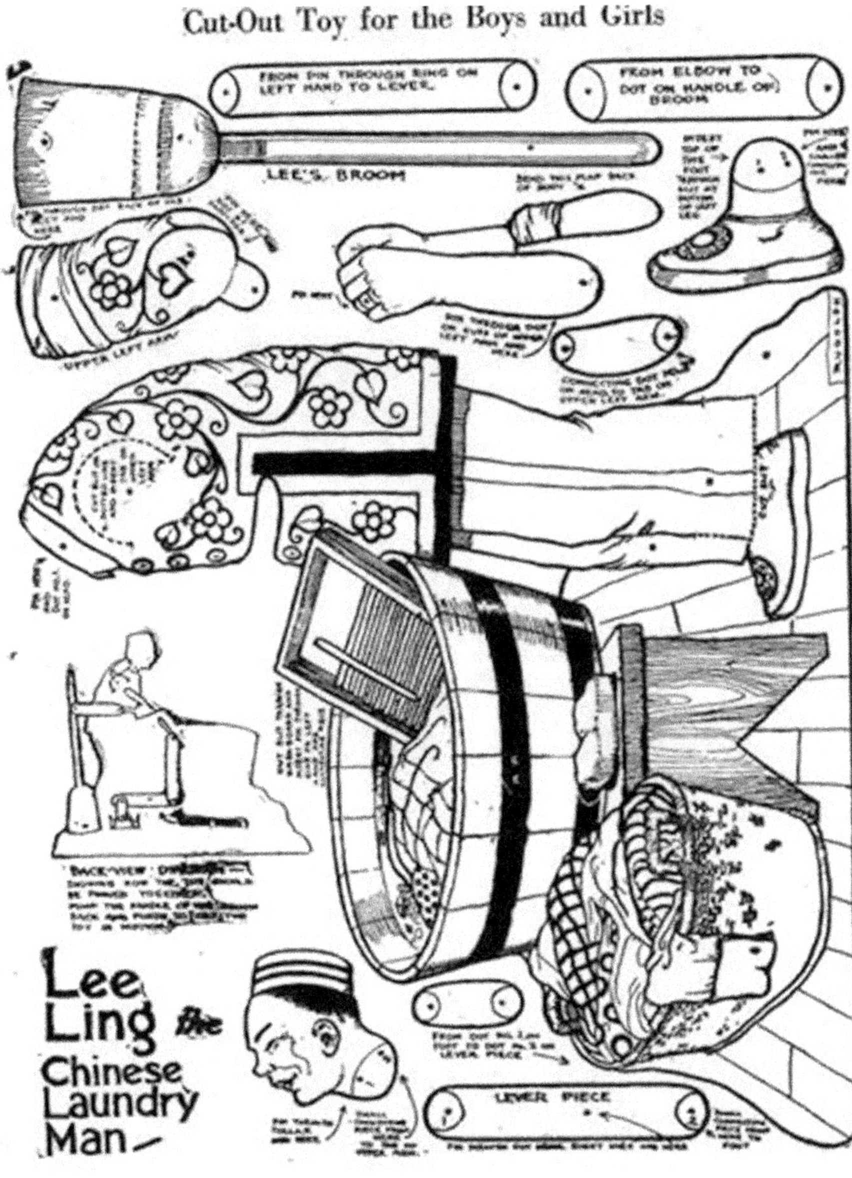

Cut-Out Toy for the Boys and Girls

FIGURE 6.4 *A 1920s cut-out toy of "Lee Ling Chinese Laundry Man."*

He closely approximates the ideal construction of symbiosis without communication" (3). Yen Sin does befriend a boy nicknamed "Mr. Bad Boy" with the enticement of the proverbial Chinese sweet lychee. Beyond his three friends—Mr. Bad Boy, the minister Malden, and the angelic Sympathy

FIGURE 6.5 *"Lee Ling Chinese Laundry Man" assembled.*

Gibbs—Yen Sin fits well into Siu's depiction: "When the American thinks of the laundryman, he usually thinks of the laundry shop where he takes his white shirts. The person and the institution are the same thing." "The Chinese laundryman" is, alas, "a thing" to Americans (13).

Toward the end of the film, Yen Sin's last act before expiring is to cut loose the scow, much to the chagrin of the community that has come to appreciate him, so that he can float back to China "pletty easy." Despite the happy ending through Yen Sin's machination and his "deathbed conversion" to Christianity, he remains a perennial alien whose home lies elsewhere. His minister friend Malden does Christianize Yen Sin's homebound scow as returning to the "Harbor" of the Lord. But the tension of Christianity and Chinese beliefs, a good Chinaman and a freak, is never truly resolved.

The happy ending for the white protagonists comes about only because Yen Sin has thwarted the antagonist Nate Snow, a homewrecker. Snow "covets [his] neighbor's wife" Sympathy remarried to Malden, after

FIGURE 6.6 *The "Chinaman" debuts in* Shadows.

her abusive fisherman husband Daniel Gibbs had been lost at sea. Snow orchestrates the return of the dead and forges Daniel's ransom notes to extort a fortune. The minister lives with the sin of having committed bigamy and sired an illegitimate child. Bed-ridden and near death, Yen Sin sees through Snow's shenanigans and forces him to confess, in a show of Oriental prophesy mixed with homespun commonsense. Yen Sin first observes his pet cat playing with a mouse before pouncing, which leads to his remark in the intertitle (Figure 6.7). The intertitle demonstrates the speech pattern of Yen Sin's pidgin with the long "e" suffixes, not to mention the absence of verb conjugation and proper syntax. As though springing from the delirium of a dying man, these words border on nonsensical gibberish to an unknowing community gathered around his deathbed.

Of course, Orientalism has long patented the collaging of nonsense and über-sense, of being muddle-headed and being the Godhead, of the trivial and the transcendent. What seems quizzical to the gathering strikes Nate Snow like a bolt of lightning, whose guilty conscience compels him to confess. This all but exonerates the minister from his sin, except that he has hidden from his family and friends what he believes to be the truth for over a year. The minister forgives Snow, nonetheless, an act of magnanimous grace that convinces the dying Yen Sin to convert. The superiority of Christianity

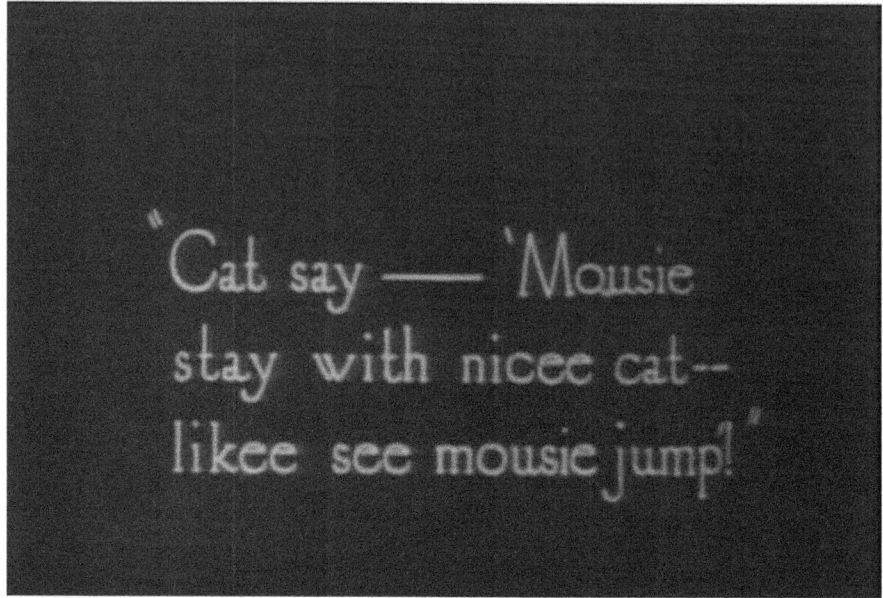

FIGURE 6.7 *Yen Sin's words in pidgin exposes Nate Snow's scheme.*

is further validated as Yen Sin struggles from his bed to unmoor the scow. Along the way, he bumps into the icon to which he used to light incense and bow down. The statuette of ancestral worship tumbling to the boat's floor, Yen Sin simply shoves it away, a gesture of indifference toward a heathen idol. But this "cutting" of ancestral ties is complicated by his dying wish to somehow drift back to the ancestral land.

This tension surfaces as well in the unconventional method of solving the whodunit by the unlikely detective Yen Sin. He reads his fellow laundryman Sam Low's message on the minister's collar, presumably written in Chinese (Figure 6.8). Yen Sin has earlier demonstrated such a four-character notation inside the collar to Mr. Bad Boy. Sam Low works in the neighboring town Infield and is recommended by Yen Sin to attend to Malden's laundry during the minister's excursion. Played by an Asian actor, Sam Low serves as the Watson to Yen Sin's Sherlock Holmes (Figure 6.9). Extras can be Asian in the Hollywood tradition, but the lead must be yellowface. Sam Low, without the hunchback and swift of foot, follows Nate Snow and discovers his treachery. This is a pattern familiar to Westerners. The comical, rotund, and fortune cookie-spewing Charlie Chan is likewise assisted in his investigation by the Number One son, more agile, spouting rapid-fire Americanisms. The yellowface Warner Oland or Sidney Toler of slant-eyed Charlie Chan fame thus commands the Number One son, played by Keye Luke or Victor Sen

FIGURE 6.8 *Yen Sin reading Sam Low's message inside a collar.*

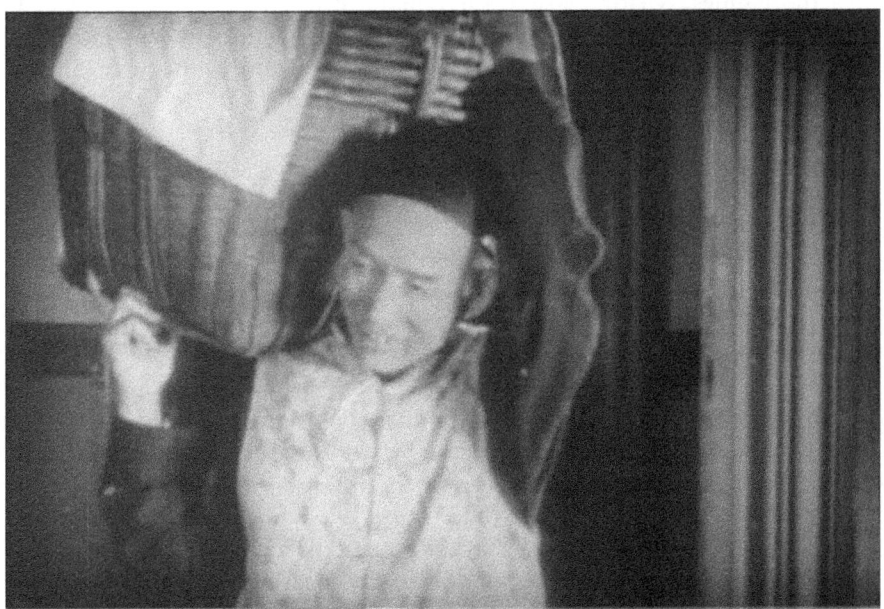

FIGURE 6.9 *Sam Low the Chinese laundryman, or Watson to Yen Sin's Sherlock.*

Yung. This casting formula applies to Oriental(ized) females as well, most prominent of which is the pairing of Marlene Dietrich's Shanghai Lily and Anna May Wong's Chinese prostitute character in *The Shanghai Express* (1932).

A coup de grâce to Nate Snow's scheme, effecting a dramatic twist in the film, Sam Low's correspondence to Yen Sin may as well be encrypted, for no one can read Chinese other than the laundrymen. Secrecy in codes is put to good use. But in Orientalist imaginary, this shadow network would lapse in no time into conspiracy and xenophobia. Charlie Chan, after all, has an evil twin in Dr. Fu-Manchu, whose Oriental operatives infiltrate every corner of the West. In Sax Rohmer's series of mystery, the yellow peril conquest of the West is only arrested, repeatedly, by Holmesian Nayland Smith and Dr. Petrie, oftentimes with the aid of Fu's mixed-race slave girl Kâramanèh, who falls in love with Dr. Petrie. Kâramanèh's betrayal of Fu is justified by her higher love for the white man. This is a narrative strategy to bolster a superior West, no different from Yen Sin forgoing his ancestral deities as a result of the minister forgiving Nate Snow.

Lon Chaney's shadow laundryman is not alone in silent films. Harold Lloyd in *Speedy* (1928) survives a street brawl with gangsters, thanks to the unexpected help from his horse-drawn trolley riders and city residents, including one Chinese laundryman, who scorches Lloyd's enemies on the buttocks with his hot pressing iron. This Chinese character is comical, but also insidious, attacking from behind. Such covert operation is consistent with the Chinese writing inside the collar from Sam Low to Yen Sin. It always contains the half-life of treachery and worse when—not if— Sinophilia degrades into Sinophobia, white love into white hate, in the public imaginary.

Exactly because the Chinese laundryman figures so closely to America, ironing out the wrinkles of its shirt and soul, American pop culture has distanced itself by caricaturing him. Exactly because the Chinese laundryman fingers our silk blouse and perhaps even underwear, exemplified by the pair of bloomers in Yen Sin's laundry basket, American pop culture has whitewashed him out of existence, bleaching out the dirt and soil from the white skin. The Chinese laundryman is the shadow America drags behind itself, like its own atavistic tail.

These century-old "perennial aliens" enjoy longevity in contemporary racism. A case in point: Abercrombie and Fitch designed a line of anti-Asian T-shirts on wide-ranging stereotypes such as Chinese chop suey restaurants, the Buddha and Buddhism, and, of course, Chinese laundrymen. Specifically, the company features a T-shirt that sports two idiotic-looking Asians in conical/comical peasant hats, soap suds, and Qing dynasty shirts with frog buttons. The caption reads: "Wong Brothers Laundry Service" and "Two Wongs Can Make It White."[5] The last phrase harks back to the tired joke on Asian infelicity over the retroflex "r," mangling the idiom "Two

FIGURE 6.10 *The cover of* The Five Chinese Brothers, *courtesy of Penguin Random House.*

wrongs (don't) make a right." The phone number for the laundry service on the T-shirt lists "555-WONG," evoking the illustrated children's book *The Five Chinese Brothers* (1938) with five brothers who "looked exactly alike." The Wong Brothers' identical features and blank grins copy those of the children's book, one of "Teachers' Top 100 Books for Children" based on a 2007 online poll conducted by the National Education Association (Figure 6.10).

Yet another Hoover advertisement mocks Chinese laundrymen, who had apparently lost their jobs to the company's washer.[6] Peering into the washer's black hole, these laundrymen crane their necks, too stupid to be aware of the ax that has already fallen: any customer's good buy equals the minority-clown's goodbye to the steam iron in his hand. Hoover's ad evokes the nativist persecution of Chinese workers around the turn of the

FIGURE 6.11 *The 1883 Missouri steam washer trade card "The Chinese Must Go."*

last century, evidenced in the 1883 Missouri steam washer trade card "The Chinese Must Go" of Figure 6.11.[7] The steam washer wears Uncle Sam's red striped trousers, which resonate with the Stars and Stripes of the United States. This image proclaims that the United States, not the Missouri steam washer alone, is kicking out the Chinese laundryman with his bag of money and his washboard. The trade card's three place names, however, belie the united front of the United States. The State of Missouri is presented as the synecdoche of Uncle Sam, assuming the nation's mantle, wearing its pants, so to speak. Yet the eviction of the Chinese laundryman involves a lopsided asymmetry, from a city to a country, from San Francisco to China. Missouri sees itself as undoing the nation's plight spreading from one specific locale, the Bay area, the beachhead of an infestation of the yellow peril.

Given the mainstream distortion and repression of such shadows, rare sightings of Chinese laundrymen from yellow photographs and newspapers in dusty archives constellate, nonetheless, into a vibrant metaphor of ethnic imagination, whereby a racist stereotype and the history of discrimination are repurposed for ethnic pride and global marketing. Graham Russell Hodges's *Anna May Wong: From Laundryman's Daughter to Hollywood Legend* (2004) traces the Hollywood star to her humble origin at a Los Angeles family laundry. Beyond biographical works, minority and Asian literature and film avail themselves of the trope of the Chinese laundryman. An Asian American classic, Maxine Hong Kingston's autobiographical fiction *The Woman Warrior* (1976) is set in her Californian family laundry. The stifling heat and the numbing work of the laundry cleanse not only customers' clothing but also inspire the novelist's quest for ethnic identity.

By contrast, Korean filmmaker Sngmoo Lee's *The Warrior's Way* (2010) is so into image-laundering—loads of stereotypes of Japanese samurai and ninja; Western gunslinger; Chinese laundryman; interracial romance; and CGI—that the film feels cartoonish, with the laundry providing comic relief. The iconoclastic, contrarian Korean auteur Kim Ki-duk casts in *3-Iron* (2004) a non-speaking protagonist who breaks into houses and apartments while the residents go on vacation, doing, among other household chores, the residents' dirty laundry in the traditional way, on the tiled bathroom floor, once even on an old-fashioned, grooved wooden washboard. The most intriguing change lies in the film's title and the implication of gender reversal. Arguably, the Korean title *Bin-jip* (Empty Room) epitomizes the female protagonist Sun-hwa's domestic abuse, a marital perversion of her profession as a nude model. In addition, the male protagonist Tae-suk, silent throughout the film, is de facto feminized, happily taking on domestic tasks. His hobby of golfing is inflated by the English title *3-Iron*, a golf club that embodies a leisure lifestyle, which masks male control and violence over others. Caught raping Sun-hwa, the abusive husband is nearly killed by Tae-suk's vengeful swings of the club. Male aggressiveness, however, is reined in by Sun-hwa, who teams up with Tae-suk and quietly soaps up the laundry to knead it on the tiled floor. The Korean "Bonnie and Clyde" brandish not weapons but soap and drying racks. The English title, along with the promotion poster hinting at a threesome, a ménage à trois, seeks to familiarize in golf lingo a foreign film for the West, not to mention eroticizing it.

In the hands of writers and filmmakers of color, be it Asian American or Asian, the representation of Chinese and Oriental laundrymen gives a new twist to the definition of whitewashing. Whereas mainstream US culture whitewashes minority experience, minorities of color resist being put under erasure. Kingston launches ethnic identity, in part, from her family laundry service. By contrast, Asian cultures are relatively immune from the experience of minority oppression in the United States. Hence, from the Asian angle, laundering as a literary and filmic motif no longer means whitewashing in the sense of being denied selfhood. Rather, Korean filmmakers of *The Warrior's Way* and *3-Iron* deploy laundering as a comic and romantic conceit, respectively. When Chinese laundry detergent Qiaobi (俏比) advertised its products in 2016, whitewashing acquires a virulent racist strain the Chinese harbor against dark-skinned people. Chinese ads do unto blacks what whites have done to "the yellow man," as *Broken Blossoms* (1919) calls its yellowface protagonist played by Richard Barthelmess. Just as whites hoist themselves on the pedestal of off-white yellowfaces, "yellows" do the same to "off-yellows"!

The 49-second-long Qiaobi commercial opens with a fair-skinned Chinese female beckoning a black male to the washer. The black male is tarred with white paint on his face and T-shirt, evoking tribal Africa's facial and body decoration (Figure 6.12). Lured by her charm, the black male draws near. He is suddenly force-fed a laundry detergent pod (Figure 6.13) and shoved head first into the washer (Figure 6.14). After the wash cycle, during which the woman sits on the lid to prevent any escape, the black male emerges cleansed and whitened as a fair-skinned Chinese male, much to the delight

FIGURE 6.12 *Chinese detergent brand Qiaobi (俏比) commercial in 2016.*

FIGURE 6.13 *The black male is force-fed a laundry detergent pod.*

FIGURE 6.14 *The black male is shoved into the laundry.*

FIGURE 6.15 *The black male emerges cleansed and whitened as a fair-skinned Chinese male.*

of the woman (Figure 6.15). This controversial Chinese commercial takes off from an Italian commercial whereby an effete, hunched-over Italian male is thrust into the washer by his mate. He who stands up from the washer turns out to be a "black stud," a muscular hulk whose metamorphosis pleases the woman no end. The stereotype of animalistic black masculinity eroticizes the Italian marketing strategy, whereas its Chinese counterpart elects to downplay, even reverse, the sex appeal of the boyish-looking Chinese male. This emasculation only highlights the beauty and attractiveness of the Chinese female. Should both commercials target women who traditionally do the family laundry, the sexual fantasies over refreshing dirty clothes and female desires diverge dramatically. Italian customers seem drawn to black virility, Chinese customers recoiled from it. A domestic chore, constituting part of age-old feminine servitude, is given a sexy spin.

Having begun with the haunting image of Sam Wah Laundry from Michigan's Upper Peninsula, I would be remiss not to close the essay with an exorcism of sorts, a final ritual of purging. Thus, it is fitting to conclude with San Toy Laundry in Park Slope, Brooklyn, New York. Corey Kilgannon reports in "He Irons, She Stitches" the moving story of San Toy Laundry (*The New York Times,* January 15, 2016). The owners Michael and Judy Huang purchased the laundry in 1983 from an "old-timer" they chanced upon at a Key Food supermarket in Park Slope. Because of Judy's "flash of kindness" in offering her spot in the checkout line to an older man, Kee-Eng Hong, who was furious after having lost his spot somehow, Hong, the previous proprietor, sold his laundry to the Huangs "for a pittance" with a singular request: "Don't change anything here." The most extraordinary part of the report is that Hong returned US$2,000 of the US$3,000 sales price, "as a good-faith gift to the next generation of immigrants determined to keep San Toy running." A New World business transaction seems straight out of an Old World that has long vanished. The Huangs have indeed kept their promise of not changing a thing, including the laundry operation, the rotary phone, and "San Toy's phone number—NEvins-8–3477—has not changed since the 1930s."

As the Park Slope location has housed a Chinese laundry as far back as 1903, it is a story of tradition, despite the fact that the host society may look askance at the "old-fashioned, Charlie Chan-style lettering on its dated sign" and more. It is also a story of the perseverance of working-class immigrants, contributing to the socioeconomic rise of the next generation and the community. At the time of Kilgannon's report, one of the Huangs's two children was a doctorate candidate at Brandeis University and the other in the master's program at Columbia University. While the road to the American Dream remains as paved with thorns as ever for Chinese laundrymen, their children have fared far better on the Eastern seaboard in the new millennium. As the émigré novelist Ha Jin puts it starkly, "the first generation was meant to be wasted, or sacrificed, for its children, like manure used to enrich the soil so that new seeds could sprout and grow" (*A Free Life* 419). Ha Jin's pronoun of "its" dehumanizes the subject of first-generation immigrants, cast in the trope of night soil in keeping with Paul Siu's theory of laundrymen as "things," the body waste from *Meiguo* ("beautiful country" or America). To borrow from pidgin substitution of "l" for "r," *A Free Life* may as well be *A Flee Life*. Ha Jin's bleakness aside, the Huangs, having never taken time off since 1983, planned at the article's end to close up shop for one week for a family vacation. May Chinese laundrymen—Sam Wah, San Toy, and more—across this great land of ours find their own little spots before being checked out from life!

7

Morphing *Bingxue*: Alchemical Poetics in Taoist *Monkey* and Nordic *Beowulf* CGI

Xue in the third tone in Mandarin means both snow and blood, among many other homophones. The common phrase *bingxue* translates literally into the neologisms of IceSnow or IceBlood. A conundrum fusing opposites of icy snow from without and hot blood from within, *bingxue* is a poetic trope for, a nexus of, mythology, alchemy, and psychology. The trio resemble one another in the focus on interconvertible metamorphosis, on the belief of larger-than-life mythical "becomings," of transubstantiation, and of psychic transference. Each of the trio hinges on narrative sleights of mind embodied in the defamililarizing poetic phrase of *bingxue*, which crosses boundaries between human and the outside world, nature and the supernatural, the sacred and the secular. Given the Romanization of Chinese, *bingxue* also bridges East and West. Given the computer-generated imagery (CGI) of global cinema inspired by Taoist *Monkey* and Nordic *Beowulf*, *bingxue* weds magic and digital technology as well.

Bingxue commences the flow in and out of the human body as well as of the earth. Snow falls on and ice shields the body of the earth. Blood from the world's heart, the internal furnace of fire and molten lava, spews out rivers of red on white snow, sizzling while freezing. Such landscape of volcanic Iceland and the Nordic is absent in the Middle Land (*zhongtu*, China) where Taoist practices evolve a strangely similar alchemical poetics based on humans' internal furnace, *dantian* in the lower abdomen. *Mjollnir*, the short-handled hammer wielded by Norse mythology's Thor, strikes and flies, resulting in thunders and sparks. This Thorean forge exists within the Taoist *dantian*, "elixir field" where the abdomen grows elixir vitae, reminiscent of Mircea Eliade's "crucible." Both Western and Eastern alchemy on transubstantiation and immortality is mythos akin to poetics that repurposes the world as an allegory venturing beyond itself, particularly human physical and psychological confines.

Norse mythology inherent in the tenth-century epic *Beowulf* meets Taoist metaphors from the sixteenth-century Chinese novel *Monkey* or *Journey to the West*. The North near the Arctic unites with the Middle of the Sinitic, jarring like IceBlood, unalienable like IceSnow. This congress of East and West takes place in the fantasy genre's addiction to CGI, deemed de rigueur in global cinema across Hollywood and Huallywood, the emerging state-sponsored tinsel town named after the second word in *zhonghua* (China) and the imago in Los Angeles.[1] Robert Zemeckis's motion-capture film *Beowulf* (2007), Sturla Gunnarsson's *Beowulf and Grendel* (2005), and James Dormer's ITV series *Beowulf: Return to the Shieldlands* (2016) resort to the full palette of ice, snow, gold and jewels, fire, and blood for a magical-cum-digital portraiture of the human, the Nordic world, and the supernatural. This approach coincides with Pou-Soi Cheang's *The Monkey King* (2014) and *The Monkey King 2* (2016) as well as with Stephen Chow's farcical *Journey to the West* (2013) and Tsui Hark's *Journey to the West: The Demons Strike Back* (2017), where the Taoist *qi* (breath) colors the entire palette, where the Nordic dragon's treasure hoard and fiery breath parallel *Monkey*'s trope of pearl-in-the-mouth and the exhalation of *qi*. A close comparative reading of the CGI episodes, particularly heroes' fights with dragons and demons, testifies to the substitution of supernormal wizardry with computer artifice. In this new millennium of science and technology, our religiosity is transferred onto the fantasy genre's virtual reality, virtual Gods.

Given the cultural chasm between *Beowulf* and *Monkey*, the double entendre of *bingxue* provides the pivot to bring them together, namely, via the concept of morph inherent in the pun of *xue* (snow-cum-blood) and in the compound formulated with *bing* (ice that either freezes rock-solid or flows and bleeds). That parentheses are called for to gloss Chinese words suggests linguistic code switching, yet another morph. Syntactically, parentheses are metamorphoses. From grammar to life in general, change defines all living things, including their end in death, which is but the stage of disintegration into ashes and dust before sprouting new life. Such cosmic morph originates in the life that Gods of various stripes breathe into clay figures—ashes and dust. The argument thus far has privileged life over death. Conceivably, death or insentience could be flipped on top, whereby life becomes a death rehearsal with all actors dreading the fall of the curtain. Either life or death, morph is the essence, which manifests itself in human practices of medieval alchemy, poetics, religions, and CGI, four areas that merge self-contradictory elements of *bingxue*. Alchemical transformations characterize both *Monkey* and *Beowulf* specifically from the inorganic to the organic. Poetics further animates lifeless words and narrative strategies. The poetics of form, such as *Beowulf*'s alliteration, apposition, and caesura as well as *Monkey*'s comic fusion of prose and poetry, shapes the content and meaning. This poetics is akin to alchemy of turning raw materials (sounds, rhymes, words, figures of speech) into gold (the poetic, the affective, the consciousness). This poetics finds its way into CGI that dominates all contemporary fantasy films, East or West, reinterpreting these classics in modern, technological, filmic terms.

This argument explores four types of morphs of opposites, epitomized by the contrasts in *bingxue*, within each work and between them: ideological, corporeal, temporal, and CGI morphs. Firstly, ideological morphs involve systems of belief: *Monkey*'s pilgrimage from China to India for Buddhist scriptures in fact veils nativist, Taoist thoughts; *Beowulf*'s Nordic, pagan mythology permeates an allegedly Christian saga. Secondly, corporeal morphs anatomize Monkey's power of *bian* (change) into seventy-two—infinite, rather—disguises. Monkey's high-low, divine-animal yoking manifests itself in his body fluids, particularly urine. This resonates with *Beowulf*'s body fluid of another kind—blood. Thirdly, temporal—temporality, temperature, and tempo—morphs go to the heart of change. Any alchemy, of the body, things, earth, and even narrative, hinges on an intervention into the progression of time. This intervention normally takes the form of speeding up by means of increased temperature and pressure, as in human *dantian* or Nordic, Welandian forge. Contrarily, this intervention can slow down or arrest the course of life by means of freezing temperature. In storytelling, such manipulation of the narrative time and space as flashback, interlace, and dream-cum-reality plays with the past, present, and future as well as heaven, earth, and hell. Finally, CGI morphs deploy light and darkness no different from temporal shuttles between heat and cold, acceleration and cessation. In global cinema, CGI visualizes the mythological in terms of computer wizardry, or machine's light show as we find in early trick films, that produces "genetic codes," even supernatural codes, out of "binary codes," to rephrase Kristen Whissel in *Spectacular Digital Effects* (2014), or that produces "special affect" out of "special effects," as Vivian Sobchack puts it in *Screening Space* (282).

Ultimately, all four morphs are driven by the romantic impulse to go beyond the human condition to reach for infinity; all of them result in melancholia, given the inexorable futility of such striving. Ideological morphs posit the porousness of systems of thought, despite overt statements of one overarching belief. Corporeal morphs venture beyond the body, temporal morphs beyond time and temperate, clement climes, and CGI beyond the mundane and human for the fantastical. These four morphs are inseparable as they overlap and morph into one another, but they are herein divided for the sake of argument. Ideology in literature comes through only by means of characters, whose corporeal bodies exist in time and shifting temperature. CGI crystallizes the contemporary method of capturing cinematically our kaleidoscopic reality, including these morphs and many more. The potential of cinematic morphs prompts Kristen Whissel to assert: "Cinematic morphs makes good on a promise that [medieval] emblem books could not fulfill: they represent the metamorphic transformations that are at the core of concepts concerning (knowledge of) the past and the future as well as the concepts of freedom and constraint that Proteus was to emblematize" (138). Despite digital morphing's dominance in visual culture, there are naysayers such as Scott Bukatman, who laments that "Morphing is an inadequate, overly literal gesture toward change without pain, without consequence, without meaning. There is something comforting, perhaps, about the stability of unstable identity, but morphing holds out empty arms" (245).

Ideological morphs

In Wu Cheng'en's sixteenth-century classic *Monkey*, China's three schools of thought, Confucianism, Buddhism, and Taoism, are intertwined. Although the story concerns itself with a Buddhist pilgrimage and portrays fake Taoist priests negatively, both Confucian and Taoist influences are clear in the fundamentally Confucian family structure of the pilgrims, from the father figure Tripitaka to his three disciples, plus the domestic servant-slave Dragon-Horse who carries Tripitaka throughout the long journey. The three disciples Monkey, Pigsy, and Sandy exhibit as much brotherly love as sibling rivalry. In addition, both the Jade Emperor's Taoist heaven as well as the Buddha's western sky resemble imperial Confucian bureaucracy with their respective network of *guanxi* (relationships) and the circulation of favors, gifts, and indebtedness. Such human transactional exchanges culminate in Tripitaka finally obtaining the sutras from the Buddha's two disciples, who resemble pranksters in giving the monk wordless, blank sutras. Discovering that by accident, Tripitaka finally acquires sutras with words by handing over his golden alms bowl, although the Buddha demurs that wordless sutras are in fact the true sutras beyond human comprehension. Chinese Zen Buddhism thrives on direct, unmediated intuition beyond intellect and speech, but it compromises with secular needs for doctrines in words and practices. Taoism also plays a key role in supernatural forces with the elixir and nectar that endow immortality, with its stress on the vitality of *qi*. In *Monkey*, a Taoist Patriarch has trained him, Laozi's elixirs empower him, and Laozi's crucible renders him indestructible with fiery eyes and penetrating gazes. Notwithstanding the plot of a Buddhist pilgrimage, Buddha's palm and gold fillet bind and control Monkey.

In *Beowulf* on the eponymous hero's slaying of monsters, the spatial and religious separations surface from the outset of the uninhabitable wasteland of the monster Grendel's "marches," "heath," and "fen" (ll. 103–104) versus the mead-hall Heorot's "loud banquet," "the harp," "the clear song of

... how the Almighty had made the earth / a gleaming plain girdled with waters" (ll. 92–93). Grendel of "Cain's clan" (l. 106), exiled in perpetuity, avenges the blood feud against Abel's (God's Chosen). Yet this Christian framework is already muddied by the notion that "Cain's clan" had been "outlawed" (l. 106). Outlawry is a uniquely Nordic concept, now imposed on Christianity by the *Beowulf* poet. The Nordic "outlaw[s]" of "Cain's clan" (l. 106) morphs into "the Eternal Lord had exacted a price" (l. 108), as if it were a Germanic *wergild*, death-price. That Grendel does not "pay the death-price" (l. 156), once again, deploys a Nordic custom of compensating for a killing. Spatially, the Nordic myth of the land mass is girdled by the tail-biting Midgard Serpent and the circular body of water.

Both Christianity and pre-Christian paganism inform Beowulf's ancestor Shield's demise. "Shield was still thriving when his time came / and he crossed over into the Lord's keeping" (p. 5, ll. 26–27). These two opening lines devoted to Shield have integrated his rise and fall, a fall that is a "soft landing" of sorts since he is said to have come into the Lord's embrace. This is followed within that stanza (ll. 28–50) with an elaborate description of Shield's ship burial, a glorious send-off for a beloved hero. However, both the elaborate funeral and the claim of "the Lord's keeping" come to naught in the way the stanza rounds off itself, almost negating everything in a bleak, nihilistic way: "No man can tell / no wise man in hall or weathered veteran / knows for certain who salvaged that load" (5, ll. 50–52). Rather than received by the Lord, Shield appears to be lost, and lost not as a hero but a mere "load" from life. That load can mean the treasure accompanying Shield's body, but it can also mean that Shield's body *is* the load, the corporeal load that disintegrates into nothingness after death. The Nordic sense of futile *wyrd* (fate) contests the Christian belief in the Lord. This tension is shown both through the life and death of Shield and through poetic linearity that disrupts the supposed progress to the Lord. The linearity is broken, Shield's unknown end throwing doubt on his beginning.

Such tension of Nordic *wyrd* and Christian faith abounds, such as Shield's great-grandson Hrothgar and his mead-hall Heorot. Lines 64–82 depict the glamour of Heorot, yet line 82 switches gear halfway through, as if right at the lull of the caesura that is gone in Seamus Heaney's modern translation, when it writes that Heorot "await[s] / a barbarous burning. That doom abided, / but in time it would come: the killer instinct / unleashed among in-laws, the blood-lust rampant" (ll. 82–85). Nordic "negative thinking" is shunned by modern preference for "positive thinking," but it appears to be their natural thought process. Birth and rise come hand in hand with thoughts of demise to medieval Norsemen. In particular, destruction is embedded within oneself: "the killer instinct" lies within the killed, as it were. In other words, one rises, only to self-destruct, only to extinguish oneself. The downfall is caused by "in-laws" related, if indirectly, to one's own blood. "The blood-lust" suggests both the thirst to dominate others by shedding their blood and the self-destructive drive to shed one's own blood. This allusion to the "in-laws" as the source of self-destruction in line 85 moves quickly to the next line's "demon" or Grendel. Figuratively, the monster Grendel becomes humans' "in-law" who will bring about human downfall. Indeed, Grendel is the heir of Cain. Cain and Abel were blood relations, so were Grendel and humans.

Corporeal morphs

From the preceding conceptual to individual level, both *Monkey* and *Beowulf* favor transformations of the body, which, by definition, venture beyond the body. Monkey's apprenticeship culminates in the Patriarch's "secret signs" of knocking on Monkey's head three times with a knuckle-rapper, walking away with his hands behind the back, and locking the door (22). The Patriarch's body language of apparent anger and reprimand sends a message that points away from that body. Such unspoken physical signs are to be deciphered only by the chosen, not to be shared by the uninitiated. As Monkey enters the Patriarch's chamber from the back door ("hands behind the back") at the appointed wee hour (three knocks), the Patriarch feigns waking up, the symbolic portal of transiting from one system to the other. As if unaware of Monkey's presence, the Patriarch recites in the manner of improvising a poem on the effects of Taoist "Golden Elixir" rather than on how the elixir is produced in the first place (23). This poem is cast as an extension of sleep, an extraction from the dream world. Yet it means to open Monkey's eyes to the occult, to awaken Monkey. The Patriarch's actual teaching comes in the form of a long poem on corporeal dynamics. The lower abdomen is believed to be the elixir field to engender alchemical "Golden Lotus" in "fierce flames." This merging of opposites resides in the metaphor of the inviolable lotus in flames, akin to the Christian symbol of the rose in flames. This can also be construed as Christ's or the Buddha's halo, fiery light emanating from the body, which is never singed. Both belong to mysticism: a rose in flames or a Christian, Buddhist saint with a halo—fire, light, and heat generated by the holy image, embodying everlastingness, never diminished, ever-replenishing. Physical matter such as the body and the light it generates lies at the heart of Genesis or any religion. After all, God's command "Let there be light!" initiates the Christian tradition of light emanating from the holy body, moving out of physical boundaries into the spiritual. As devices for the sacred aura, the halos are joined by stained glass windows in the architecture of Christian churches and the gold leaf and shining tempera in medieval book illustrations. CGI is but the most recent body-expansion technique, continuing the pictorial and visual tradition of halo, gold leaf, and tempera.

In keeping with the Taoist yin-yang symbiotic doctrine, the Patriarch immediately follows the "haloed" lotus with a warning against the perils of internal fire. The three calamities he narrates include two originating from within the body: a fire "springs up from within, and consumes the vitals, reducing the whole frame to ashes" (24–25). A wind "blows from below, enters the bowels, passes the midriff and issues at the Nine Apertures" (25). The forging of the golden lotus lies within the body, which becomes a forge. Its destruction lies similarly within the body.

Monkey's rite of passage concludes in a rather dubious dismissal. Showing off his magic tricks to fellow disciples, Monkey is expelled by the Patriarch, who worries that he may give away the secret of transforming into a pine tree! Yet pines encapsulate precisely his long apprenticeship under the Patriarch, aimed at enabling Monkey to extricate himself from any tight spot and to overcome any obstacle: aging turned into immortality; Monkey's seventy-two transformations to exit any danger; his Cloud Trapeze to flee; his body hairs to clone and impersonate. Monkey is the symbiosis of opposites: a hyperactive monkey born out of an unmovable stone; a change into a static pine tree that is a Chinese symbol of longevity, which moves, ironically, through time; the restless monkey who shows great constancy in his devotion to the Buddhist pilgrimage, the "short leash" of the Buddha's golden fillet on his forehead notwithstanding (27).

Such Taoist balancing of contradictions informs one of the quintessential moments in *Monkey* that leads to Monkey's subjugation, the turning point of what can be facetiously titled "Buddha Palm with Monkey Pee." Despite all his power, Monkey finds himself trapped by the Buddha's palm and subsequently by the fillet that shrinks to crush his skull whenever his master Tripitaka recites the Buddha's Fillet Tightening Chant. This is one of the universal figures of speech for control, no different from the American expression "under one's thumb":

> Monkey came at last to five pink pillars, sticking up into the air. "This is the end of the world," said Monkey to himself … He plucked a hair and blew on it with magic breath, crying "Change!" It changed at once into a writing brush charged with heavy ink, and at the base of the central pillar he wrote, "The Great Sage Equal of Heaven reached this place." Then to mark his disrespect, he relieved nature at the bottom of the first pillar. (75)

First of all, the translator Arthur Waley stumbles when he writes "at the base of the central pillar" because the Chinese original simply reads "on the central pillar." "The Great Sage Equal of Heaven reached this place" is an incomplete translation: the latter half is *daoci yiyou* ("reach here a trip/journey," literally). The word *you*, in particular, circles back to the novel's title *Xiyouji* (*Journey to the West*). It turns out that Monkey's signature on the pillar dooms him for a much longer trip or pilgrimage to India in the West, but not before a five-hundred-year imprisonment under Five Element Mountain. "Reach here [in his] trip" becomes almost ironic since Monkey is going nowhere from that point on, either a prisoner for five hundred years or a prisoner for the duration of the pilgrimage with the fillet locked on his forehead. Arguably, the five pillars mark the end of Monkey's journey of independence: he is to be entombed under the pillars and to be reborn as a servant to Buddhism.

Monkey's cry of "Change!" is akin to the spell of "abracadabra" in English when magicians perform their tricks on stage of making their assistant vanish or levitate. That "Change!" is *bian* (變) in Mandarin. Monkey's hair plucked from his head turns into a Chinese ink brush to sign "The Great Sage Equal of Heaven" on the Buddha's, as it were, middle finger. This change takes place above Monkey's head "on the middle finger," a self-aggrandizement for all to see from afar. But another change is taking place below: Monkey empties his bladder "at the bottom of the first pillar." Such metamorphosis transpires not only through his head aspiring to reach the sky but also through his male organ to discharge tension of another sort. *Bian* signals the inflation of Monkey's ego to "The Great Sage Equal of Heaven," but *bian* also implies the homophone for urine (便). In tongue-in-cheek classical Chinese, *bianzhe, bianye* (變者,便也, "what is known as change, it is but urine"). Urine is the product of the body's biological process, similar to those occurring in physical and metaphysical, chemical and alchemical, realms. Thus, two transformations arise simultaneously, one from Monkey's head, the other from his penis. His head is full of himself, his bladder full of urine. Monkey writes his name in two scripts, one with his brush and the other with his penis. Both are one and the same—masculinity or manhood to mark out and claim his possession. Power and pee are almost interchangeable. Indeed, relieving oneself constitutes the animal instinct of marking territory, no different from his signature on the central pillar. Monkey's writing strives to be an emperor's carving to mark important sites across imperial China, but it could be construed as modern vandalism or graffiti. Territorial markings of an emperor denote his power, which deconstructs itself when the self-appointed next emperor—Monkey—displays his bestiality by peeing.

Monkey's motive in relocating his two pieces of writing from the third pillar to his urinating at the base of the first pillar, or the ball of the thumb, is intriguing. While locating the vainglorious self-advertising of his name on the tallest third pillar for all eyes to see, he moves the traces and stench of his biological and animalistic urge to the fringes, on the bottom of the first pillar, the fleshiest bulge of the five pillars or Buddha's palm for all noses to sniff. Consciously, he announces himself in words, visually, to the eyes of humans and Gods. Subconsciously, he announces himself in smell, olfactorily, to all animals and demons from below. Marie-Louise von Franz in *Alchemy* (1980) theorizes the duality: "Symbolism handed on by tradition is … rationalized and purged of the scurrilities of the unconscious, the funny little details which the unconscious tag on, sometimes contradictions and dirt," or, in this classical novel, Monkey pee (16). Franz in fact notes that "the urine of an uncorrupted boy [before puberty] … has something magical in it" (48). Since Monkey retains his child-like innocence, his pee carries magical properties, the smell of stench nothwithstanding.

In contemporary filmmaking, the classical novel's pairing of the high and the low enlivens films of high seriousness such as *The Monkey King* and *The Monkey King 2*, on the one hand, and, on the other, films of parody and farce such as Stephen Chow's *Journey to the West* and Tsui Hark's *Journey to the West: The Demons Strike Back*. The finales of the former set of serious films, along with those of many others, choose to close with a bang and not a whimper. The drive for the maximalist in global cinema via special effects (for the special affect of godlike sublime) results in the uniformity of deploying the Buddha Palm as the ultimate coup de grâce with Chinese characteristics, a nativist icon of alleged Chineseness yoked to global cinema's aspiration for overreach, resulting in formulaic overkills. Figure 7.1, a still from *The Monkey King 2*, shows the moment when the Buddha Palm is poised to crush the White-Boned Lady. Figures 7.2 and 7.3 capture similar points in *The Monkey King* and *Journey to the West*. By contrast, the latter parodic films almost poke fun at the solemnity and power associated not only with the Buddha Palm but also with any established order in general. Chow and Tsui play with and caricature the Buddhist and filmmaking systems as if they are relieving the systems of excesses of self-inflation, albeit deploying the Buddha Palm for the same purpose of the superlative.

Corporeal transformations in *Beowulf* are evidenced by the dragon.[2] In a nutshell, the dragon's fiery breath etherealizes its poisonous blood in a transubstantiation process between its heart and lungs. Whereas the spewing of fire does not exactly reveal the source, its quenching does.

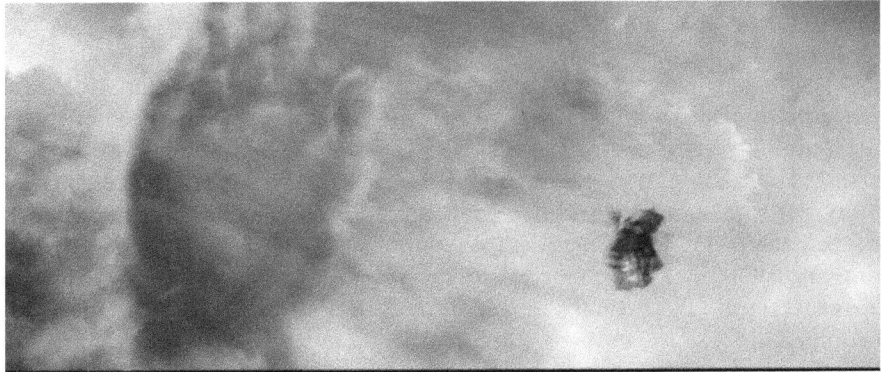

FIGURE 7.1 *The Buddha Palm in* The Monkey King 2.

FIGURE 7.2 *The Buddha Palm in* The Monkey King.

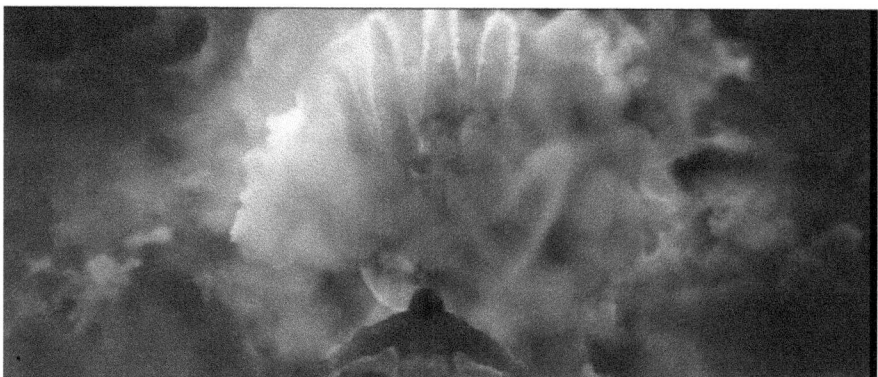

FIGURE 7.3 *The Buddha Palm in* Journey to the West.

Robert Zemeckis's motion-capture, hence exclusively computer-generated, *Beowulf* pinpoints the moment as Beowulf severs his left arm à la Grendel in order to swing deeper into the dragon's gullet to pluck out its heart. Once he does, fiery blood gushes from the wound, instantly extinguishing the flames from the dragon's mouth (Figure 7.4). Multiple morphs are arrested in that figure: the changing of natural and corporeal elements, body parts of one heart and two arms, hero and monster, the living and the dead. Before this finale, Beowulf encounters for the first time his son the dragon in Grendel's mother's cave/womb with a vagina-shaped opening in Zemeckis and Chris Ryall's graphic novel, a tie-in to Zemeckis. About to be expelled from the cave by the dragon's torrent of flames like menstrual blood in Chris Ryall, Beowulf jumps for his life, a sperm whose service is no longer required. Zemeckis's film also shows the next scene of Beowulf's

FIGURE 7.4 *Zemeckis's* Beowulf *with the dragon's fiery blood gushing out.*

FIGURE 7.5 *Beowulf escapes from the dragon's fire in Zemeckis's* Beowulf.

narrow escape, prostrated on the ground, the tongues of fire right above him (Figure 7.5). Ryall's graphics come with the dragon's onomatopoeic roar of rage "RRAAAGHH!," capitalized on the fire itself. Ryall strives for such a sound effect to simulate Zemeckis's film with a soundtrack, a coupling of sound and sight absent in the original text, whose Old English eludes most readers anyway. This feature of film (and) sound, specifically in CGI episodes, merits close scrutiny, particularly in *The Monkey King 2*'s *erhu* (two-stringed Chinese violin) solos.

Mircea Eliade's *The Forge and the Crucible* (1956) provides an alchemical rationale for the dragon's morphs among three states of matter, from the solid gold it hoards as its raison d'être to the fluid blood coursing through its veins and to the gaseous breath emitted to incinerate human bodies, combination of solids and fluids, into ashes and air. The internal circulation intersects with the external one in an ever-changing process. Eliade writes that "Ores 'grow' in the belly of the earth after the manner of embryos. Metallurgy thus takes on the character of obstetrics. Miner and metal worker intervene in the unfolding of the subterranean embryology: they accelerate the rhythm of the growth of ores" (8). Humans who most hasten, even replace, the working of time on the ore are, of course, blacksmiths and alchemists. In the Middle Ages, ores were believed to be "generated by the union of two principles, sulphur and mercury." Eliade further quotes A. Daubrée's translation of *Bergbüchlein*: "in the place of mercury, they presuppose a humid, cold and mucous matter, without sulphur, which is extracted from the earth as its sweat and by which, with the copulation with sulphur, all metals are said to be engendered" (Daubrée 387 quoted in Eliade 48). Fiery sulphur and liquefied mercury maintain a perfect balance in the dragon's blood, mercurial within yet sulphurous once let out.

This valorization of alchemy informs both the dragon's body leading to nothingness and Beowulf's body leading to fame. In the hero's visualization of his own possible demise, Hrothgar's mead-hall turns into Grendel's meat hall. Indeed, Heorot boasts of abundant mead, honey wine with spices, but no food, except human flesh consumed by Grendel. In lines 442–455, Beowulf contemplates his own demise, to be cannibalized by Grendel. Beowulf leaves specific instruction as to his Weland-made chain mail rather than his bones. The body is worth less than the names of Beowulf as well as of the legendary blacksmith Weland. As Weland forges the armor that lasts through time, so does the hero Beowulf make his name. The romantic, religious impulse for timelessness pulsates in the making of the hero's armor and the making of the hero's name. The magical transformation in the forge likens itself to that on the battlefield. This has already taken us to temporal morphs.

Temporal morphs

Temporality stands for both temperature and the duration of time, which is always wedded to temperature and the elements. Whereas heat or rising temperature engenders life forms, hatching animals, gestating fetuses, and ripening ores and metals in the bowels of the earth, cold or dropping temperature brings about the opposite to life, death or cessation of life, which is but a stage in the cycle of nature. The abbreviation of temp denotes the temporary nature of all living things as well as dead matter, for life and death are forever in flux, relentlessly morphing. Indeed, time marks Monkey's rise as well as fall. Waiting for the right hour of the night to visit the Patriarch for secret teaching, Monkey counts his breaths: "There is no watchman to beat the watches or call the hours. The best Monkey could do was to count his incoming and outgoing breaths" (23). Counting breath (*shuxi*) is a Taoist and Buddhist meditation practice that fuses the finite physical existence with the infinite air, earth, and the flow of time. A simple act, so repetitive as to be hypnotic, taps into cosmic multiplicity. As such, Monkey bides his time for the rise, yet his fall is also marked by time. During his five-hundred-year imprisonment, Monkey is given iron pills to appease his hunger and smelted copper drops to quench his thirst (77). Arguably, Monkey undergoes cruel and unusual punishment, which serves as a second gestation melding him with iron, copper, and other materials in the womb of the earth, reminiscent of his first gestation in a rock "worked upon by the pure essences of Heaven and the fine savours of earth" (11).

Along with temporality and temperature, temporal morphs include a third kind of change, namely, that of tempo, of narrative shifts. This narratological gear shifting is most pronounced in, so to speak, trippin' in *Monkey*. Trippin' is the 1970s slang to describe a hallucinogen-induced altered state of consciousness. Getting high on psychedelics such as LSD allowed Aldous Huxley and Jim Morrison, among others, to enter "the Doors of Perception," which, of course, replicated nocturnal dreams, daydreams, and even spiritual epiphanies and cognitive awakenings. Four centuries prior to the modern "amenity" of chemical substances, characters in the Chinese classic *Monkey* already venture in and out of a dreamland adjacent to, accessed through, their quotidian reality and mindset. Such back and forth resembles an out-of-body trip taken by the dream self, a trip that takes off like a musical variation, a wrinkle in the life course of the real self.[3] Of course, a Freudian approach would not view the heaven and hell in dreams as parallel universes beyond oneself. Rather, they are subconscious longings and fears projected outward, externalized.[4]

The pun of trippin', however, brings us to the rhetorical, stylistic formula of *Monkey*'s characters stumbling in their dreams and waking up. They slip up often because they are pushed from behind. Trippin' oneself or getting tripped up becomes the proverbial glitch in what appears to be a normal routine. Dreams and nightmares come to a halt, as characters awake to heightened, deepened awareness of their trip to the West and into their own soul. Like a Freudian slip, this glitch opens the sesame of a peephole onto the hermetic, reputedly fail-safe, system. Trippin' out is the way in. Accordingly, *Monkey*'s characters stumble upon the truth, coming face to face with themselves.

During the pilgrimage, Tripitaka has a dream visitation by the Crow-Cock King, who was pushed into the well but had been preserved by the Dragon King "with a magic pearl" (191) for three years. At the end of his appeal for help, the phantom Crow-Cock King stumbles and wakes Tripitaka up. Such dream sequences constantly reprise with variations throughout *Monkey*. The emperor of the Tang dynasty, Taizong, intercedes on behalf of a dragon king, who beseeches Taizong in a dream. Taizong hence engages his minister Wei Cheng in a chess game to prevent the righteous Wei, capable of crossing into the spiritual realm, from beheading the dragon king. Wei dozes off in the midst of the game and executes the dragon in his sleep. Unable to fulfill his promise, Taizong falls ill and dies, yet he arrives in the netherworld equipped with Wei Cheng's "recommendation letter" to give to Wei's confidante serving as an official in hell. This confidante manages to return Taizong from the yin to the yang world by adding two strokes, thus twenty years to his lifespan and reign on the throne, in the registry of the living and the dead. Both heaven and hell are conceived in human terms, with *guanxi* or interpersonal connections playing a prominent role. On the cusp of his return, Taizong languishes by the river in hell engrossed in two golden carp "leaping in and out of the waves," the very pursuit between the two kings, himself and the dragon king, in and out of the living and the dead. Only when Taizong's horse is pushed and "its rider [falls] into the river" is he repatriated (107). This interplay of dream and reality informs *Monkey* in particular and the journey of life in general, a dream and an allegory that culminate in the awakening or nirvana from life.

The two brush strokes added to Taizong's lifespan echo Monkey's own dream vision. Arrested by ghosts and taken to hell in his sleep, Monkey strikes his lifespan of 342 from the registry, a most striking strikethrough and a numinous numeral that would look like this: ~~342~~. After all, Monkey does not erase the number but simply cancels it. The number does not vanish, only rendered inoperative. This paradox points to death being stricken from the book of life: death is killed; dreams overwrite life. The random number of 342 becomes predestined doubly, not just as the lifespan but as its denial. By the same token, the designated eighty-one calamities of the pilgrimage are a script already written waiting to be fleshed out by the pilgrims. Abstract numbers are to be filled, lived by humans.

The narrative strategy of modifying the temporality and the tempo of the story emerges in *Monkey*'s trippin' as well as in *Beowulf*'s interlace. John Leyerle in "The Interlace Structure of *Beowulf*" has identified *Beowulf*'s narrative style as interlace that interweaves two threads of the story like braiding two strands of hair into one queue. In temporal terms, the *Beowulf* poet intersects three instead of just two strands. When he is queried as to his identity, his answer is first contextualized by the past (the rise and the name of his father) and by the *wyrd* (fate) in the future (the fall as in the mead-hall Heorot "awaiting its burning" and as in Beowulf's demise). The present is less a fleeting moment in time, mechanically determined by the clock. Rather, the present merges in a river of time, almost a mythical time where past, present, and future fold into one another. This sets the stage for many episodes later where the effect or the end precede the cause or the beginning. Time is less chronological, sequential than fused, circular. Compared with the modern sense of mechanical time, Beowulf's world experiences time as if from a bird's-eye view, untethered to the present.

What appears to modern eyes to be digressions becomes John Leyerle's interlace. The *Beowulf* poet practices interlace or montage as he presents the scop, or court singer, singing the praise of Beowulf. Note the cinematic transition from "many a warrior / gathered, as I've heard" (57, ll. 836–837) with their galloping horses (57, l. 863) to "Meanwhile, a thane / of the king's household, a carrier of tales" (59, l. 866), as if it were a crosscut or montage to synthesize a mental picture of "C" comprising both rise and fall from the picture of A (horses) and the picture of B (the king's singer in Heorot singing of Beowulf as well as "Sigemund's exploits" l. 874). In the midst of his performance in honor of Beowulf's triumph over Grendel, the scop segues into a cautionary tale of doom and tragic end of the dragon-slayer Sigemund (father of the true dragon-slayer Sigurd in the Germanic myth), with the secret of his nephew-son Fitela (59). In Germanic mythology, Fitela is the son of the incest between Sigemund and his sister Signy. This reprises the Nordic interlacing of rise and fall, of heroism and its dark side. Rather than a tangent or digression, it is an interlace, a counterpoint, a montage, of the heroic and the tragic, of glory and impending end. The dragon-slayer Sigemund has a secret of shame, just as the Grendel slayer carries the seed of time that will age and defeat him in the end. The scop's storytelling provides a longer view, a collective memory of the vanity and *wyrd* (fate) of humanity. The montage or interlace effect of A+B=C is part of *Beowulf*'s poetics, an alchemy of mental images aiming for certain psychological effect.

Beowulf's digressions are frequently triggered by material objects, fundamentally different from modern emplotment by means of action or deeds. Yet objects imply deeds or past wars and debts in Old English. Having killed both Grendel and Grendel's mother, Beowulf returns to the Geatland and rules for fifty years after the king Hygelac was slain. The story of Hygelac's demise has already been narrated in a flashback prompted by an object, the "torque of gold" (83, l. 1195) Hrothgar bestowed upon Beowulf in appreciation of the slaying of Grendel. This treasure is in turn given to Hygelac upon Beowulf's return to the Geatland. Hygelac's "neck-torque" (83, l. 1211) is thus a gift stained with invisible blood, part of the war spoil taken from fallen enemies, now Hygelac among them. Hygelac's fall is not only foreseen in the torque's "rise" or in its being offered to Beowulf, but the fall of the Geat king also appears later in a flashback, when the current king Beowulf contemplates his own demise before taking on the dragon. Beowulf's demise is in a further flashback and elaborated on as Wiglaf, Beowulf's successor, explains how the Swedes would now avenge Hygelac's slaughter of the Swedish king, now that Beowulf is slain. Numerous flashbacks interweave the present moment, the impending doom in the near future, and conflicts in the past. Even the neck-torque's glorious debut comes with its bloody end prophesized. *Beowulf*'s is a poetics that goes against the passage of time in a reversal of cause and effect: first the present, then introduce the cause of the present, which lies in the past. But the future of certain doom is constantly foreseen and visualized, by the *Beowulf* poet, Heorot scops, Beowulf himself, and the Geat woman elegizing after Beowulf's death (207, ll. 3150–3156), so much so that the future destruction must be a prospect widely accepted by the medieval audience.

CGI morphs

With its magic wand of binary light and shadow, zero and one, CGI standardizes, stylizes, and, truth be told, "levels" Nordic, Taoist, Tolkienian, neo-medieval, or classical myths. CGI means mainly the manipulation of light against darkness, or lit shapes against a studio's green screen to be digitally altered, all for the effect of magic to substantiate the trio of morphs explicated above—ideological, corporeal, temporal. Lightning or thunderbolts are designed to enlighten, to provide an elevated discourse for filmic climaxes. In the context of Huallywood (Hollywood wannabe, aka, Beijing-directed soft power via global cinema), however, CGI aims to lighten, whiten, and whitewash yellow (off-white) faces and tales that gravitate, unwittingly, to global hegemony of Anglophone white culture by means of Hollywood and American popular culture. Although designed to show smooth transition from one image to the next, digital morphs represent ruptures. In Roger Warren Beebe's words, "the morph as a rupture in narrative (a sort of punctuation or suspension of narrative in a moment of sublime spectacularity) and as a rupture in a greater historical narrative (a way of marking a turning point on the way to a posthuman cinematic form and affective regime)" ("After Arnold" 161). Beebe sums up that the morph means "a suspension in the progress of the narrative" (166).

As a method of high-tech alchemy, CGI enables the trio of morphs to break out of ideological compartmentalization; to transgress against the confines of the self as well as space, evidenced by the fantasy genre's de rigueur cross-dissolves; and to subvert temporal tyranny in slow motion, fast forward, time-lapse cinematography, and logically improbable visual spectacles. CGI is our millennium's new bottle for the old wine of imaginary metamorphosis, from Ovid's *Metamorphoses*, to Aztec shaman transformation into falcon or jaguar, and to Chinese dragons containing features of different animals to indicate that it is forever changing. These features include deer antlers, snake scales and body, chicken or eagle claws, and other body parts. CGI's formulaic climax of cross-dissolves harks back to the Chinese dragon as a being-cum-becoming, despite the sacred, iconic, even perfect pedestal on which the Chinese elevate it. The dragon's perfection is instantly called into question considering the Chinese proverb of *shenglong jianshou bujianwei* (You see the divine dragon's head, but not the tail). Usually taken to mean the dragon's indescribable shape and unimaginable power, it conceivably points away, like Monkey pee on the Buddha Palm, to the makeshift, hodgepodge nature of China's self-proclaimed image of "heirs of the dragon," a totemic, obscure lineage from time immemorial.

In comparison to the realistic depiction of human characters, CGI in fantasy films is reserved for nonhumans, principally Gods and demons, especially the latter since they rationalize fight scenes that require digital wizardry. To rephrase Blake's penetrating insight of Milton in *Paradise Lost*, the plot of fantasy films trudges "in fetters" when it moves mortals on earth, whereas it takes flight "at liberty when of Devils & Hell." The prose then soars into poetry. Given its position at the cusp of digitalization and entertainment, computer science and technology are "of the Devil's party," literally in the visualizing of the beyond, "without knowing it." To illustrate, note the multiple ironies embedded in that one film still of the White-Boned Lady spinning a web under her loom to entrap Tripitaka in *The Monkey King 2* (Figure 7.6). Before taking leave of his master, Monkey has encircled Tripitaka in a protective ring, once again CGI disguised as magic. The CGI of a spider's web coming from the White-Boned Lady's fingertips represents her demonic power; technology in global cinema stands in for premodern magic. The web comes on the heels of her life story, as if figuratively spinning a yarn, a sob story, to move Tripitaka emotionally and to move him physically out of Monkey's protective ring. An *erhu* solo, especially its vibrato, plucks the heartstrings, a refrain of the theme music ringing from the opening credits to the end, punctuating key private moments. Herein lies the irony of virtual reality, which is fantasy spun by digital trickery. Nonetheless, her yarn happens to be her true life story of having been the human sacrifice to vultures and gods to end a famine. Tripitaka is moved and, of his own volition, moves out of his sanctuary because the White-Boned Lady confesses her trauma and pain. Tripitaka becomes vulnerable because she has shared her own vulnerability, a strange entanglement and

FIGURE 7.6 *The White-Boned Lady spinning a web in* The Monkey King 2.

kinship of the predator and the prey to be continued in the prolonged inter-karmic romance between the two.

In addition, weaving used to be a traditional feminine task to clothe and swaddle in warmth her family and loved ones. The loom is a matriarchal heirloom for women deprived of any claim to heirs; it is a material object that intertwines female labor and disenfranchisement, one that looms large over history (his story) like guilty conscience. But the White-Boned Lady subverts it to execute her insidious, literally underhand, conspiracy to enshroud the victim with the spider web spun from her fingertips. The spider web has long been associated with spider demonesses bent upon sucking dry, "bleeding," the masculine life force. Hence, the White-Boned Lady symbolizes the female avenger for the injustice inflicted on her and on women at large. The moment when threads, which are but computer-generated filigrees of light, sprout out of her fingertips is accompanied on the soundtrack by a Tibetan monk's otherworldly chordal chant to signal supernatural power. A quiet CGI moment of relative stillness proves far more fruitful than its conventional high-velocity, high-octane counterparts such as an explosion, avalanche, titanic clash, and whatnot.

In its opening credits, "authentically Chinese" music instruments of *erhu*, zither, tambourine, and others proffer a sense of Chineseness. But when the opening credits culminate in the film title, the soundtrack has eased into decidedly Western orchestral, grandiose film music that is taken for granted in global cinema. The *erhu* functions as the portal into exotic, epic fantasy. The *erhu* solo returns when, by the loom, the White-Boned Lady confesses to Tripitaka her life story, juxtaposed by the crescendo of CGI special effects, of the sound effect of orchestral music and magical chordal chant, and of femininity. Convergence of visual, sound, and gender aims to create an over-the-top phantasmagoria. The pattern is set musically and thematically: going small, local, and "authentically native" Chinese first, followed by going big, technological, and global.

Solo performances of the *erhu* come as the sole musical instrument for confessional moments and emotional highs, to convey the sound of the soul. Yet in this sense of alone-ness, singularity is as constructed and forged as the *erhu* itself, the musical instrument allegedly embodying Chineseness. Meaning literally "two-stringed barbarian music instrument," the *erhu* hails from Central Asia, outside of China. Further afield, the film music is composed by Christopher Young, a Caucasian, and *erhu* solos are credited to Karen Han. Trained at Beijing's Central Conservatory of Music, Han is responsible for snatches of *erhu* music in *Men in Black 3* (2012), *Star Trek* (2009), and *Pirates of the Caribbean: At World's End* (2007) as well as in China-themed *The Joy Luck Club* (1993) and *The Last Emperor* (1987). Given that the *erhu* has two strings and the hands that move them come with myriad skin colors, the duet of Chineseness and non-Chineseness fluctuates like chordal chants of two harmonic vocal registers, or like the White-Boned Lady the victim and the vampire. *Erhu* music is a recurring motif, initiating a global audience to an exotic locale with exotic sounds in the opening credits, which fade seamlessly into Western orchestral music. Needless to say, the grand sound of Western orchestras is closely associated with fantasy films' epic, CGI spectacles from *The Lord of the Rings* onwards in recent memory. Do *erhu* solos serve as the soles, the bottom of the foot, or the foundation and the soul of Chineseness? In any event, the *erhu* of the opening credits and of alleged Chineseness sets the stage for the film to market itself in global cinema.

All the action sequences are trademarks of CGI. The showdown between Monkey and the White-Boned Lady reaches a turning point when she conjures up from underground tentacles of bones and skulls, shafts of "dark light" from herself as the alchemical "black sun" (Figure 7.7). To counterattack, Monkey splits himself right down the middle into multiple images to torpedo her avatar of a mammoth skeleton with nearly perverse golden accessories of a tiara, epaulettes, and multiple rings, a spider's six-legged lower body to boot (Figure 7.8). Both his self-splitting and her self-cloning are the two sides of the same CGI light show, either through Monkey's fiery light or through the White-Boned Lady's dark light. This light show continues in the concluding inter-karmic romance between Tripitaka and the White-Boned Lady. About to be crushed by the Buddha Palm into ashes, the White-Boned Lady is saved by Tripitaka giving his own life. In a nebulous world cast in northern lights, again the light show of CGI, the White-Boned Lady converses with Tripitaka, predictably accompanied by the *erhu*. A contrite White-Boned Lady gestures in a thousand-armed Goddess of Mercy Guanyin pose (Figure 7.9) before slashing herself to prevent Tripitaka's sacrifice (Figure 7.10). CGI serves well this long

FIGURE 7.7 *The White-Boned Lady's "dark light" from below in* The Monkey King 2.

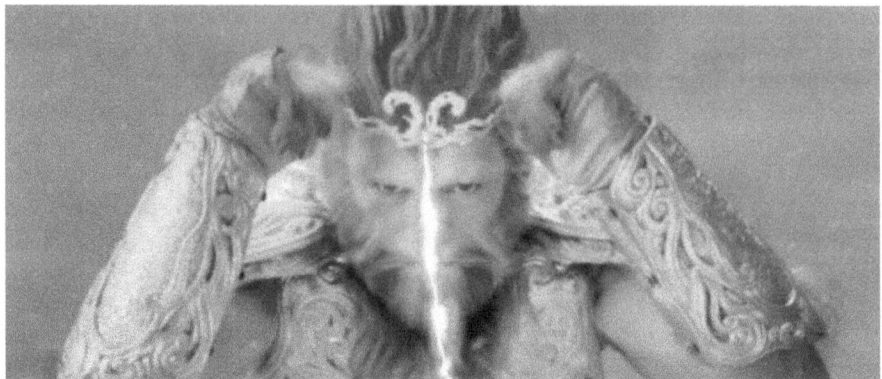

FIGURE 7.8 *Monkey self-splitting in* The Monkey King 2.

FIGURE 7.9 *The White-Boned Lady's Guanyin pose in* The Monkey King 2.

FIGURE 7.10 *The White-Boned Lady slashing herself in* The Monkey King 2.

goodbye, a melodramatic Platonic romance between two self-sacrificing characters, a romance "with Chinese characteristics," to borrow a phrase from current Chinese propaganda. This is followed by the "bromance" of tears as Tripitaka exhorts Monkey to kill him in order to save the White-Boned Lady's soul.

All these CGI morphs in the conclusion are motivated by the Buddha Palm with the voice-over threatening to turn the White-Boned Lady into "nothingness," "ashes" (Figure 7.1). Specifically, the Buddha says "*huazuo wuyou, huifei yanmie*" (turn into nothingness, with ashes blown away and the smoke extinguished). This is most extreme, as an existence, albeit demonic, is made to vanish without a trace. The Buddha's threat of pulverizing the demon comes as the divine justice against her sin and transgression. Tripitaka's compassion, however, compels him to sacrifice himself for her sake. Ashes, the tiniest granules of matter and the least significant, turn out to drive the strange romance of Tripitaka and the White-Boned Lady. Both willingly give up their lives to spare the other from the Buddha's wrath. In fact, by conceding to Tripitaka's plea, the Buddha Himself has shown compassion.

Conspicuously, action sequences in Zemeckis's *Beowulf* are also packed with CGI techniques: Beowulf's duels with Grendel, with Grendel's dam, and finally with the dragon. Contrary to *The Monkey King 2*'s repressed romance, *Beowulf*'s action involves two kinds: making war or making love, both engineered by inner drives, prompting the actors to take action to realize spatial and/or corporeal desire with the aim of eliminating the existence of the enemy or of eliminating the existence of one's sexual desire. Both desires seek to effect changes, to demand their own extinction, through killing of the foe out there or killing of one's own urges in here. *Beowulf*'s love scenes, therefore, resemble warfare, exemplified by Grendel's "dam" (female parent of an animal) melting Beowulf's phallic sword with a mere touch (Figure 7.11).

FIGURE 7.11 *Grendel's mother melting Beowulf's sword in Zemeckis.*

James Dormer's ITV series *Beowulf: Return to the Shieldlands* encapsulates this duality in its characters of Skinshifters, the so-called Mudborns who morph between human disguises and their true monster shapes. These dissembling monsters are rarely pure evil. Skinshifters debut with the spy Koll, who is coerced by a human, Hrothgar's in-law Abrecan, to assassinate a key Heorot official. Captured and in shackles, an enraged Koll changes to his monstrous shape when he learns of his wife's death sentence for his crime. In other words, wrathful monstrosity springs from human love. Similarly, the good healer Skinshifter Elvina takes on her monster form, first of all, to rescue Beowulf, her lover, from the stake and, secondly, to rescue Grendel, her son, from the Heorot guard's blade. Figures 7.12, 7.13, and 7.14 show three cross-dissolves as Elvina changes back to human with Grendel holding his injured arm in the background. A monster surely, but as Frank McConnell argues in "Born in Fire," "the word, 'monster,' derives from the Latin *monere*, to warn; but *monere* itself probably derives from the Indo-European root which also generates the Latin word, 'to show.' The monster, in other words, is both a warning and a spectacle" (232). Both Koll and Elvina shape shift in order to save their loved ones. The cross-dissolve presents them in a terrifying, freakish image, which is motivated, ironically, by love. The paradox of form and motive harks back to *The Monkey King 2*'s prolonged battle between the two enemies of Monkey and the White-Boned Lady bent upon annihilating each other. Although this battle of seeming hate concludes in Monkey's favor, with the aid of the Buddha Palm, it leads into Tripitaka's chaste love for the White-Boned Lady.

FIGURE 7.12 *Elvina in her Mudborn form in* Beowulf: Return to the Shieldlands.

FIGURE 7.13 *Elvina as half-human cross-dissolves to become human in* Beowulf: Return to the Shieldlands.

FIGURE 7.14 *Elvina cross-dissolves to become human in* Beowulf: Return to the Shieldlands.

An overly long romantic story of self-sacrifice perhaps, it demonstrates a tendency similar to *Beowulf* of mixing love and hate, humans and freaks.

For maximal global appeal, filmmaking East and West seems to favor extremes, not only the "extreme sports" CGI proliferates on-screen but also the extreme settings of morphing *bingxue* of fire and ice, of volcanic eruption and arctic deep-freeze. *The Monkey King 2*, for instance, sets a multitude of fights in snow, entirely out of context of the classical novel. The Nordic *Beowulf*, of course, finds itself in its natural element of ice. Inspiring both works is our millennial pursuit of heroic savior in an endless war on terror. The worst of times, after all, wishes for the best of times by way of a miraculous delivery. To that end, the West boasts of a long tradition of tragic heroes, who aspire to great things and fall due to certain tragic flaws. Beowulf, for one, died because of having gone it alone against the dragon, a king more concerned with his fame than with the welfare of the Geat tribe. Zemeckis's Freudian spin sexualizes the fundamental tragic tenor of the two kings' failing. By contrast, Monkey is comic, parodic, child-like, and asexual, diverging drastically from the Western notion of hero. Nonetheless, palpable similarities bridge the two hemispheres in terms of a shared alchemical poetics of ideological, corporeal, temporal, and CGI morphs.

8

China's Orient in *Fan* de Siècle Culture

This chapter turns the tables, from whites' Orientalizing of "off-white" characters to China's version of "off-yellow," darker-hued characters. China's Orient unfolds against the backdrop of President Xi Jinping's 2012 slogan "China Dream," which captures poetically his nation's millennial rise, and which cloaks spatial, discursive expansion as a mere elevation in height.[1] This beautiful dream of world peace and harmony under the reign of a New China marshals and martializes non-Han minorities within China's borders and, for lack of a better term, Asiatic humanoids without. To apply Edward Said's East–West power dynamics in *Orientalism* (1978) to the East and, specifically, to the majority Han Chinese vis-à-vis other Asiatics, China's discourse of fiction and film comes to silhouette itself against Orientalized non-Han minority populations and cultures as well as against other Asiatics embodying in their humanoid image—freakish or idealized via computer-generated images (CGI)—as much repulsive evil as alluring romance. Vested in China's Orient is both exoticism and horror. Contemporary popular culture is replete with examples. Ang Lee's *Crouching Tiger, Hidden Dragon* (2000) sets the stage for millennial China's love affair with Muslim Uighurs and borderland deserts, an eroticism over the Silk Road's origin of Xinjiang or China's "Wild West." Jiang Rong's *Wolf Totem* (2004) and Jean-Jacques Annaud's 2015 film adaptation not only relocate the setting to the Inner Mongolian grassland but also revise and sentimentalize mass reeducation of urban youth during the Cultural Revolution.[2] Even earlier, Dai Sijie romanticizes young lovers sent down to the hinterland of Sichuan mountains with Balzac, classical violin, and a local "little Chinese seamstress" in his eponymous novel and film (2001, 2002). Dai's incongruous splicing of the West's high culture and the indigenous ingénue exoticizes the Maoist purge for his original Francophone and subsequent Anglophone readers. Esoteric Tibetan sky burial notwithstanding, Joan Chen's *Xiu Xiu: the Sent-Down*

Girl (1998) paints a far bleaker picture of an urban youth peddling her body to local officials in exchange for her return to the city—to no avail.

China's Orientalism fantasizes non-Han Others as well as China's own past, only re-purposed, re-invented. In relation to non-Chinese, Jing Wu weaponizes the predatory trope of a wolf in *Wolf Warrior* (2015) and its sequel for patriotic fervor along China's opium-infested southwestern borders as well as in what Howard French dubs "China's second continent" of Africa. In relation to China itself, this collective re-imagining from the post-Mao era delves into history in the synecdoche of tomb robbing in a series of internet literature and film. Such transforming of Maoist national trauma ranges from internet novels *Ghost Blows Out the Light* and *The Secret of the Grave Robber* to the 2015 films *Mojin—the Lost Legend* and *Chronicles of the Ghostly Tribe*. *Mojin* et al.'s ancestral Chinese ghosts join hands with *Wolf Warrior*'s Asiatic humanoids of drug fiends and traffickers, Caucasian mercenaries included, as Chinese heroes' monstrous foil. In these franchises of novels and films, the serial nature of China's Orient, charming and perilous at once, bespeaks a new empire's repetition compulsion, a soaring dream tied with a kite's umbilical cord to haunting nightmares, which arise out of one's own neo-dynastic zeal and capitalist market forces.

Instead of fin de siècle denoting the Aesthetic, art for art's sake movement at the end of the nineteenth century in the West, *fan* de siècle diagnoses China's ruptures as it plunges into the twenty-first in a graphic memoir, an internet novel, and in films, all crystalized in the word *fan*. The long memory of an octogenarian Rao Pingru's graphic memoir *Our Story* (2013) subconsciously reiterates the leitmotif of food, or *fan* (飯), literally "rice" in Chinese yet generalized as meals. The good times and sweet memories run up against the bad Maoist years with empty stomachs. The absence of details of those lean years contrasts sharply with the plenitude of the past. If one China is remembered fondly in great specificity, Rao buries the Maoist China in the oubliette of his family history—an Other disavowed by the Self, an Orient splitting within the Orient. Whereas Rao represses the haunting ghost of yesteryear, Tianxiabachang's sensational tomb robbing internet novel *Ghost Blows Out the Light* (2006) and two film adaptations (2015) satiate and feed the fantasy of millennial Chinese fans. The Red Guards and their revolutionary fanaticism justify archaeological expeditions into China's dynastic and Maoist past as well as a national psychological revisioning. Since the subtle distinction between "-n" and "-ng" endings oftentimes eludes non-English speakers, these fa*n*s to a man grow a "g" into wolfish or vampiric fa*ng*s, a people's "teething" in the celebration of jingoistic nationalism in *Wolf Warrior* and *Wolf Warrior 2*. The three-way splits of China comprise Rao's *fan* or food; millennial fans consuming as well as being consumed by tomb-raiding virtual reality; and discursive fangs of moviegoers savoring *Wolf Warrior*'s triumph over drug traffickers along China's borders to the sequel's over pandemics and coups in Africa.

An octogenarian's graphic memoir *Our Story*: Two Maos of China

Rao Pingru published his Chinese-language graphic memoir *Pingru Meitang: Wolia de Gushi* in 2013 at the age of ninety-one. In memory of his wife of six decades Mao Meitang, the bulk of illustrations were done after her death in 2008. Among the graphics that were dated, most came after 2008, except three from 2003, 2005, and 2006 (292–294). The English translation by Nicky Harman, *Our Story: A Memoir of Love and Life in China*, was brought out by Pantheon in 2018. Harman and Pantheon retitle the memoir for the English-language global market, cashing in on the millennial China fad and the romance genre. Indeed, Rao's is a heart-wrenching love story with Mao Meitang through years of hardship of the Second World War, the civil war, and Chairman Mao Zedong's ruthless purges disguised as revolutionary campaigns. In particular, love and life with his spouse Mao persevere despite having been "unloved" by Chairman Mao and subjected to labor reform and reeducation in a figurative death-in-life from 1958 to 1979.

While the Chinese subtitle *Wolia de Gushi* does mean Harman's *Our Story*, the phrase *"wolia,"* a local variant of *woliang* in Mandarin, is far more intimate, slangy than "our," given that the southern accent all but pinpoints the couple's hometown of Nancheng, Jiangxi. Harman could have translated it as the more vernacular *Me and You* rather than *Our Story*. The local specificity in the subtitle's heart-warming turn of phrase *wolia* endears itself to native-speaking readers. This may be inspired by Rao's fellow octogenarian, even nonagenarian, Yang Jiang's memoir *Women sa'er* (*Us Three*) on the family bonding amidst Maoist adversity of Yang, her eminent scholar husband Qian Zhongshu, and their daughter Yuanyuan. Should one Romanize Yang's Chinese title as *Women san*, then the title would approximate *The Three of Us*, losing the informal tone of the retroflex *Sa'er*. Slurring *san* (three) as *sa'er* is the equivalent to dropping the "ng" in "liang," both betokening the closeness of the loved ones, so close in fact that they have dispensed with the formality of Standard Mandarin pronunciation, that they have bent the rules and "loosened" their tongues amongst themselves.

"Our Story" of Rao and Mao, however, parallels their un-story or no story under Chairman Mao. One Mao is Rao's lifelong love, with whom the memoirist had shared fond memories of Chinese cuisine throughout southern China in the late 1940s and early 1950s; the other Mao ripped apart their family, sending Rao and their sons to faraway labor camps, eating them alive for two decades. The remarkable minutiae of the octogenarian's memoir on the couple's travels and food tasting abruptly fall in the late 1950s into what journalist Louisa Lim calls collective amnesia when Rao, an ex-Kuomintang (or ex-Nationalist) officer, was sent from Shanghai to a labor camp in the province of Anhui in 1958, where Rao languished until 1979. With only a passing nod or two at the dispersal of his family and the scarcity of food, Rao offers the barest of a testimony on having been swallowed up by Mao's China for twenty-two years, so sketchy that it pales in comparison to Yang Jiang's memoir *Six Chapters from My Life "Downunder"* (1981). This may be unfair, though, in view of the prominence of Qian Zhongshu. A revered essayist and scholar in her own right, Yang Jiang can afford to chronicle their years of reeducation through labor. Rao, having been an artillery officer in the Kuomintang army, must have endured endless struggle meetings, group criticisms and shunning, and more, which do not even grace the memoir in passing, except that his sons suffered, having inherited "bad elements"— bad blood, as it were—from their father.

Throughout Mao's campaigns, Rao and Mao are no longer connoisseurs of delicacies; they *are* the delicacy for the Chairman. In the post-Mao China, Rao reunited with Mao, only to witness her steady decline, plagued by diabetes and dementia. An octogenarian's long memory synthesizes *youwu* (presence/absence, existence/nonexistence) of two Maos: one, "Mother of [My] Children" (*haizi de ma* in Chinese), he would fain never forget; the other, Father of the State, he feigns to have already forgotten. They have come to chart the axes of Rao's life: one was his love by his side; the other his Red Sun shining above and smoldering yet from the grave.

In contrast to the millennial romanticizing and fantastic revising of Maoist trauma, exemplified by Tianxiabachang's (pen name of Zhang Muye) internet novel *Ghost Blows Out the Light* and its film adaptations, Rao excels in factual unpretentiousness, dedicating his graphic memoir to his late wife. Thoroughly experiential, Rao's memory is highlighted by *fan* or food, a key dimension of Chinese culture in general, and of Mao-induced famines in particular.[3] This is entirely opposite to the fantasy-driven internet novel and CGI-glutted films. Rao indulges in sweet, pun intended, memories of having partaken local cuisine across southern China. The novel *Ghost Blows Out the Light* and both film adaptations trade actual reminiscences, including Rao's gustatory ones, for a virtual extravaganza. The visual and auditory spectacle substitutes for "body memories" of the smell, taste, look, and sound of local cuisine.

Rao's title page is illustrated by two rice bowls. The following page shows two hometown delicacies from Nancheng, Jiangxi, subsequently glossed as "Tiger Skin Duck" in a bowl and "Cassava Meatballs" in a bamboo steamer (36). Childhood memories of Rao's parents are represented, revealingly, by their respective rice bowl. Dinners with family members sitting at a round table recur throughout, all marked out by a caption next to each character. The first such drawing lists twelve figures (22). Any cursory examination would suggest that Rao is an amateur hobbyist, drawing out of personal interest and to commit to memory what has been lost. Far from pursuing artistic perfection, Rao creates drawings that resemble a beginner's trial and error, utterly in need of mature craftsmanship. The lackluster, child-like drawing may well be the draw Pantheon is betting on for the English-language market. The simple, unskilled lines and colors portray a China mysterious with a dark past, yet also ingenuous and seemingly at peace with itself. The Chinese and global readership embraces Rao's graphic memoir for the tone of lighthearted tranquility despite the turmoil of modern Chinese history that has engulfed the Raos.

Assuredly, part of this sense of equilibrium comes from the gastronomic leitmotif, which readers anywhere in the world would find appealing, particularly when the foodstuffs hail from an ancient culture renowned for its cuisine. The array of famous Nancheng dishes continue with Lye Zongzi Dumplings and Soup Vermicelli (29), Mid-autumn Mooncakes (32), Small Fries, and Bones (38). Not only are these dishes pictorialized but the de facto recipes are explicated in the accompanying pages, all intertwined with childhood memories of his family and various festivals. This contextual richness, to a certain degree, compensates for the reader's inability to taste the food. Rao came to know Mao Meitang as a child in Nancheng and the nearby town Nanchang. One tiny memory lapse is intriguing, given the self-imposed two-decade amnesia later on in this chronological narrative. Meitang had a "brave and quick-witted" escort to school, who chased away Meitang's bullies. "Meitang told me the maid's name," Rao writes: "but unfortunately I cannot remember it now" (60). Rao's authentic voice comes through in not being able to recall a minor character, an "extra," in their lives, whereas Rao skips two decades, the prime years of the couple with toddlers and infants, without as much as a word of acknowledgment. Self-censorship over persecution, pain, and guilt over a growing family entails that a writer must refrain from even alluding to self-censorship.

Nancheng dishes then give way to Nanchang delicacies, as Rao unites with Mao in her city. Nanchang boasts of Ovenside Sesame Cake (120) and Cantonese food (140–141). While serving in the Kuomintang army, Rao and his fellow soldiers partake "stir-fried shredded pork and greens, eggs fried with garlic chives" chased down with "baijiu liquor" (130). After their marriage in 1948, they avail themselves of China's culinary abundance in their travels: Xuzhou's pears (160) and *youtiao* (fried breadsticks 161); Zhangshu's generous portions of "shredded pork and garlic sprouts" and "minced chicken soup" (174); Liuzhou's "teeming fishes congee" (182); Guiyang's zongzi and "Cantonese style sweet and savory midmorning snacks—chashao pork buns, zongzi, paper-bag chicken and sticky rice chicken" (186); Anshun's communal "hot pot" (191), "garlic-chive pies" (193), the Miao (Hmong) minority's "chestnuts" (196), rice noodles (198), and grilled corn cobs (201). A litany to make any mouth water! So into food are the Raos that they attempt to open their own noodle restaurant in the 1950s in Nanchang, only to fold in six months. Despite the business debacle, the Raos help themselves to Nanchang's *guotie* pot-sticker and deep-fried bean curd (219).

A publishing house editor in 1958, Rao is summarily sent to Anhui "to do Reeducation Through Labor" (249), toiling ten years to build a dam, another ten on a gear factory floor, a promotion of sorts from outdoor to indoor labor. This coincides with Mao Meitang carrying "bags of cement on the construction site of [Shanghai's] Natural History Museum" (255). Chapter 6, "You Ask Me When I Will Return," is the only one out of the seven chapters on the two-decade black hole of their lives. This chapter continues the focus on *fan* or food, yet in a dramatically diminished way. If eating gives joy pre-1958, they can no longer afford this luxury for the next twenty-two years. Food becomes a matter of survival.[4] Meitang helps plan Rao's "three-day action plan for six cents' worth of food coupon," basically on "a [daily] saucer of pickled cabbage" (264). Consistently, Rao's writing spices hunger and misery with fun and hope. Even the pathetic "action plan" with square grids demarcating Day 1, Day 2, and Day 3 vertically and breakfast, lunch, and dinner horizontally is so absurd that it is almost hilarious, especially when inside the nine grids are the same saucer and a tiny pinch of salt. Making a joke out of desolation is, of course, a survival strategy. Stricken by edema in 1959, with a swollen abdomen and stick-like legs, Rao takes comfort in the timely arrival of Meitang's parcel of cod-liver oil, to which he attributes his speedy recovery. Father in a labor camp and mother in a community workshop, the Rao children must fend for themselves by kneading their own dough to make pancakes. The fourth son deftly crafts a pistol out of his share of dough, out of which the second son bites off "the pistol barrel" (267). Losing both meal and pistol, the fourth son bursts into tears, a moment of grief that happens to be comical as well. Rao thrives on such balancing of tears and laughter, except the restrained and understated style rarely betrays extreme emotions.

This is the reason Rao focuses on *fan* or food, exactly because millions died of starvation in the late 1950s and 1960s. Food means life, even when lives are being devoured. His tongue would rather speak of what has passed through it into his body than what his body has passed through in the maws of Mao. The ritual and symbolism of eating, however, have changed beyond recognition in the hands of those coming after Mao, who reimagine, as Tianxiabachang and like-minded filmmakers do, historical traumas as escapist virtual reality. Whereas Rao buries the ghosts, post-Mao writers and directors raise them, reveling in a phantasmagoria of the past to usher in "the China Century." There is another way to conceptualize the key difference between Rao and others. Rao used to be the eaten and tries to dissociate from that visceral pain of having lost so much. In the post-Mao Darwinian "Socialism with Chinese characteristics," quite a few artists would rather see themselves as the winner, the eater, in control of a challenging future, albeit haunted by the past.

Ghost Blows Out the Light for the China Century to unspool, like a film

The wildly popular Chinese internet novel *Ghost Blows out the Light* opens with "Grave robbing isn't sightseeing. It's not reciting poems, nor is it painting. It can't be that elegant, leisurely or respectful. Grave robbing is a skill, a skill that requires destruction." The author Tianxiabachang echoes, in a thinly-veiled rewording, Chairman Mao's famous saying, part of the sacred Little Red Book of the Cultural Revolution clutched in every Red Guard's hand. Mao's Holy Writ endorses a certain degree of violence, part of any armed struggle. Indeed, rebels who won through bloodshed in 1949 became the People's Republic of China; rebels who won through bloodshed in 1776 became the United States of America. Mao's prophecy of blood goes:

> A revolution is not a dinner party, or writing an essay, or painting a picture, or doing embroidery; it cannot be so refined, so leisurely and gentle, so temperate, kind, courteous, restrained and magnanimous. A revolution is an insurrection, an act of violence by which one class overthrows another.

Just as Chairman Mao justifies violence as class insurgency, so does Tianxiabachang inflict on netizens the mind-numbing mediocrity of a sprawling fantastical narrative of tomb robbing. Both masters take from the haves to consolidate their hold on power—Mao's in the 1960s across China; Tianxiabachang's across the millennial Chinese-language cyberspace. Most revealingly, the pen name of Tianxiabachang means, literally, "under heaven supreme singing," the monopolizing drive of wish-fulfillment apparently quite agreeable to his fans. The derivativeness of Tianxiabachang's opening resonates with Chairman Mao's. Far from an original thinker, Mao himself spins off from Frederick Engels's "On Authority" (1872): "A revolution is certainly the most authoritarian thing there is; it is the act whereby one part of the population imposes its will upon the other part by means of rifles, bayonets and cannon."

Given that hero or strongman worship runs amok in today's world, *Ghost Blows out the Light* and its on-screen reincarnations suggest repression and Gothic haunting as the national psyche feels compelled to excavate and revise its history. Consistently, a neo-imperial, global capitalist expansion, reminiscent of the nineteenth-century British Empire and the twentieth-century American Empire, presents itself as a reaching out to the non-Chinese other and a reaching in to China's own Maoist and dynastic past. Both forms of China's overreach proceed in the name of love and bonding rather than self-interest and material gains.

Mojin: The Lost Legend, directed by Wuersha, is one of the two films in 2015 based on the internet novel. Both films consist of escapist fantasies into the Gothic and underground history, fraught with dynastic and Maoist violence. Just as China is on the rise and expanding globally, these films dive into the past and subconsciousness. The forward-looking, growth-oriented millennial China is shot through with a backward-looking, Gothic imaginary of tomb raiding. The internet novel went viral in 2006, tapping into the restiveness of a changing system from the collective communist ethos to a capitalist profiteering drive. The quest for wealth aims at the global market out there; however, tomb raiding redirects down into the ground right here, or a bit off-center, in the remote borderlands of Inner Mongolia and Xinjiang. Instead of gold and material treasures, the Hitchcockian MacGuffin in *Mojin* is displaced onto a life-giving Equinox Flower to bring back the loved one, who perished during the Cultural Revolution. Rather than the drive for money, this film turns the enterprise of tomb robbing into a wish fulfillment to compensate for loss and guilt over the past. Apparently a quest for material wealth, the tomb raiders are portrayed as yearning for lost love, their heart's desire outweighing profit. Déjà vu, all over again: this duality is similar to turn-of-the-last-century robber barons Carnegie, Rockefeller, and others becoming philanthropists or to millennial US tech tycoons monopolizing the global market through unscrupulous business practices while setting up foundations to fight world hunger and epidemics.

The opening voice-over by the protagonist played by Kun Chen narrates the origin of *Mojin*. The strange English title comes from *Mojin Xiaowei* (摸金校尉, captains charged with prospecting for gold in tombs or, simply, tomb robbing), the dignifying military rank granted to tomb raiders by Cao Cao of the Three Kingdoms of the first century BCE. The chaotic times with scarce resources compelled political and military leaders to generate revenue by taking not just from the living but also from the dead. Tomb raiding became one quick way for riches. The attribution of *Mojin* to the historical villain Cao Cao, defeated by Liu Bei and his two sworn brothers, by Tianxiabachang in the internet novel is intriguing, consistent with communist China's *shanzhai* (rebels' or bandits' mountain stronghold) mentality. That Cao Cao has been notorious comes to justify *Mojin*'s non-conformist revolt. After all, the Maoist communism has always valorized itself as the righteous, iconoclastic insurgents against corrupt orthodoxy, filled with revolutionary zeal and passion against a moribund, oppressive tradition. This can be seen in *Ghost*'s chapter 1 when the narrator's father is said to have squandered the family fortune, a common motif in communist Chinese literature on the ills of feudal China to be supplanted by communism. This is a literary conceit shared by many, for instance, the opening to Yu Hua's *To Live* (1992), where the protagonist Fugui in his debauchery gambles away the entire fortune accumulated through generations.

In keeping with the communist rebel image, Mao Zedong's regime prided itself on the fifty-thousand *li* (one third of a mile) Long March of 1934 to 1935, which charted the escape route from southern to central China under the Nationalist crackdown. Mao also aligned his regime with historical autocrats such as the First Emperor of Qin and rebels such as the peasant revolt of *Huangjin* (Yellow Scarves or Yellow Turban). Tianxiabachang evokes the communist DNA of insurgency to subvert common decency and respect for the dead, creating an alternative code of respectability through camaraderie, youthful devotion to communist equality, despite the fact that they engage in the desecration of the dead beyond the pale.

The Mojin team's slogan of "united and live, divided and die" harks back to The Three Musketeers's "All for One, One for All." Much of this film is derivative, including the internet distribution, going viral in China because it taps into the universal human need for fantastic escape from the hardship of life while reflecting that hardship. Historically, that hardship stems from mass migration and persecution of the Maoist years. In a millennial China with the Great Helmsman still deified, that hardship continues in the cutthroat competitiveness, contributing to a widening gap between the haves and the have-nots, no different from the socioeconomic injustice in an advanced capitalist economy like the United States.

This internet novel is highly imitative, borrowing from the Western film genre of grave robbers whose "day jobs" are archaeologists and aristocrats. These include university archaeology professor-turned-swashbuckler Indiana Jones (Harrison Ford) in Steven Spielberg's *Raiders of the Lost Ark* (1981) and *Indiana Jones and the Temple of Doom* (1984); "Lady" Lara Croft (Angelina Jolie, or Alicia Vikander in the 2018 remake) with wall-length book shelves in *Lara Croft: Tomb Raider* (2001, 2003); and the archaeologist Rick O'Connell (Brendan Fraser) in *The Mummy* trilogy (1999, 2001, 2008). These protagonists combine professional expertise with action hero's larger-than-life daredevil stunts. This thin line between intellectual elite and common thief also lies between above- and underground, or between conscious reality and subconscious make-believe. Yet the expertise of Hollywood's Western archaeologists are substituted by the Chinese mystical *feng shui* (geomancy) tradition passed down to Mojin members, including their Mojin Amulet (boar tusk or ivory), Mojin Compass with Taoist Eight Trigrams, Black Mule Hooves to halt zombies or *da zongzi* (sweet rice-filled bamboo leaves), and their superb kung fu skills. In general, book knowledge is replaced by secret knowledge or esotericism close to mysticism.

The Mojin team consists of Hu Bayi, his given name pointing to his birthday on August 1, which is the Foundation Day of the People's Liberation Army (PLA). Yet his nativist, nationalist, liberation army-ish flavor is spiced up, exoticized, eroticized by Qi Shu's Shirley Yang, with her English given name. Despite her Lara Croft look, with the same kind of slim, curvaceous physique, the same kind of outmaneuvering of men, Shirley constantly reverts back to feminine hysteria or girlish temper tantrum, particularly when she pretends to care less about Hu's life and death, only to storm back to scream "liar!," which betrays her feigned indifference. This female guile thoroughly punctures itself at the end when the daredevil Hu sacrifices himself to save her by tying her down, much to her dismay, in the coffin. Hu means for the coffin to float out of the cavern fast filling with water. With the coffin lid opened in safety and Shirley wailing inconsolably over the loss of her love, Hu suddenly materializes in front of her eyes as if playing a prank on her. Shirley bursts out in a girlish, nasal whine between anger and relief. When he hesitates over putting the equivalent of an engagement ring on her finger, Shirley pouts and accuses Hu of not being a *yemen*. *Yemen* used to be a typical northern Chinese address for men, which also means "lords" or "masters." The pair of lovers are accompanied on the tomb-raiding adventure by two clownish characters. These two additional Mojin team members are Wang Kaixuan or Lord Kai, played by the comedian Bo Huang; and the cartoonish, *xiangsheng* (traditional standup comedy performance of a duo's crosstalk) actor Da Jin Ya or Grill speaking in a rapid-fire, high-pitched voice or screaming in fear.

In terms of time and space, both the film and the internet novel belong to genres that point to the future, with films' high-tech CGI and internet novels' new form of fan-based dissemination of content. Yet the narrative structure is nostalgic and escapist. A pattern of having the cake and eating it, too, emerges. Sci-fi-style virtual reality embellishes historical revisionism of the Maoist past. Archaeology of dynastic ruins comes hand in hand with video game sequences or underground CGI scenes shot against the studio's green screens. Whereas the conventional wisdom has the past as the known and the future as the unknown, the past of the novel and the film is distorted, repressed, and unknown, with the future quite predictable.

The millennial film has an overture of tomb raiding, where the protagonist Hu Bayi's voice-over opens with Mojin's origin and the codes of conduct governing such enterprise. Specifically, a candle is lit by the coffin about to be opened. If the candle dims or is extinguished, the title of the internet novel suggests that the ghost has blown it off. This means that no matter how close the raiders are to the treasure, they must desist. Yet this filmic opening's voice-over of ghost extinguishing the light circles back to the internet novel's opening with its allusion to Chairman Mao, perhaps *the* apparition looming over all. Reading the two openings together, one can argue that the Founding Father Mao with his ten-year holocaust of the Cultural Revolution and other devastating campaigns constitutes the phantom of the nation, which continues to haunt millennial China. The China Century must negotiate with Mao's legacy, the sin against millions of Raos included, keeping the communist *xianghuo* (ancestral incense) lit and burning, while exorcizing the national trauma. This psychic trick ultimately accounts for the rage that is the internet novel: it succeeds in simultaneously acknowledging and disavowing, exhuming and entombing, "what hurts," which is Fredric Jameson's term for history.

As the candle flickers, Hu realizes the deceased is so well preserved that it is none other than Hu and Kai's young love or "old flame" Ding Sitian of the Cultural Revolution years. The light eventually goes out, just like the young Hu and his comrades' past, only to throw, figuratively, a dark light on the Mojin team's imminent reentry into the same royal tomb in Inner Mongolia and their own "memory palace." Indeed, when Kai chances upon the way to the mausoleum in the distance, the lay of the land resembles the profile of a pregnant woman lying supine (Figure 8.1), as if taking a page out of the 1885 *King Solomon's Mine*'s twin peaks called Sheba's Breasts that leads to the treasure. This colonial, masculinist, and Eurocentric conquest of "virgin land" resonates with the unveiling of Ding's face in a stone sarcophagus suspended midair with chains like neural synapses and blood vessels. Just as Kai uttered "Ding …" when he witnessed the landscape from afar in Figure 8.1, Hu confronts, in a close-up, Ding's "angelic" face long buried within himself. From the Euroscape surveilled by Kai to Hu's neuroscape, the expedition to Inner Mongolia ventures into the past and the protagonists' suppressions.

Symbolically, Ding's given name Sitian (thinking of sweetness) draws from communist China's slogan *yikusitian*, remembering the misery of past feudalism and thinking of the sweetness of present socialism. Yet this sweet girl played by Hong Kong actress Angelababy veils or inters under her pretty mixed-race face China's past trauma; moreover, her Western-sounding stage name of Angelababy belies the pure nativist fervor that her Red Guard character personifies. This overture is like a promotional trailer: intense, action-packed, quick cuts, soundtrack leading to the plot

FIGURE 8.1 *The treasure's location in the profile of a pregnant woman in* Mojin.

gradually unfolding. This overture ends with the disbanded Mojin team peddling Chinese curios on the streets of New York in the 1980s, judging from the quaint station wagon with wood trim on the sides and the gigantic mobile phone, amidst inner-city decay of piles of trash and black youths breakdancing. Mojin has indeed retreated, not only from that one venture but from tomb raiding altogether, so much so that they have left China for New York.

To enlighten Shirley on Kai's return to Inner Mongolia in search of the Equinox Flower (*bi'an hua*, the flower on the other side of the river), which Kai had promised to retrieve for Ding Sitian, Hu explains the Maoist years in a series of flashbacks. Kai's journey intends to fulfill the promise decades ago as well as, subconsciously, to bring Ding Sitian back to life, for the flower is alleged to have the power to revive the dead. A flashback takes us to the 1960s or 1970s when the young are dispatched to the remote borderlands to labor and learn from the people. Revisionism is at work as the young men and women embrace their mission with joy and passion, when in reality it is a banishment from the cities and their families, as Rao Pingru's *Our Story* discreetly hints at. The team of Mao's youths transgressed against Inner Mongolia's deities; the Cultural Revolution's dictum of Demolish Four Olds led the zealots to smash stone guardian statues on the prairie as well as those underground in Japanese Army armory tunnels. Hence, the flashback, in an infinite regression, goes from the movie viewers' twenty-first century back to the Mojin team's present of the 1980s, to the team's past of the 1960s, to the Japanese Army's 1940s, and finally to an unspecified, remote dynastic past. Spatially, it ranges from New York to Inner Mongolia to underground tombs, the last location occupying the latter half of the film.

The Mojin expedition is commissioned by a cult leader Ying (implying yin for dark, occluded as opposed to bright or Yang, which happens to be Shirley's surname) Caihong with a Global Mining Company front. Ying is sick with brain cancer and desperate for the panacea of the Equinox Flower. It is significant that, with her eyes one blue and one black, Ying leads an entourage headed by two lieutenants, a white male and a Japanese girl fighter Yoko, à la *Kill Bill*'s Gogo Yubari played by Chiaki Kuriyama. Both Yoko and Gogo don the fetish, soft-porn high school uniform and miniskirt. Derivativeness can be rather convoluted. Here Quentin Tarantino's Orientalist girl fighter is copied by a Chinese film for a heavy dose of Japanese malice by way of Hollywood. The Equinox Flower is alleged to have passed down from a nomadic Khitan princess, so the non-Han others are fully exploited: Inner Mongolia, the nomads' belief system, Khitan's Gothic tombs and mystical alterity.

The nativist horror, aka, horror "with Chinese characteristics," shows in the zombies named after Mid-Autumn Festival's *da zongzi*, sweet rice-filled bamboo leaves, to be temporarily halted by black mule hooves. The Equinox Flower is also held up like a Chinese ancient round mirror, reflecting back or triggering the guilt-ridden Hu and Kai in an attempt to reunite with Ding. The nativist characteristic fully emerges in the cavalier use of trigrams, the key to mysticism, which is the unknown anyway, subject to manipulation. Hu reads the suspension bridge's pieces of wood as long bars versus broken bars that formulate the trigrams. Hu further forecasts the location of the tomb through his compass not so much of the magnetic north but of a Chinese Eight Trigrams (bagua).

The Khitan Princess's Equinox Flower is so named to suggest the division between two halves, as much between life and death as between the equal length of day and night as the sun crosses the Equinox around March 21 and September 23. Humans on earth either go up into the sky or the future or go down into the earth or the past, except such tomb-raiding tales mix the two. Going down for treasures of the dead requires soaring up via the technological flights of CGI and special effects. Ding sacrificed herself to allow Hu and Kai to lift off in the elevator to escape from the underground explosion, only to have them returned to the exact spot to relive the past. The film itself is also divided in two, with more scenes above ground in the first half and almost all underground in the second half. Location shots in New York and the prairie are replaced by green screens and computer-generated cave scenes, moving from the open space to studio virtual reality.

Chronicles of the Ghostly Tribe, directed by Lu Chuan, exemplifies well one constant complaint of Western viewers: the plots of Chinese films are perennially messy. The story zigzags and jumps; incongruous filmic elements mishmash. Characters materialize in the narrative and then vanish. *Chronicles of the Ghostly Tribe* is no exception. Yet the convoluted plot reflects, in fact, the torturous Chinese history and national psyche behind the popularity of a mediocre, almost kitschy, internet novel and its filmic afterlife. The Ghostly Tribe symbolizes China's own painful history, expunged yet still lingering, if only subconsciously. A schematic sketch of the plot, however, is in order.

In *Chronicles*, the protagonist Hu Bayi volunteers for and survives a suicide squad in the late 1970s, tasked to investigate "unidentified creatures that could alter history" deep inside a Kunlun Mountain, Xinjiang, archaeological site. Hu came to lose all his comrades, including the archaeologist Professor Yang Jialin and his daughter Yang Ping, Hu's beloved. An allegedly history-changing, epoch-making event initiates the hyperbolic, apocalyptic, and propagandistic rhetoric typical of Maoist China, which prided itself on being the most righteous and "rightest" form of government, among other superlatives. The term "suicide squad" (*gansidui*, literally, dare-to-die team) signals voluntary martyrdom for a patriotic cause, evoking the agitprop martyr Lei Feng and others, rather than terrorists like today's suicide bombers. Such military terminology as the suicide squad manifests the overall militarization of the film. China's top secret Bureau 749 is entrusted with the mission of investigating such inexplicable, almost supernatural, occurrences, suspected of being conspiracies against China. The code name of Bureau 749 is in keeping with those of covert spy agencies, exemplified by Great Britain's MI6, or of fictitious spies, exemplified by 007. Acronyms and numbers are deployed in naming to create a mysterious aura. Hu is eventually recruited by 749.

Similar to *Mojin*'s opening voice-over by Hu Bayi, *Chronicles* commences by going back in history, not as remote as *Mojin*'s dynastic past but twentieth-century, mostly communist, archaeological discoveries. Played by Taiwan's Mark Chao with traces of his Taiwanese accent, Hu Bayi narrates the chronological excavations from the loaded moniker of a "dragon corpse" find in 1934, jumping to 1956, 1972, 1974, and then 1978's Kunlun Mountain. The exact dates and widely-publicized digs, especially the 1972 *Mawangdui* mummy with her flesh intact, dating back to the Western Han dynasty (206 BCE–AD 9), lend credence to the fantastical setting of the film. This historical progression also brings the audience to the Red Guard-style Model Beijing Opera song and dance in the Kunlun desert to incentivize soldier-workers suffering from altitude sickness at the excavation site. Such musicals of revolutionary zeal all flop, so to speak, hiding subtle critiques of Maoism. The Kunlun oil field workers' Model Opera halfway through the film ushers in monsters. A bereft Hu on the train finds his fallen comrades singing in chorus, which evaporates like a mirage. The cast features *Mojin*'s Hu Bayi, comic Wang Kaixuan, and Yang Ping (later named Shirley), with the addition of Professor Yang, a mysterious librarian Mr. Wang, and Captain Sun.

As soon as the suicide squad enters the underground cavern belonging to the eponymous Ghostly Tribe, the squad comes under attack from prehistoric dinosaurs, firebats that incinerate whoever comes into contact with them, avalanches, and other disasters, all CGI. Despite the brevity of their acquaintance, Hu has fallen in love with Yang Ping, while Professor Yang plays a strange matchmaker role. Yang all but commands them to join hands in the Ghostly Tribe's cavern to open the Demon Pagoda's gate in hopes of releasing all the tribesmen imprisoned by their antagonist, the human king Prince Yi from time immemorial. The convoluted plot later reveals that in Yang Ping's body flows her mother's Ghostly Tribe blood, which will lead to self-immolation in her prime on account of Prince Yi's curse. The only way to save her is to have Yang Ping and Hu, descendant of Prince Yi, jointly break the curse. That Hu is elevated to the other half of undoing Prince Yi's spell suggests he is more than a mere descendant: he is the bona fide heir apparent. Intent on saving his daughter, Professor Yang is oblivious to the side effect of unleashing all the monstrosities into the world. This catastrophe is thwarted by Captain Sun who throws himself on the Tribe's flame to extinguish it. One of the phantom keepers of Prince Yi's vault, Captain Sun sacrifices himself to prevent the opening of what is the equivalent of Pandora's Box.

Prince Yi's curse that brings about spontaneous self-combustion of the Ghostly Tribe members when they reach forty or fifty years of age merits a closer look. To apply communist iconoclasm to this conceit, setting fire to the Ghostly Tribe turns them into sacrificial lambs or martyrs in the tradition of book burning and knowledge suppression by the First Emperor of Qin in history and by the futuristic *Fahrenheit 451* (1953). The Emperor of Qin, of course, buried alive scholars; dystopian fictions routinely emplot the hunting down of dissidents or dissident thoughts. This explains one of the most touching moments in the film when characters fail to touch: Yang Ping's mother puts up her hand on the windowpane to match with her husband Professor Yang's on the other side while being burned alive by Prince Yi's curse (Figure 8.2). Yang Ping's mother manifests no ghostly evil, but human love. Ghosts are more human than humans, especially when Professor Yang covers their young daughter's eyes to shield her from witnessing the human torch that is her mother and also from the fate that awaits her when she comes of age. Having inherited her mother's human compassion, Yang Ping herself uses up all her Ghostly Tribe's gifts, as if burning herself up, to revive dead comrades: Hu Bayi, Professor Yang, and Captain Sun of the suicide squad.

Having survived the cavern, Hu is mysteriously whisked away from Bureau 749 by a library director Mr. Wang. Rather than the head of a Beijing library, Wang is the master keeper of Prince Yi's vault, of which Captain Sun is but one. Throughout Hu's stay at the library, Wang secretly plies Hu with Professor Yang's academic publications on the Ghostly Tribe. Ironically, Prince Yi's chief guardian exposes Hu to, rather than shields Hu from, the Ghostly Tribe nemesis. The deepening of Hu's knowledge of the Tribe coincides with the lengthening of his hair from the closely cropped army days as well as with the "flaring up" of an old shoulder wound inflicted by

that burns us to ashes at a certain age.

FIGURE 8.2 *Yang Ping's mother burned alive while trying to touch Professor Yang in* Chronicles of the Ghostly Tribe.

firebats. Wang finally reveals his true identity, while offering the sage Taoist-Buddhist counsel like an incantation: "Arising [*sheng* or life] may not be arising; extinguishing [*mie* or death] may not necessarily be extinguishing," thus subverting the binarism of life and death. This is a fusion resonating with, though not equivalent to, the Western expression of death-in-life and life-in-death. The first half of the counsel on "arising" is in vernacular, spoken Chinese (*baihuawen*), followed by the second half inching toward classical Chinese (*wenyanwen*). Compared with the first half's conversational *buyiding shi* ("may not be"), the second half's *mie weibi shi mie* contains *weibi*, an in-between expression straddling classical and vernacular Chinese. Akin to archaic biblical language that lends authority, *weibi* elevates the rhetorical register of what is already a Taoist-Buddhist maxim synthesizing all binary oppositions, Arising and Extinguishing included.

Likewise, the film's dichotomies of human versus ghost, ancestral spirit versus evil spirit, above- versus underground, consciousness versus repression, are cast into doubt. The less apparent pair of East versus West is similarly wedded. While Wang's chant draws closer to Eastern inductive synthesis than to Western deductive analysis, the consciousness-altering tone echoes the film's apocalyptic aura. The epic, grandiose absolutism befits China's self-image as the millennial superpower with a decisive role in human and world affairs, yet it smacks of the Messianic-Marxist predestination hailing from the West.

In terms of CGI embodiment, good keepers of the vault, such as Captain Sun and his fellow terra cotta-style warriors, are just as much "light show" as ghostly monstrosities. Both are specters produced by technology. The two protagonists evince similar blendings. The good Yang Ping doubles as the Ghostly Tribe's leader Shirley. Hu witnesses the merging of the two, once again a light show in front of the Demon Pagoda (Figure 8.3). Note the contrast between the two images. On the one hand, the Ghostly Spirit flows in midair in an erect posture, with frontal nudity and symbolic depravity. On the other, in the PLA's army uniform, especially the erstwhile leggings or puttees, betokening purity and sacrifice, Yang Ping lies supine and unconscious. What happens next is evidently a case of possession, literally, as the Spirit, later renamed Shirley, takes over Yang Ping's mind and body. By shooting Shirley in the finale to avert the hostile takeover of the world by the Ghostly Tribe, Hu kills Shirley to bring back Yang Ping before she expires. Mr. Wang's paradoxical axiom even applies to the enemy's last breath: a dying Shirley overlaps with an arising Yang Ping. Yang Ping returns to bid a sappy farewell to Hu: "*nishi shanliangde, zhengzhide, ke'aide*" (You are good, righteous, lovely). This convergence of horror and romance in a melodramatic mode teeters on kitsch, ripe for parody with the refrain of "de" (of) to make a string of adjectives in the Chinese language. To appreciate the farcical potential in Chinese, one can embellish the translation as the purple prose of "You are goodly, righteously, lovely." What is heart-warming and tear-jerking to the Chinese may be sidesplitting to the Westerner.

FIGURE 8.3 *The Ghostly Tribe's leader about to merge with Yang Ping in* Chronicles of the Ghostly Tribe.

Lest I belabor the obvious, the female protagonist yokes an exotic English name with a common Chinese name. In fact, her first name Ping could mean duckweed (萍) or ordinary (平), both denoting inconsequentiality. The English name highlights the otherworldly fantasy over China's Wild West of the Xinjiang desert. Hu Bayi, on the other hand, conveys nativist nationalism in that his name Bayi commemorates his birthday on the Founding Day of the PLA. Hu in his crew cut contrasts with his long hair during his long hibernation at the library. More importantly, Hu's body undergoes the same kind of metamorphosis, as does Yang Ping's floating corpse in Figure 8.3. To be precise, Hu is singed repeatedly by the old shoulder wound from firebats. The X-ray reveals mutations of Hu's shoulder bone structures (Figure 8.4). Yang Ping and Hu have been mongrelized as both human and ghost. Yang Ping's Other is Shirley. Likewise, Hu straddles the pure innocent self with Prince Yi's blood coursing through his veins and the contaminated self with the curse of firebats. Both firebats' victims and the Ghostly Tribe die of self-immolation. The firebats burn up human beings, just as Prince Yi's curse torches the Tribe members. Syllogistically, the firebat passes onto Hu Bayi the very curse his ancestor Prince Yi placed on the Ghostly Tribe. Ultimately, the two sides resemble each other more than they differ. This is the source of Chinese films' proverbial messy plot. Rather than Western logic of causal, linear analysis, the Chinese favor a more synthetic, cyclical methodology. While *Chronicles* pits humans against ghosts, the two are inextricably entwined, just like Arising and Extinguishing. China's pain from the Maoist past is projected out, dissociated as the Ghostly Tribe. That China's Other is but its own repressed Self comes through vividly in the attraction and repulsion between the two protagonists as well as within the split halves of each protagonist.

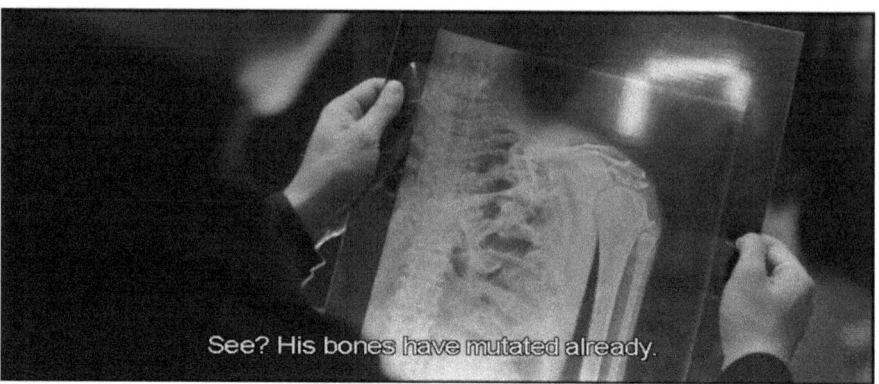

See? His bones have mutated already.

FIGURE 8.4 *Hu Bayi's shoulder bone mutation as a result of firebat scorching in* Chronicles of the Ghostly Tribe.

The naming of the archvillain as the Ghostly Tribe (*guizu* 鬼族) carries great historical implications. China or *zhongguo* (literally, the Middle Kingdom) has long viewed itself as the center of the world, hence alluding to neighboring non-Chinese as ghostly subhumans. The most salient example is the Japanese ghosts (*riben guizi,* 日本鬼子). Yet the film's Ghostly Tribe doubles as both the non-Chinese Other and the Chinese Self, the latter repressed and displaced externally. This psychic maneuvering stems from the Chinese history and consciousness. Priding itself as owning the twenty-first century, China must juggle its past and future. Moving toward its pivotal position on the world stage, China has to, nonetheless, contend with its memories of Maoist excesses as well as with the contemporary reality of the growing chasm between the haves of the coastal urban areas and the have-nots of the rural hinterland, no different from American tribalism of the coastal elite versus the rust belt, whites versus blacks, the north versus the south, the immigrant versus the native-born, and other socioeconomic and racial fault lines. Put bluntly, the Ghostly Tribe may well be China itself, gazing back from a dark mirror of the past, of the underbelly, and of its own repression. China's dilemma resembles that of the United States plagued by alleged fake news, "Build the Wall," and "Make America Great Again." To be a superpower entails warring not just against others but against the part of oneself that is bottled-up, forever haunting, though, like one's own shadow.

Wolf Warrior across Southeast Asia and Africa

Jing Wu's *Wolf Warrior* (2015) and *Wolf Warrior 2* (2017) feature a Chinese Rocky-Rambo combo in a global battle theater that concludes in kung fu-boxing finales, showcasing not only heroism "with Chinese characteristics" but also military hardware and technological prowess. In *Wolf Warrior*, the daredevil Leng Feng wages war against the drug lord Min Deng along China's southwestern borders, traditionally called the Golden Triangle adjoining Thailand, Laos, and Myanmar's mountain ranges with soil and climate perfect for the growing of opium poppies. The emplotment of narcotics is historically loaded since the Qing dynasty collapsed both under the weight of thousands of years of dynastic-tyrannical corruption and under British colonialism spearheaded by the two Opium Wars in the mid-nineteenth century, heralding what communist China dubbed "a century of national shame" until, of course, the rise of the Red Sun.

Ramboism with a Chinese twist arrives with ham-fisted, propagandistic overtones of the history of the PLA and of patriarchal tradition. The overture consists of a dramatic action sequence of Leng Feng shooting dead Min Deng's little brother despite having received the order to retreat. Leng defies the order to save a comrade injured and groaning on the ground, a heavy-handed reprise of his father's dilemma of mercy killing in the Sino-Vietnamese War in 1979, which has led to the father's lifelong guilt and withdrawal. It is implied that Leng's father had completed his mission of bringing an urgent dispatch back to the headquarters only after having fulfilled the comrade's wish of mercy killing. The comrade's plea "Make it quick" smacks of martyrdom from a *di* (young brother) to his *ge* (elder brother), putting the mission above sworn brotherhood. The very notion of brotherhood signals the responsibility to the larger family of the Chinese nation, for which martyrs sacrifice themselves.

Faced with the same dilemma, not once, but twice, Leng manages the second time around to strafe and fell a nearby tree trunk to shield the wounded soldier. This is the formula of one-upmanship that underlines the New China's "upgrade" in technology and in national spirit over the Old China and its failings. As though debunking a hundred years of national shame, Leng rises above his father's choice of either shooting the comrade or abandoning him. Throughout Leng's precision shots at the same bullet hole to eliminate the person in hiding, Min Deng is kept apprised of his brother's last hour via cell phone images. Visual representation through surveillance technology constitutes the film's narrative modus operandi, as both the bad and the good guys, the latter being the PLA commanders, enjoy live feeds of the action in the field through cell phones, body cams, drones, and satellites. Big Brother's panopticon eye controls the unfolding of the plot on-screen as well as the unfurling of nationalist passion off-screen.[5]

The best—and the worst—of examples comes from the conclusion of *Wolf Warrior 2*. Trapped under a reinforced concrete pipe, Leng stretches out his cell phone to transmit live coverage of the rebels' massacre of Chinese and African employees at a Hanbond (China-owned) factory (Figure 8.5), which enables the Chinese Navy cruiser commander and his staff to witness

FIGURE 8.5 *Leng Feng's cell phone transmitting live coverage of the rebels'
massacre in* Wolf Warrior 2.

FIGURE 8.6 *Chinese Navy cruiser commander witnessing the slaughter in* Wolf
Warrior 2.

the slaughter in real time on their ship's LED screen (Figure 8.6). The
bloodbath is accompanied by the soulful hymn of "Amazing Grace," sung
by the mother of Leng's African godson Tundun, one of the besieged Leng
has promised Tundun to rescue. As committed to saving Tundun's mother
and all the other hostages as Leng is, the commander anxiously awaits his
superior's order. When it finally comes through, the commander screams like
a madman to launch the precision missiles, based on nothing more than the
coordinates of Leng's cell phone, to eliminate every single one of the Western
mercenaries and African rebels, apparently with no collateral damage—the
amazing grace of smart bombs made in China.

This may be the worst of examples not so much because of the
ethnocentric wishful thinking as the sloppy slippage between characters'
Chinese words and English subtitles. The oral report from the staff to the

commander diverges from the subtitle's translation. The oral report in Chinese says: "We've received the order from our superiors" (我們得到上級的命令 *women dedao shangji de mingling*). This suggests to the Chinese audience that Beijing has issued the order of intervention to save human lives. The subtitle shifts away from a Chinese chain of command in view of the English-speaking global audience: "We've received the authorization from the UN." It is debatable whether the United Nations would authorize such a high-risk military action in the first place. In addition, the naval armada with aircraft carriers and destroyers flies Chinese flags. When the armada first appears on the screen, the caption in Chinese informs the audience that the ships receive orders from the Central Command to evacuate overseas Chinese. This points to a Chinese military operation for Chinese civilians rather than for Africans.[6] Indeed, splashed across *Wolf Warrior 2*'s domestic Chinese-language advertising is a slight revision of a classic Han dynasty commandment in bright red, rendered herein in an archaic biblical voice: "Whosoever transgresseth against China (*zhonghua*) shall be slain however far he may run." This opening salvo of the publicity campaign mirrors the film's closing shot of the front and back cover of a fictitious People's Republic of China (PRC) passport, the back cover inscribed with a vernacular prose reprise of the classic literary phrase, an inscription nowhere to be found in any PRC passport.

Contrary to the caption and what the Hanbond factory manager announces, Leng promises to bring all out to safety. This manager is the only Chinese character with gray hair, a sign of aging and insidiousness in a millennial China idolizing strength and youth, a millennial China "headed" by a Politburo of senior citizens, all of whose hair is dyed inky, shiny black. This manager instructs and proceeds to physically separate Chinese to be transported by the helicopter from African employees, who are to be left behind. The manager causes a tear-jerking scene when interracial couples, mostly Chinese males and African females, cling onto each other. The manager is then vetoed by Leng who says in Chinese that women and children will evacuate on the chopper, whereas men will leave together on foot. Switching to mangled English, he simplifies the two-prong instruction: "We leave together." Such filmic fissures are myriad: between what characters say in Chinese and in English, between what characters say in Chinese and what the subtitles say in English.

To avenge his brother and to hold China hostage with a biochemical weapon that targets solely Chinese genes, Min Deng employs foreign terrorists led by one Oldcat (Tomcat in film websites such as www.imdb. com) played by the Briton Scott Adkins. Herein lies yet another Chinese characteristic of Jing Wu's Ramboism. The finales of both films involve Leng's kung fu duels with the West, embodied by Oldcat and Big Daddy, played by the New Yorker Frank Grillo, in the sequel. Although the subheading is "*Wolf Warrior* across Southeast Asia and Africa," the casting of white villains symbolically thrusts China's wolf fangs into the representative bodies of the West. Thus, Leng engages with Oldcat in a showdown at the Golden Triangle border. In their skirmish, Oldcat rips off Leng's red shoulder badge that declares, in English, "I fight for China," and scoffs at Leng's elite unit of Wolf Warriors as "boy scouts." To don the shoulder badge of Red China is perhaps rich with associations for Chinese but for non-Chinese, this "fashion accessory" is rich, preposterous. That bright red in the shape of a shield defeats the whole purpose of Wolf Warrior members wearing camouflage in the subtropical forest. The English wording of "I fight for China" also modulates the patriotic message since the global lingua franca intends the proclamation for the world's eyes beyond the confines of a domestic viewership.

The discrepancy of receptions aside, Oldcat's mockery enrages Leng to the extent that he pushes the knife at his throat back at Oldcat to kill the opponent. Such dramatic reversal comes to pass as well in *Wolf Warrior 2* when Leng realizes Big Daddy shot his lover Long Xiaoyun with the silver bullet that has guided his search for Long's killer across Africa. Leng's fury springs not only from personal vendetta but also from Big Daddy's slight against "inferior" Chinese, a taunt akin to Oldcat's "boy scouts." Big Daddy's words make it not only personal but also cultural. Both white antagonists' provocative words unwittingly shift Leng into overdrive, with his adrenaline pumping, because their insults touch on Leng's and China's raw nerve of "a century of national shame." Whereas what Big Daddy says associates him with Western imperialism, what he does immediately brands him as one of the kung fu genre's archetypal villains. In hand-to-hand combat, Big Daddy deploys an underhand fighting technique with *anqi* (dark or hidden weapon), arrowheads thrusting from the fists. This *anqi* harks back to Jet Li's rival with a razor swishing along in his long hair in *Once Upon a Time in China* (1991), or to Jade Fox's blades sticking from the soles of her shoes in *Crouching Tiger, Hidden Dragon*. Repeatedly stabbing Big Daddy with the silver bullet to avenge Long and China, Leng whispers into his dying enemy's ear that the history of defeat and inferiority is "fucking history" (*Natama shi yiqian*, Figure 8.7). "That's so fucking yesterday" befits the Chinese curse word (*tama*) and the vernacular "*yiqian*" (before) more than the subtitle's overly formal "That's fucking history."

"History be damned!" is Leng's send-off for Big Daddy in *Wolf Warrior 2*. However, Leng taps into the very history of communist China unabashedly in *Wolf Warrior* when he runs out of bullets and clamps on the bayonet. By striking a forward thrust tableau with his rifle and bayonet against a phalanx of Min Deng's army at the border, Leng evokes the hackneyed mise-en-scène of Model Beijing Operas' fearless martyrs, fighting to the last breath. This individual bravado enacts long-standing propaganda, although it soon leads to an incredulous contravening of military etiquette. Flatulent excess has a way of deflating itself into travesty. What constitutes a moment

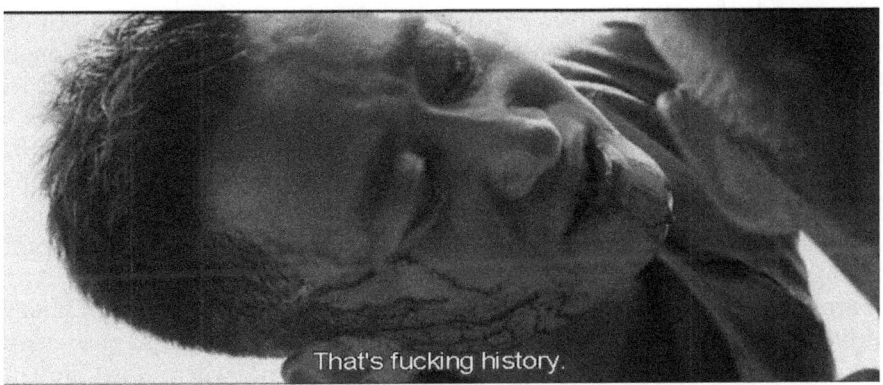

That's fucking history.

FIGURE 8.7 *Leng Feng whispering into his dying enemy's ear in* Wolf Warrior 2.

for applause in China lapses into a moment for laughs in the West. As the Wolf Warrior Special Forces commander, along with Deputy Commander Long Xiaoyun, arrives to congratulate Leng who has arrested Min Deng single-handedly, the commander salutes Leng first before Leng returns the salute. This outrageous episode reverses military ranks, but it thrills the Chinese audience perhaps because one feels a salute is due the hero. To any patriotic audience, the ridiculous exchange is somehow justified by the fallacy that Leng *is* China.

Such communist self-valorization imbues the films. When one African American mercenary engages in a mortal combat with Leng in *Wolf Warrior 2*, he professes confusion as to what exactly Leng is fighting for, now that he is discharged, harking back to Oldcat's rubbing of his fingers to indicate his gun-toting motive of money. Leng replies between clenched teeth: "Once a Wolf Warrior, always a Wolf Warrior." This resonates with the mutual military salute and self-introduction of their serial numbers and units between two former People's Liberation Army fighters, Leng Feng and the Hanbond factory security chief Lao He, a retired PLA officer who rediscovers his wartime glory in the ensuing fight. These Chinese saviors come to the aid of Chinese and African workers at a moment when they are abandoned by African authorities, the United Nations, and the US marines. Dr. Rachel Prescott Smith, played by the mixed-race and bilingual Celina Jade, puts her trust in the US embassy and marines, who are no-shows amidst the crisis. America does show, however, in Celina Jade's quasi-Caucasian features and fluent English, no different from the paradox of communist purity vested in the "mixed-blood" of Angelababy in *Mojin*. Leng Feng literally means cold front, one that heralds Chairman Mao's prophecy that "the East Wind is prevailing over the West Wind." Individual heroism is put in the service of a collective and communal obligation. "One wolf cannot defeat a lion or a tiger," Wolf Warrior commander informs Leng, "but a wolf pack can be invincible." This conjures up the Maoist catchphrase that the United States is but a paper tiger in the face of the Chinese populace. Through blood-curdling violence a New Red China is born, the films broadcast to the world.

Jing Wu's films were so successful that each engendered its own spin-off. *Extraordinary Mission* (2017) and Dante Lam's *Operation Mekong* (2016) emulate *Wolf Warrior* in terms of the setting of the Golden Triangle. The archvillains in these films are mostly overseas Chinese drug lords, who soon change to foreign adversaries in their sequels with global aspirations. Any nationalist expansion by definition does not stop at the borders: China's millennial dream looms large over parts of the world, Africa in particular. China in Africa energizes Jing Wu's *Wolf Warrior 2*, where an Africa in conflagration is to be saved by the lone Chinese hero and, ultimately, by the Chinese military might. It is significant that the hero has adopted an African godson, protected African employees of Chinese factories, and cultivated a vaccine through the petri dish of his own body. Dante Lam's *Operation Red Sea* (2018) likewise sets the rescue mission of overseas Chinese, in addition to Arabs and others, by the Chinese Special Forces *Jiaolong* (Water Dragon) in the Red Sea and a fictitious Arab or North African country. Although heavily derivative, Bing Tan's *China Salesman* (*Deadly Contract* 2017) tweaks *Wolf Warrior 2*'s "gunboats" and kung fu into business acumen and high-tech wizardry, complemented by the fading star power of Steven Seagal and Mike Tyson. The Aikido master and the boxing champ may well constitute a sales pitch in China but they look like caricatures of their youthful selves to American eyes. The erstwhile stars' Chinese market appeal looks downright bizarre in the context of global cinema. Likewise, China's self-image in these films seems somewhat nineteenth century and colonial to the rest of the world. Similar to his military counterpart, the China salesman overcomes tribal conflicts and repeated French hostile takeovers, while rescuing an African girl from what appears to be the ritual of clitoridectomy and winning the hand of the French business representative Susanna. Ironically, nativist romance favors pairing Chinese heroes with Western(ized) objects of desire: Shirley, Celina, Angelababy, and a very fair-skinned blonde Susanna. Killing white men closes with getting white or white-ish girls. The climax of *China Salesman* is reached when the salesman, finding no UN flag, raises a PRC flag instead to ensure safe passage through hostile fire. Better still, why not let the white girl do the hoisting first on behalf of the salesman and of China? (Figure 8.8) Such spectacle reprises Leng Feng's victory lap, so to speak, when he escorts the convoy to the United Nations safety zone by flying a PRC flag (Figure 8.9). The national symbol becomes a symbol of peace as the New China fashions its own identity vis-à-vis its Orient of ethnic minorities, Asiatic neighbors, Africans, and others. *Wolf Warrior 3* is slated for release in 2019, forecast by a tag-on trailer after *Wolf Warrior 2*'s closing credits. This trailer of sorts

FIGURE 8.8 *Flying a People's Republic of China flag to ensure safe passage in* China Salesman.

FIGURE 8.9 *Leng Feng flying a People's Republic of China flag to ensure safe passage in* Wolf Warrior 2.

shows the hostage Long Xiaoyun surviving Big Daddy's gunshot wound yet with a knife pressed against her throat reminiscent of Jihadi John and ISIS beheading, a miraculous half-resurrection to guarantee the wolf pack's longevity. Which alternate universe will it take its Chinese fan(g)s to in Leng Feng's next mission? Space, the final frontier, probably, as in *The Wandering Earth* (2019) casting Jing Wu as the astronaut-martyr?

9

An MSU-within-MSU: Mandarin-Speaking Undergraduates Writing "Chinglish"

With the exponential rise of Mandarin-speaking undergraduates in recent years, a school was born within Michigan State University, an MSU-within-MSU, a foreign branch campus, as it were, in the midst of MSU's East Lansing campus. In other words, foreign branch campuses may be upon us, on our shores rather than off. The University's international student report in 2018 states that "Chinese students could account for as much as 9.9% of the entire student body and as much as 66.1% of the international student body." Indeed, walking across the university grounds or Wells Hall, in particular, where large, general education classes take place, one catches snatches of the crisp Beijing accent as well as its variants from throngs of Chinese students. One rarely hears them struggling with English, though, as they never seem to be engaged in dialogue with American classmates. Nor does one hear American students groping for words to practice Chinese with them. The two MSUs thus orbit each other from afar, self-segregating with their own kind—American or non-American—in class selection and in other social circles.

At the risk of generalizing, a large number of this mini-MSU are paying customers to help keep afloat the university in economic woes since this Midwestern state's recession and the near-collapse of Detroit's automobile industry, the Big Three. One US higher education observer, Rahul Choudaha, even wonders whether international students have been herded like "cash cows." Such sources of revenue have been drastically curtailed as a result of the Trump administration's nativist America First policies. Stephanie

Saul reports in *The New York Times* that "schools in the Midwest have been particularly hard hit—many of them non-flagship public universities that had come to rely heavily on tuition from foreign students" ("As Flow of Foreign Students Wanes" Jan. 2, 2018). Since MSU has had a sterling "global brand recognition," that is, until the twin eruptions of Donald Trump and pedophile Larry Nassar, it continues to benefit from, in Saul's words, "foreign student enrollment, which now tops a million at United States colleges and educational training programs, and supplies $39 billion in revenue."

As customers are always right, particularly those with deep pockets, why should Mandarin-speaking undergraduates inconvenience themselves with daily conversations in an alien tongue, with which they may have the vocabulary and expressions of a teenager or younger? Why should they step out of their comfort zone, and experience self-doubt, hesitating over words, frustrated by their peers' turns of phrase? But that is supposed to be the whole point of their overseas study: to be immersed in an academic environment not just for a diploma but for critical thinking and empathetic imagining in the form of academic English. Practically, however, instructors find themselves negotiating the ideals of liberal arts education inherent in the macro-MSU, on the one hand, and, on the other, the micro-MSU's objective of returning home to China with a piece of paper ready to be mounted on the office wall.

I have had the good fortune of teaching a handful of Chinese students majoring in education and Teaching English as a Second Language (TESOL) in my Asian American literature classes as well as hundreds of Chinese students in disciplines such as Business, Hospitality, Accounting, Economics, Computer Science, and Engineering in required Integrative Studies in Arts and Humanities (IAH) classes with or without teaching assistants. I have also taught summer online courses to scores of MSU students, most of whom apparently having returned home to, or "summering" in, China. I volunteered to teach IAH general education courses for the simple reason that since these international students were not about to take my upper-level English classes, I felt compelled to move toward the mountain, to take on required IAH courses favored by Chinese students, courses usually shunned by some of my colleagues. Evidently, certain faculty members self-segregate, too, if they can manage. Teaching the large swath of Chinese students how to write academic English, with its attendant critical skills, is the right "rite of passage" in any institution of higher education. Looking back at their writings in, for lack of a better term, "Chinglish" and looking forward to more of the same, I wonder if this rite is conducted in the right way after all. This mini-MSU certainly lies within MSU but it may not be *with* MSU in terms of this rite of passage because, as all such rites go, it involves pain and hardship, with Spartan return. MSU sports' rally cry of "Go Spartans!" may sound like an ironic pun to those who see but meager yield in any investment in English for Academic Purposes (EAP). As career-oriented as American students, these Mandarin-speaking students are practical and perceptive in favoring ESP over EAP. ESP stands for English for Specific Purposes rather than Extrasensory Perception. English for Specific Purposes represents highly professionalized English in specific careers, such as Business English or Hospitality English. If anything, ESP means the exact opposite to Extrasensory Perception; the acronym suggests English for Simple People. Accordingly, English becomes a means to a practical, capitalist end, oblivious to the wealth of cultural capital inherent in any language. To broaden student perception of English as a mere means to a professional end, I propose a two-pronged approach: on the one hand, a balanced, comparative curriculum of Eastern and Western texts; on the other, an incremental yet uncompromising immersion in critical thinking and empathetic imagining.

Given that the IAH courses I have volunteered to teach and plan to teach are "Asia and the World" and "Area Studies and Multicultural Civilizations: Asia," a large number of Asian, particularly Chinese, students have enrolled in them. I have no idea how much influence my Chinese-sounding name has had in student decisions. I have emphasized the "and" in course titles so that they would not become Asian-centric, as so many are, taught by Asian researchers required to take on large, gen-ed courses. I have tried two models. The first one conducts a comparative study of key cultural icons that travel across space and time. We begin with mythical dragons shared by East and West. The dragon has long been the symbol of imperial China and Chineseness, as in the sixteenth-century classic *Monkey* (*Journey to the West*) and in Ang Lee's *Crouching Tiger, Hidden Dragon* (2000). By contrast, the tenth-century Old English epic *Beowulf* features an evil dragon and other monsters, which serve to elevate the heroism of the dragon-slayer. Maximal dragons then shrink into minimal germs in our new millennium, where science and technology have not so much retired mythical dragons as secreted their modern spawn in the form of carriers of global pandemic and paranoia, in Stephen Soderbergh's *Contagion*, K-Horror *The Host*, and anime *Spirited Away*. Given the global breadth in our literary and visual texts as well as in class discussions with peers from other backgrounds, students ideally acquire transferrable analytical skills as they cross cultures in business, science, education, and other majors.

The second model focuses on "Cool Outlaw and Lawman, East and West, in Words and Pictures." Cool outlaw in both East and West has been hot, firing up public imagination from medieval Robin Hood ballads and *Outlaws of the Marsh* (*Shuihu Zhuan*) to millennial cannibal Hannibal in Thomas Harris's *Red Dragon* and tomb robbers of Chinese internet fiction and film. Law-abiding readers and moviegoers project their discontent and rebellious impulse onto outlaws. Such transgressive flirting is counterpointed by a fascination with lawmen, be it the rational genius of Sherlock Holmes or Robert van Gulik's yellowface Judge Dee, not to mention Detective Dee in Hong Kong swordplay films. Indeed, the thin line between outlaw and lawman, violence and justice, cold-bloodedness and passion, East and West is so blurred that it begs the question of such distinction in our global village. This course pairs satanic serial killers with godlike serial detectives, represented in both fiction and film. The latter hails from Hollywood and Huallywood, the tinsel towns bathed in the Californian sun or soft-powered by Beijing.

Right from the outset, my syllabus acknowledges the challenge of such cross-cultural balancing. Walking the tightrope suspended between the set of scales of lawlessness and law, East and West, how do we, groping like the blindfolded Lady Justice from the West, wield the Buddhist, Manjusri sword of wisdom to shear through the illusion of differences, the fallacy of universality? Does this question suffer from mixed metaphors from two opposite systems? Does it upset logical binarism and imagistic consistency? How to reconcile something that is both cool and hot, both medieval and trending now? Such is only the beginning of our breach into the ever-morphing conceptual and artistic imagination.

My pedagogy in either scenario is to bridge East and West, rather befitting international students' overseas studies. This would not alienate English-speaking American students, for over half of the course content relates to the Anglo-American, Western culture. Moreover, the language by which the intellectual pursuit unfolds is their native tongue. These IAH courses walk on a tightrope, poised between familiarity and strangeness, depending on each student's perspective and background knowledge. Put in the trending lingo of ethnic food, my course, pun intended, serves an East–West fusion fare, which culture purists in the English or East Asian departments may dismiss as a state of stomach-churning ConFusion. To purists, I play a Con game of Fusion. But fusion is far more appetizing for a mixed American and non-American clientele than a course on, say, Chinese films, which can be taken without ever stepping outside of Asia itself, or a course on American films, which would recruit fewer international students.

In terms of curriculum, I experimented by opening the course with Anglo-American versus Chinese text. The first scenario moved from *Monkey* to *Beowulf* because *Beowulf* was so unfamiliar even to American students, although some of them had read excerpts in high school. *Monkey*, by contrast, was an integral part of Chinese cultural literacy, while remaining fun and entertaining to others. *Monkey* has the added advantage that Chinese students immediately identify themselves with the mythical protagonists in a novel more appropriately translated as *Journey to the West*, to India, to be exact, for Buddhist sutras. Students' difficulty with English and America crystalizes in Monkey's gold fillet worn like a cursèd crown, one that contracts to cause what I facetiously term as "Monkey's Migraine," as well as in the myriad monsters lusting after the longevity-giving flesh of Tripitaka,

Monkey's master. Monkey's migraine encapsulates overseas students' psychological stress. Perhaps unbeknownst to most Chinese students, cannibalistic monsters may well embody universities coveting "cash cows." Visual representations in book illustrations, archeological finds, graphic novels, and, of course, films and TV series bring these classic heroes alive, albeit in a commercialized and somewhat compromised fashion.

The second scenario reverses this East to West trajectory, initiating from Robin Hood to *Outlaws of the Marsh* because the Sherwood outlaw is universally known. *Outlaws*, on the other hand, presents daunting challenges. Even to young Chinese students, this fourteenth-century novel may as well hail from a foreign country of a distant past, fraught with outlandish events of facial branding of criminals, of a mass killer who happens to be the beloved legendary tiger-slayer Wu Song, of a roadside inn that butchers its guests for dumpling stuffing, and more. The physical and the metaphysical, the textual and the ideological, intertwine in a disconcerting way in *Outlaws* for modern readers, East or West.

Consistent with the mission of ConFusion, the first scenario strikes me as "Teaching *Wyrm* to Dragon Seed." In *Beowulf* written in Old English, the key word "*wyrm*" means worm, snake, and even dragon. This range of connotation is being transmitted to Chinese students, or Dragon Seed, in Pearl S. Buck's antiquated usage. Buck may not be that far off considering China's self-image as *longde chuanren* (descendants of the dragon). *Wyrm* is then modernized as "germ," as in germs of insights, embryonic ideas germinating, about to materialize. Conceivably, this germ is also the virus that contaminates in Soderbergh et al.'s xenophobia. The online portion of my hybrid courses relies on (mis)communications, trans-Pacific even in summer online courses, worming along fiber optic internet lines or spreading through airborne digital signals.

When I first taught the IAH course, I had a rude awakening going through week one's discussion posts online: most students might not even be aware that they were writing ungrammatical and awkward "Chinglish" rather than English, as if they had simply Google translated from Chinese! In contrast to Anglophone writers deliberately concocting Chinglish for their fictitious yellowface characters, Mandarin-speaking undergraduates compose what they believe to be English, which in the worst-case scenarios takes after pidgin or creole. To riff on one of President Xi Jinping's favorite slogans, students posted English "with Chinese characteristics." Indeed, they could only know that what they had written was not good English if they had known what good English sounded like. This fell into Donald Rumsfeld's "unknown unknowns—the ones we don't know we don't know." Indeed, had the students had any inkling of what they had dashed off, would they have published it to the whole class via MSU's online platform D2L? This commenced a long and ongoing editorial and proofreading career that I had never envisioned for myself. There was little chance to address student ideas, which were cluttered, mangled by Chinglish. Just to sort out the language itself took up all my energy. When I noted the ills of "Chinglish," students in denial complained to IAH administrators, who in turn warned against my coinage of this inconvenient truth that would not go away even if we look away.

In addition to questionable English, another common denominator is the didactic tone. Writing invariably carries a moralistic purpose to better oneself, not so much in demonstrating one's proficiency in critical analysis as in vowing to work hard for academic and social advancement. Part of the responsibility surely lies with MSU itself. The drive to increase revenue to compensate for state funding cuts for the past few decades may have led to loosening of admission criteria. Language skills take years of dedicated work; there is no short cut. This has created the parallel universes of two MSUs on campus, each keeping the other at arm's length. "Good fences make good neighbors," including invisible linguistic walls, paid for by China. However, MSU and peer institutions also pay a heavy toll for such mutual self-segregation, despite having been thrust together by circumstances and bureaucracies.

Given the extraordinary struggle with the English language that I witnessed in these posts, I decided to drastically shorten the paper length to make it more realistic. Rather than papers, I opted for short, detailed analysis of well-chosen themes, textual passages, and/or film stills. These short assignments favor quality over quantity. The trade-off is this: students need to carefully proofread and edit their papers or to have them so edited by professionals at the school's Writing Center and ESL Writing Lab before submission. Submitted papers must be grammatical and idiomatic, lest they receive a failing grade. I even went so far as to provide specific examples. Not surprisingly, quite a few papers copied the exact arguments of my samples. To soften the blow of requiring international students to seek editorial help from the Writing Center to ensure their writing was in Standard English, I added that I empathized with their dilemma. The ultimate goal for all students was the ability to write Standard English without any assistance, which was, after all, the very reason for crossing the ocean to come to the United States. Should international students feel offended by my "telling it like it is" with respect to awkward Chinglish and such, I urged them to keep in mind that I, too, had crossed the ocean and I, too, have been wrestling with the two-headed beast of my native and adopted tongues, my mother and stepmother tongues, whenever I type—even now.

Practically, this rule of editing and proofreading is nearly impossible to enforce. Students complained that they could not get an appointment at the Writing Center. More devastatingly, the MSU Writing Center and the ESL Writing Lab insisted on an absurd "mantra" of "We don't do grammar!," as if they were engaged solely with higher aspirations, such as the student's idea, narrative structure, imagery, voice, and so forth. No one was asking for grammar lessons; rather, students simply needed to be told whether their sentences made sense. If not, how to revise them? For foreign students who had difficulty writing a lucid sentence or an organized paragraph, these so-called writing professionals behaved like instructors at a driving school who refused to teach basic techniques of driving. Instead, these professionals claimed a mission of, say, itinerary planning to stunning vistas of Grand Canyon or Yellowstone. How to drive to the tourist site, it appeared, was entirely the instructor's discretion.

This is why an unforeseen editorial and proofreading career would persist as long as I volunteer to teach IAH courses. Should I pass along subpar Chinglish as the Writing Center does? After all, like a game of Chinese whispers, what the next MSU instructor has to contend with in terms of the student's proficiency in English would no longer be my concern. Should I opt for multiple-choice questions and in-class group projects without any writing to grade, as many classes do? Given the exorbitant fees levied on international students, double that of in-state students, it is unconscionable to play the liberal game of "anything goes" under the assumption that Englishes of various stripes from the Commonwealth are equally good as the global lingua franca. First of all, Mandarin-speaking undergraduates are not subjects from the British Commonwealth, who might have attended English-language schools back home, who might have grown up bi- or tri-lingual. The liberal notion of global Englishes constitutes one end of the TESOL spectrum, the other end being English-only monolingualism. Both are extreme positions: the latter is unequivocally racialist; the former is disingenuous. By embracing Englishes indiscriminately, liberals profess a progressive tolerance of differences in race, accent, culture, and language usage. Their color-blindness and tone-deafness are not only patronizing but ignore the fundamental power dynamics inherent in skin color and accent. Ultimately, it either is or is not Standard English that communicates effectively. To play with English, to tease out global Englishes, a foreign student must first master the master tongue, even if it entails a period of unease and disorientation, even if it means being temporarily enslaved by the rules and conventions of the English language.

My "red line" of nonstandard Chinglish should not be critiqued from a US minority perspective that valorizes nonstandard speech acts, such as Black English or Spanglish. Unlike people of color born and raised in the United States, Chinese international students arrive from elsewhere, paying steep fees for slots in US institutions of higher education. Commensurate with their financial investment, Chinese students ought to dedicate themselves to getting *in* linguistically and culturally in the first place. This is diametrically opposite to US minority politics, where the oppressed communities of color assert their identity, including pride in their dialectal variants against the tyranny of the majority discourse and white privileges. Mandarin-speaking undergraduates need to acquire the alien tongue rather than cling onto the mother tongue as if they have never left the motherland. Historically, only colonialists never deign to strive for native fluency of the colony's language. On the contrary, colonists recreate their homeland in "The Heart of Darkness" or in the Crown Jewel of Hong Kong. The MSU-within-MSU suggests a new strain of neo-imperialism, whereby Mandarin-speaking outposts of a new empire insist on their cultural inviolability, despite the irony of their pilgrimage to the West. A paradox exists in Mandarin-speaking undergraduates' centrifugal and centripetal pulls. In public spaces across the MSU campus, they exhibit arrested, even regressive, linguistic habits, huddling together with their own kind, a contradiction to the appearance of mobility in their flight to the United States, in their slick Mercedes-Benzes, in their loud and assertive Beijingnese. (One sports car sports a Michigan license in the rear and a Chinese one from the province of *xiang* [湘 Hunan] in the front!) Nonetheless, isn't an American student dropping the course with a preponderance of Chinese names, or an American instructor not taking on such a course, practicing self-segregation as well?

To combat Chinese students' defensive self-ghettoization, a limbo that refuses to see itself as such, I mount a two-pronged strategy in IAH courses: not only interlacing Eastern and Western texts but also immersing students in a pedagogy of critical thinking. The latter deploys an incremental approach, from shorter close reading and general introduction to lengthier and more in-depth analysis. Both exercises insist on immersive reading, interactive activities via film stills and queries, and, ultimately, independent thinking. To lead by examples, I upload online analyses of passages or thematic explorations. I try to write in the lucid, even graceful, academic English worthy of Norton Anthology's introductory materials prior to specific excerpts from the English literary canon. I do so because during my tenure teaching, lecturing, and conferencing across Asia, in China, Hong Kong, Macau, Taiwan, and South Korea, the constant refrain from students and some faculty has been that they have felt most at home in such introductory materials in Norton, in comparison to literary criticism of various stripes of a more individualistic and insightful nature. The comfort level may in fact stem from the fact that such introductions are, by definition, more informational than insightful, hence conforming to Asian pedagogy in favor of rote memory and collective consensus. This is counterproductive to independent thinking. But that ultimate goal depends on gradual changes, particularly when foreign students may not even have a solid grasp of the foundational tools of words and expressions for cultivating insights. Imaginative flights out of set parameters would have to come later.

While operating in a political neutral ground, an instructor has an easier time advocating the necessity of critical thinking and empathetic imagining. Yet any material that questions Chinese—or any students'—ideological frame of reference or ethnocentric self-image invariably meets with immense challenge, the course objective of critical self-reflection notwithstanding.

My second model of "Cool Outlaw and Lawman" concludes with a unit on two internet novel-inspired Chinese films: *Mojin: the Lost Legend* and *Chronicles of the Ghostly Tribe*. Both are 2015 film adaptations of the tomb-raiding novel *Ghost Blows out the Light* (2006). Desecration of the dead ought to belong to outlawry or lawlessness, except it becomes heroism and romance.

I initiated the unit with a short excerpt from Edward Said's classic *Orientalism* (1978). Said theorizes that the West justifies colonialism by constructing the Other, the Orient, which awaits a civilizing, Christianizing mission. In the new millennium, China on the rise creates its own Orient, like the erstwhile Saidian mirage, to define, psychologically, China itself and to legitimize its expansion as self-defensive in the face of external threats. In such tomb-robbing narratives, China's Orient lies underground, treasures and dangers either from the distant dynastic past or from the recent Maoist past. The present tomb raiders are armed with Taoist esoteric knowledge as they fall into the rabbit hole of erstwhile nomadic tribes' royal tombs in Inner Mongolia. In addition, the filmic flashbacks cut to the protagonists' 1960s Red Guards passion answering Chairman Mao's call to "go down to the countryside," the very borderlands where the tombs reside. A historical revisionism transpires in the novel and films' representation of the non-Han or ethnic minority dynastic past and, most poignantly, of the Cultural Revolution, which was a ten-year de-cultural holocaust.

In preparation for each text, I always upload Reading, Analysis, and Assignment well in advance, while counseling students to do their work *in that order*. My advice stems from the fact that when I was growing up in Taiwan and bombarded by daily tests, not to mention the traumas of nationwide entrance examinations to high school and to university, I and fellow students were taught a "trick" of skimming through the answers to multiple-choice questions first before reading the questions because it might save time, particularly if the question were factual in terms of date, name, or event. According to this logic, time-consuming reading comprehension is secondary to identifying the right answer in as little time as possible. What might have been right there and then is decidedly wrong here and now. My courses are not a timed exam. The order of Reading, Analysis, and Assignment aims to invite students to come up with their own interpretation of literature and film, which is the very purpose of US institutions of higher education with its dual emphases on critical thinking and empathetic imagining. Before buying into my analysis, students are encouraged to develop their own argument by joining reason from the left half of the brain with imagination from the right half. By crossing the ocean to attend a US university, international students are one of US now. They are in the process of fusing the East and the West into one. If the student were a native-speaking American student, taking this course would take him/her out of the US into THEM, for much of the class materials breach the tribalist walls of our global village.

This unit on two popular tomb-raiding films has challenged Chinese students' self-perception, so much so that in-class discussions have been awkward and uncomfortable, and student evaluations fell below the usual positive results, despite the fact that critiques of Chinese films have been tempered and juxtaposed by similar instances of US ethnocentrism, exemplified by twentieth-century Ramboism and twenty-first-century Trumpism. Whereas such course materials trigger little to no emotional resistance to an American-majority class, a Chinese-majority class reacts strongly to what it perceives to be China bashing. This brings up the issue of academic freedom inherent in critical thinking for instructors and students alike. Should instructors be engaged in a bit of empathetic imagining to see things from the Chinese perspective? Should instructors self-censor materials that impinge on students' "safe space"? Should they offer spoiler alerts, inviting students to close their ears and minds to materials they might dislike? Critical thinking, after all, is never entirely objective, governed as much by reasoning and rationality as by one's positionality and self-interest. How exactly to balance the need for critical thinking and the concern over student disaffection? How to join the Western head with the Chinese heart, or the other way around, given the body's and mind's instinctive qualms over and revulsion against foreign objects?

Student writings on what some Chinese students perceive to be this unit's "Sinophobia" provide an unsettling freeze frame of a closure for my courses. This concluding freeze frame captures certain Chinese students staring, unblinkingly, back at me. This uncomfortable "staring contest" is further aggravated by how the fad of technology use in online and in-class settings facilitates or incapacitates self-reflection. Online courses have done away with face-to-face contact altogether. So is technology the virtual avatar enabling students and instructors? Or is it the phantom limb in denial of empathetic failures on both sides? All such evolving questions remain the conundrum at the core of any interaction between the two MSUs and, by implication, the two hemispheres of the world.

10

Ishiguro's White Dolls

Anglo-Japanese Nobel laureate Kazuo Ishiguro launched his career with a Japanese and ethnic stage—two 1980s novels set in Japan and/or with Japanese characters, only to switch inexorably to a mainstream (white) fictional universe. Ishiguro's about-face evokes Walter Benjamin's "angel of history" hurling into the future with his face "turned toward the past" ("Theses on the Philosophy of History" 1940). More pointedly ethnic than Benjamin's philosophy, though, Ishiguro's oeuvre manifests variations of the orphan syndrome of Westerners of Eastern descent: neither truly Western in the eye of the West for "having come from elsewhere"[1] nor truly Eastern owing to the deficiency of heritage language, culture, and memory. Belonging to neither compels Ishiguro to split his whiteface characters into both, akin to an insecure child—Kathy H. the clone in *Never Let Me Go* (2005)— cuddling her imaginary doll, subconsciously projecting her vulnerable self, now hugged and loved by a parent-like imago, all parties apparently white. Who is the object "me" in a title that ends either with an exclamation or a question mark, either with a falling or a rising pitch? Who is the invisible subject "you" being addressed or appealed to? They are one and the same in this one-person act dangling between a command and a plea.

Whereas the clones' initials disown them from any genealogy, they have been consistently visualized as white, as in Vintage Books' lily-white cover girl fronting Ishiguro's novel and in Mark Romanek's 2010 film adaptation. Why do the initials exorcize as a matter of course any non-English-sounding surname, hence people of color like the author, in spite of the fact that the protagonist Kathy H. exhibits in abundance *kokoro* ("heart," even though familiarized and Anglicized), the Japanese sensibility of indebtedness to and intuition for others?[2] The novelist and the reader see what they wish to see—whiteness.

Yet irony abounds in Ishiguro's white dolls. Straddling the roles of adult protector and protected infant, Ishiguro's whiteface characters, nonetheless, are haunted by ethnic residuals: the "dusty" white bone Chinamen and "racy" romance at Darlington Hall (*The Remains of the Day* 1989); the British detective's Shanghai boyhood playmate Akira (*When We Were Orphans* 2000); the blind American diplomatist's spy doppelganger Matsuda (*The White Countess* 2005); East Europeans as the racial other in *The Unconsoled* (1995) and *Nocturne* (2009); the samurai-style duel among Anglo-Saxon medieval knights (*The Buried Giant* 2015); and the unceasing waves of mourning and guilt. Ishiguro's brilliant career of ethnic passing has purged bilingual double-tonguing that Asian North American writers practice and exploit. While Ishiguro reinvents himself, shedding the Fanonian "Japanese skin" to assume "white mask," millennial ethnic writings are Ishiguro writ small, whereby each work's bilingual overture teases with foreign words in Romanization from foreign bodies, yet settles in presently to the American English of off-white—yellowish—American characters.

Although discouraged by an Ishiguro who prefers universal, cosmopolitan, and aesthetic interpretations, a number of critics seem determined to find Japanese motifs in the post-Japanese stage, which covers pretty much the last three decades. Barry Lewis in *Kazuo Ishiguro* (2000) critiques the racial bias inherent in deploying *bushido* to analyze Stevens in *The Remains of the Day* (24) or "playing the Japanese card" (25), yet Lewis himself mentions "Japanese motifs." His first two "Japanese" novels, Lewis maintains, "are delivered with the same slow, atmospheric nuances he admires in Kawabata" (19). Citing Anthony Thwaite's "In Service" from *London Review of Books*, March 18, 1989, Lewis finds "distinct Japanese characteristics (such as indirectness) in Ishiguro's work, however much he may disclaim them" (10). Lewis further adds: "Two specific Japanese motifs in *A Pale View of Hills* (ghosts and suicide)" (20), so much so that Ishiguro is likened to a "ghost writer …. departed from the text, leaving only a handful of haunting images and a reverberant silence" (36). In terms of Japanese cinema, Lewis notes that Yasujiro Ozu's "preference for plotlessness clearly aligns him with Ishiguro." It should be the other way around, of course, as Ozu predates Ishiguro by decades, possibly exerting influence over Ishiguro's narrative style (69). In *The Buried Giant*, the prolonged "take" on samurai in stasis prior to springing into sword fights comes straight from Akira Kurosawa's *Seven Samurai* (1954), *Yojimbo* (1961), and other swordplay films.

Cynthia F. Wong in *Kazuo Ishiguro* (2000) cautions against interpreting his two early novels "according to paradigms of his 'oriental' heritage" (2), on grounds of Ishiguro's insistence on imagination. Contrary to her own admonition, Wong pinpoints Japanese sensibility *momo no aware*, "'the sadness of things' or 'sensitivity to things'" in Ishiguro (29). Wong considers any "realistic references to the history of either Japan or Britain [being] secondary to the emotional lives of his protagonists" (20). What if such "emotional lives" as *momo no aware* stem from the repressed childhood trauma of leaving Japan for Britain? Would Ishiguro be a Nobel laureate had he stayed in Japan without the dislocation and had written in Japanese? Surely a moot, hypothetical question, yet what is an intrinsic, taken-for-granted, even clichéd quality within one native context acquires added value of freshness, rarity, even exoticness once transported to a foreign context. Like currency, the exchange rate of symbols predictably favors the hegemonic party to the marginal. Ishiguro's novels buried with this gigantic, albeit unseen and unnamed, Japanese sensibility exemplify such an asymmetrical floating literary world. In *Kazuo Ishiguro and Memory* (2014), Yugin Teo also describes Ishiguro "as a writer of the Second World War" (10), comparing *A Pale View of Hills* to *Hiroshima Mon Amour* (1959). Needless to say, Alain Resnais's film is set in Japan, the interracial romance being a metaphor for the two theaters of war in Europe and Japan. Of the myriad Second World War films, Resnais's is chosen for its Japaneseness. But no critic as yet seems keen on examining Ishiguro's oeuvre through the lens of diasporic whiteface performance with its obsessive-compulsive fixation on monolingualism and Englishness, a whitewashed body of work where ethnicity is all but erased.

What Ishiguro engages in can be broadly described as Asiasplitting, one word instead of split into two to underscore the paradoxical, tortu(r)ous nature of this psychic maneuver. Not to mince words, the mind cleaves or severs its Asianness while cleaving or clinging onto that which is cleft. This conundrum of diaspora is universal, traced all the way back to Psalm 137: "And they that wasted us required of us mirth, saying, Sing us one of the songs of Zion. How can we sing the Lord's song in a strange land? ... If I forget thee, O Jerusalem, let my right hand forget her cunning. If I do not remember thee, let my tongue cleave to the roof of my mouth." Held captive by the rivers of Babylon and commanded to entertain the captors with sacred songs, Jews take an oath of never abandoning or cheapening Jerusalem on pain of paralysis or silence. Yet this vow of silence has to be sung in a tongue that not only has to move, to un-cleave from the roof of the mouth, but increasingly do so in the adopted tongue of the strange land. The ancestral tongue has become estranged for generations in diaspora. This biblical quandary befits any artist in diaspora expressing what is repressed, or repressing even as s/he expresses. That Ishiguro is a master of the English language with indiscernible traces of Japanese demonstrates the paradox of monolingual English-speaking whiteface "poor creatures" and their off-white creator (*Never Let Me Go* 233).

Asiasplitting invokes the term hairsplitting, denoting an obsession over devilish details, but it also calls up the phenomenon of atom-splitting, the chain reaction that leads to nuclear fission. Splicing the analogues of hair and atom, Asiasplitting suggests a fleeting psychological frisson like a short-circuit, a power surge, that effects cosmic change. The infinitesimal and the trifling turn infinite and transcendental. Asiasplitting is consciously or subconsciously practiced as Anglo-America of Asian extraction lays and hatches its sp(l)itting image, psychic repression projected out, or imago that doubles as the undesirable and the heart's desire.

Psalm 137 vouches unwavering attachment to the homeland in language that bespeaks self-alienation, the body's detachment from the mind. Biblical tropes of ineffectual hand and tongue foreshadow the obsessive compulsive disorder of Ishiguro's white-doll characters staring at their own hands at the most devastating moments. These creatures' inability to recognize their own hands mirrors the creator's whitewashing and Asiasplitting, a feat so accomplished that he may well be the whites' token Japanese doll, the 2017 Nobel laureate for literature. Such recurring hand imagery invariably leads to the nightmarish, Kafkaesque narrative most memorable in *The Unconsoled*, a strand that has continued unabated throughout his distinguished career.

This head-hand severance begins in the 1983 short story "The Family Supper," if not before. A less veiled Ishiguro pens a story of a Japanese prodigal son returning from California to Japan and to a traditional, authoritarian father, whose wife has possibly committed suicide by partaking "fugu," the Japanese delicacy of puffer fish that is poisonous if not properly prepared. The Orientalist stereotypes of postwar Japanese suicides, ghosts, and haunting take a page from Ruth Benedict's unsettling *The Chrysanthemum and the Sword* (1944), which depicts the United States' Pacific War enemy as a mongrelized contradiction of aestheticism and abomination. The son's return to Japan, seen through Benedict's white lens, crystalizes Ishiguro's dilemma: he must marshal the master tongue of English, which is part of him now, to embody the ancestral land already off-kilter when channeled by English and its linguistic and conceptual frames. "Fugu" is a rare sighting in Ishiguro of the Japanese language, a strategic placement of foreign words to accentuate the exotic Japanese practice of consuming poison either to cheat or to embrace death. The homecoming of an Anglicized native son on—and, indeed, off—the page constitutes a welcome cognitive estrangement for English speakers, who see their sense of unfamiliarity reflected in the characters' distance from their own bodies and family. Not just the California-tainted son but the traditional father evinces the exact self-alienation at the closing of the story: "For some time my father seemed to be studying the back of his hands." Part of his own body, like his son and Japan's postwar changes, is defamiliarized, an apt metaphor for the disparity between the content of fading Japaneseness and the form of dialogue in fake English between Japanese father and son. Given that knowing something "like the back of your hand" is to know that thing well, Ishiguro subverts the integrity of the Japanese character by turning an English idiom on its head, hence destabilizing the medium of English as well. The more the creator owns the master tongue, the deeper his creatures suffer self-dispossession.

Ishiguro is not unique in the recurring motif of betrayal or, rather, self-betrayal, a minority complex shared by ethnic writers on both sides of the

Atlantic. In his dubiously titled *Native Speaker* (1995), Chang-rae Lee baldly confesses through his spy protagonist Henry Park: "In every betrayal dwells a self-betrayal" (314). The pioneering Asian American novelist Maxine Hong Kingston likewise embeds guilt in her narrator's vampiric self-image: "I had vampire nightmares ... Tears dripped from my eyes, but blood dripped from my fangs, blood of the people I was supposed to love" (220–221). Shedding tears for the loved ones while shedding their blood results in self-hate. Both Ishiguro's "back of his hands" and Kingston's vampire fangs draw from Western tropes in English, the very act symbolizing a departure from one's alleged origin. Ethnic writing explores and exploits oneself and one's community for the mainstream audience, who harbors a deep-seated curiosity for multicultural tales, tails of color pinned to a white body.

While Ishiguro manifests this whiteface, yellow skin split or eye-hand dis-coordination throughout his corpus, it does not necessarily have to be this way. Conceivably, two tails of color can intersect, bypassing altogether or at least minimizing the proverbial white donkey. Iranian auteur Abbas Kiarostami's Japanese-language film *Like Someone in Love* (2012) eerily resonates with Ishiguro's whiteface masquerade. A Japanese college student in Kiarostami works as a prostitute on the side and is enchanted by a senior client's painting. A 1900 oil on canvas *Training a Parrot* by Chiyoji Yazaki depicts a Japanese woman in a striped kimono on the right gazing and supposedly training a parrot in its swing and vines on the left. The retired, possibly pedophiliac, sociology professor muses aloud as to whether the woman is teaching the parrot or the other way around, given that the parrot's beak is slightly open and the woman's mouth demurely closed. The mise-en-scène further disrupts the customary give-and-take, command-and-obey, relationship between the owner and the pet, with the parrot placed above the woman's eye-level, crouching down to cast a bird's-eye view at her. The two red tassels hanging from its perch swing sideways, the only diagonals in a painting of straight lines, the only bright color in a painting of muted dull greys, yellows, and greens. The oblique tassels suggest that the perch is in motion, in action, as opposed to the static passivity of the woman.

The vertical split between a Western-style parrot on a roost amidst vines and a Japanese woman in a kimono also lends itself to a cultural interpretation. The Meiji-era Japan sought modernization and Westernization in the same breath, just like a parrot imitating human speech. The motif of emulation mirrors a Japanese artist's Western oil painting techniques. But the Western art tradition serves to express a Japanese conundrum. Intertextually, Kiarostami complicates the painting by the very fact that an Iranian is making a Japanese-language film. After the retiree's commentary, an academic exercise in words, the prostitute enacts. Reminiscing that her grandmother used to liken her to the woman in the painting, she animates her memory by striking the same pose beside the woman in the painting,

FIGURE 10.1 *The painting* Training a Parrot *in* Like Someone in Love.

rolling her hair up into a similar chignon (Figure 10.1). Her modeling dangles between, on the one hand, a nostalgic, bittersweet moment with a client who doubles as a caring grandfather and, on the other, a professional repetition like the oldest of rituals, be it language acquisition or sexual gratification. What remains muddled, however, is who plays the person versus who the parrot; what is human and Japan and, as the film title intimates, "in love" versus what is not—on the canvas as well as on the screen.

Ishiguro shares this ambiguity over self and other. The theme of self-alienation reprises with the trope of hand, unwittingly harking back to Psalm 137. *The Remains of the Day* that catapulted Ishiguro to stardom culminated this estrangement. Lord Darlington's staff come to the realization of their menial status whereby they merely provide labor as no more than hired hands to the aristocrats, professional dignity of butlers and housekeepers notwithstanding. Stevens the butler, his father, and Miss Kenton the housekeeper find themselves scrutinizing their own hands at various points of near schizophrenia. Stevens's father examines his hands before he dies, wondering if he has been a good father. Miss Kenton "glance[s] down a second at her hands" (215). Stevens is not even aware of his own tears as the body continues the routine of service, with the hands pouring after-dinner liqueur for guests.

In *When We Were Orphans*, the whiteface novel that is closest to home, Japan, Ishiguro persists in deflecting the homing instinct onto the International Settlement of Shanghai, China, on the eve of the Second World War and onto the Japanese childhood friend Akira, doppelganger to the

Sherlock-esque protagonist Christopher Banks. The boy Akira's speech pattern without verbal conjugation, verbs, or articles is the only time when Ishiguro dabbles in a foreigner speaking English or pidgin. To suggest, as Barry Lewis does in *Kazuo Ishiguro* (2000), that Stevens "speaks English as if it were a foreign language" elides working-class emulation within one linguistic system, on the one hand, and, on the other, non-native speakers' herculean challenge hailing from another linguistic system (94). Stevens does speak in a stiff, affected manner, particularly when he subconsciously assumes the persona of Lord Darlington at a countryside pub, yet that is a far cry from Akira's broken English.

One daring adventure undertaken by the playmates Banks and Akira is the foray into the Chinese servant Ling Tien's room to steal a bottle of "magic lotion" (101) that transforms "severed hands into spiders" (97). Children's fear turns an alien with "a cap and a pigtail," who happens to be a Shanghai native, into a macabre magician (95). Their imaginations run amok, associating severed hands and multiple fingers with spiders' legs. The freakish chinoiserie lifeforms are as far removed from Englishness-cum-Japaneseness as possible. When the adult Banks returns to Shanghai in search of his parents abducted some thirty years before, this childhood quest becomes a nightmarish dress rehearsal. Venturing into Chapei, the slum warren adjacent to Shanghai's affluent International Settlement, Banks deludes himself into believing that the Japanese soldier he has chanced upon is Akira. The soldier's atrocious English is about the only similarity to Banks's childhood friend. This soldier turns out to be a traitor, according to Colonel Hasegawa, but one who has warmed to a Banks on the verge of delirium. Concerned for Banks's safety in Japanese hands, "Akira" volunteers to teach Banks Japanese in the event of his absence or death: "'*Tomodachi*,' he said. 'You say. *To-mo-da-chi*.'" The only Japanese lesson in Ishiguro's corpus, *tomodachi* means "friend," now anatomized as much by the unfamiliar syllables as by the staccato delivery of the syllables. While each sound struggles to connect with the next, both the teacher and the student burst into "uncontrollabl[e]," near hysterical laughter (279). Truncated foreign syllables are spit out from a whiteface's Asiasplitting. As the soldier is subsequently arrested by his fellow Japanese, Colonel Hasegawa accuses him of having given "information to the enemy." This intimates the minority complex of succeeding by turning its back on ethnicity. The colonel comforts Christopher: "it is wise not to become too sentimental." However, he "faltered on this last word, so that it came out as 'sen-chee-men-tol'" (296), perhaps the only occasion beyond the two Akiras where Ishiguro ever attempts the Japanese accent. Even in his two early "Japanese" novels, neither the Japanese expat protagonist in *A Pale View of Hills* (1982) commits any grammatical or syntactical misstep in English nor does the Japanese father in *An Artist of the Floating World* (1986) ever slip in his speech in fluent English. Both are whiteface, as native-speaking as any other of Ishiguro's characters. The half-hearted, sentimental gesture of "sen-chee-men-tol" defeats itself since Hasegawa, no different from his counterparts of a Chinese officer, a Chinese elderly man, and other non-English characters, speaks exquisite English elsewhere. There is in fact no chorus of voices in Ishiguro, whose characters are all allegorical Everyman manifesting psychological complexes of mourning and loss in the global lingua franca.

Just as the soldier Akira conducts a crash course of Japanese for Banks in Chapei, the boy Akira seeks to comfort Banks over his parents' quarrel by pointing to "the slatted sun-blinds" and quoting a Japanese monk: "we children ... were like the twine that kept the slats held together .... bound not only a family, but the whole world together" (77). Cast in Banks's recall, Akira speaks fluently and with deep meaning. An oxymoron of a word, "twine" is singular yet it suggests entwined strands, twoness, or a twin. "Twine" contains within its very spelling the twin of doppelgangers. But when the adult Banks repeats that advice to another police officer, it has been altered: "We're the twine that holds together the slats of a wooden blind" (144). "We" are professional detectives, no longer "we children." Detectives have arisen as the twine for wooden blinds. Sun-blind is a compound word that conjoins opposites, sunlight and darkness, particularly symbolic as it is attributed to a monk from Japan, the Empire of the Sun, whereas the counsel resurfaces several times removed as wooden blinds, as though the sun has "set" into its facsimiles, not even living wood but wooden, dead wood. The word play evolves in sophisticated figures of speech in English, in spite of the alleged source of a monk from the Empire of the Sun.

Whereas a novel has a way of dubbing Japanese voices, Ishiguro's screenplay of Shanghai-themed *The White Countess* cannot but have the Japanese actor who plays the spy Matsuda speak in elegant, if accented, English. Bidding farewell to his twin, the blind Jackson, on the eve of Japanese military takeover, Matsuda laments that destruction is "in the nature of things," the Law of Nature dictated by that very mastermind of invasion. Turning back before exiting the door, Matsuda muses: "Let me put to you something of a personal nature." As he takes his leave, Matsuda bows "in wishing you every good fortune." The Japanese bow to a Jackson who cannot see suggests muscle memory that is distinctly Orientalist, his elegant English notwithstanding. A chasm opens up between the mind expressing itself in English and the body inured in Japanese body language, conjuring up age-old Orientalist representations of perennial aliens, despite a Westernized façade, speech included. How doubly reconfirming it is for Anglo-American readers: a Nobel laureate of Japanese ancestry advances the deracinated, universal human condition of mourning and loss; furthermore, he countenances, elects even, the stock image of Oriental schizophrenia between mind and body! Given the constancy of whiteface characters dissociated from their own hands as well as themselves, it would be rather dull had Ishiguro named every protagonist in his novels "Everyman." But that allegorical streak runs throughout Ishiguro's corpus, evidenced by the post-Arthurian *The Buried Giant*, a giant so buried that it is nowhere to be found like the haunting off-white doll in the heart of all his whitefaces.

The lop-sided Orientalist whiteface ventriloquism at times culminates in a fine duet of East and West. In the closing moments of *The White Countess*, this duet becomes literal. Jackson, his beloved white countess, and her daughter Katya flee Shanghai on a sampan, where a fellow refugee, an Asian trumpeter, plays a melancholic tune to the accompaniment on the soundtrack by an *erhu*, a two-stringed Chinese violin. The visual and the auditory, reality and dreamscape, East and West circle back to halfway through the film when Katya peeks into a shadow magic box. The vision Katya witnesses foreshadows their boat ride, with two blond characters and their girl dancing on a sampan drifting against Chinese architecture on the riverbank, the roof ridge of which undulating like a flying dragon and the boat floating like a phoenix. Only in a sonic, dialogue-less dream vision does East and West wed so seamlessly. Once awakened into Ishiguro's characters, they adopt an Anglophone monotone. Ishiguro's indiscernible, accentless whitefaces unfold in a monolingual writing style that has stood him in good stead but that is decidedly not the choice of the bulk of his Asian North American counterparts.

By no means is Ishiguro alone in whiteface performance. Contrary to his other novels, Chang-rae Lee adopts a white protagonist in *Aloft* (2004), albeit haunted by his late Korean wife. The symbolic flight from race appears to crash in the end. Katie Kitamura's style in *A Separation* (2017) resembles the Nobel laureate's quiet pensiveness, with measured long sentences, braced further with long insertions between dashes. Like Ling Ma's *Severance* (2018), Kitamura dispenses altogether quotation marks for dialogue, rendering the novel a long meditation by the nameless protagonist, the widow of feckless, philandering husband Christopher. Ridding an ethnic novel of code-switching dialogue is a step toward deracination, where every character is a whiteface, ventriloquized by the English-only author. Akin to the post-1980 Ishiguro, Kitamura's faceless narrator has no racial markers other than the Japanese-style restraint, yet another whiteface narrator devoted to total self-erasure, which only deepens masochistic guilt and shame. Ishiguro seems to lead the way into a literary utopia of color-blindness in the twenty-first century, taking point for the privileged minority squad so whitewashed as to be blind to their tokenness.

Whereas Ishiguro's Japanese slips of *"To-mo-da-chi"* and the like are few and far between, Asian North American novelists populate various points on a spectrum of ethnic representation via the ancestral tongue. There exists no Korean words in Suki Kim's *The Interpreter* (2003), but the immigrant parent characters are murdered because they turn Immigration and Naturalization Service (INS) informants on, thus traitors to, their own community. Kim even capitalizes on the absence of Korean: "When he says 'nothing' in Korean, the word leaves an echo, the peal of hollowness" (148). The Korean word "nothing" is subsumed within English, calling attention as much to the voidness of the word as the passing of the parents. The hollow echo amplifies a nothing-within-nothing effect.

Close to the "nothing" end of the spectrum, Jung Yun's *Shelter* (2016) disorients from the outset by means of a single Korean phrase the protagonist Kyung Cho fails to comprehend: "*Aboji gad chi shuh suh.*" The Korean mother character is either appealing to the protagonist for help: "Your father hurt me" (16) in a family history of domestic violence or she is pleading on behalf of her husband: "Your father is hurt" (40). Horrifying violence, domestic as well as in the hands of robber-rapists breaking into the parents' house, is doubly shocking because the characters are neither sheltered by the castle of their home nor do the family members share a common language. Ironically, the American success story of owning a single family house and commanding the English language masks abuse behind the walls and alienation from one another and even from oneself, ancestral roots included. The effective use of Korean in Yun is a one-off, in fact, as both parents survive the ordeal to speak in impeccable English, leaving their Bosnian and fellow rape victim Marina to struggle in pidgin. Just as Ishiguro's Matsuda does a Japanese bow while enunciating a fine turn of phrase in British English, Yun recycles the stereotypical schizophrenia of Asian bodies—the Korean immigrant husband's physical violence and the wife's passive submission—versus American English coming out of those bodies. Imagine the code-switching heteroglossia should Yun persevere in linguistic ambiguities! However, the real reason to the English-only fictitious universe of Ishiguro et al. may simply be that their talents lie elsewhere, probably not in the way of doing voices, absent a musician's ear and a linguist's competence in transcribing uncanny sounds, once so soothingly familiar to the child or to the fetus.

It is no accident that on the other end of the spectrum with a profuse sprinkling of the foreign language, those novelists are mostly of Chinese descent, to the extent that the style verges on Chinglish. With the millennial rise of China, literary deployment of Chinglish seems fitting as superpowers engage in a war of words. Gish Jen has long attempted that in *The Love Wife* (2004) with myriad and maze-like four-character Chinese idioms, Romanized and glossed in various fonts and boldface. The dizzying and at times erroneous smorgasbord is justified by new arrivals bringing China and Chinese to an English-language fictitious universe.[3] Madeleine Thien tries her hand in *Do Not Say We Have Nothing* (2016), where a relative escapes the Tiananmen Square massacre to bring generations of family lore and a Sinophonic slant to the young Chinese Canadian protagonist. Thien's urge to reconnect with Chineseness is so palpitating that it results in an overzealous primer of beginning Chinese, with blunders right from the start. The sprawling cast of characters requires a genealogy, a family tree, before the novel begins. The family tree is entitled in Chinese *Jiapu* (family register/ music score). *Pu* means to pun on both the record and the Western classical musicians persecuted during Maoist campaigns. Yet the Chinese character *pu* (鋪 store) Thien uses should have been *pu* (譜 register/score). A glaring mistake that is but decorative chinoiserie to English speakers, the family register, nonetheless, lies at the heart of Thien's story. The family register unwittingly becomes a family shop in Thien's Chinese word choice.

Thien's opening pages continue this primer to the Chinese language, yet by degrees the story "rights" itself into the genre of Asian North American bildungsroman. Similar to many other Asian American bildungsromans, Thien's novel is Ishiguro's career trajectory writ small. In any given Asian North American novel, the opening pages set the stage of ethnicity through tropes of ancestry, oftentimes the immigrant (grand)parents and their pidgin, only to graduate to Asian American identity formation almost exclusively in the master tongue. What Ishiguro undergoes from a short Japanese phase to a never-ending whiteface phase is what each individual Asian North American novel goes through. In Thien's case, after over 450 pages of family saga of torture and persecution, the novel concludes with the musician family's possible reunion in a remote Gobi Desert sanctuary, a happy ending of sorts marred by yet another misnomer: "宇 (yu) which meant both *room* and *universe*" (457), implying that the family's humble abode would be their self-contained universe. In all likelihood, Thien mistakes the homophone 寓 (apartment) for 宇 (universe). The former is indeed used in *gongyu* (公寓) for apartment or room, broadly speaking. Even in simplified Chinese, 寓 rather than 宇 is used for apartment. On a narratological level, the coupling of Maoist savagery and the beauty of Western classical music evokes the traditional Taoist symbol of yin and yang, dark and light, striving for a balance. This compensatory strategy also motivates Dai Sijie's romantic escapist novel and film *Balzac and the Little Chinese Seamstress* (2001, 2002), where the urban youth, lugging his suitcase of Balzac and classical violin, is sent down to the Sichuan countryside. Jiang Rong's *Wolf Totem* (2004) reprises that with Jack London's *The Call of the Wild* (1903) and Tchaikovsky's *Swan Lake* amid Inner Mongolian grassland. Western high culture serves the wronged intellectuals as their security blanket, so suggest a Malaysian Chinese Canadian Thien, a Chinese émigré in France Dai, and a Chinese novelist Jiang.

The impulse to flaunt bilingual expertise is keener in certain Asian North American novelists than Chinese expatriate novelists. Of the latter group, Ha Jin rarely makes a song and dance over his mastery of Chinese. He demonstrates instead how he has come to master the English language. By contrast, Jade Chang's *The Wangs vs. the World* (2016) may as well be retitled as *Jade Chang vs. The English-Speaking World*. Chang's excessive showing off of her language skills so overwhelms the story that the "versus" spells doom for reader reception. Wang is a common surname, but it also means the king, the royalty. Chang's princely parade of Chinese names, history, words, phrases, customs, and whatnot fall on deaf ears of her intended audience in the West. Chang's and Thien's Chinglish is the verso (back side) to Ishiguro's recto (front side) of whiteface, or the other way around. As we move into the twenty-first century, "the China Century" according to some pundits, the war of words will escalate. On this side of the Pacific, the mainstream white audience has come to relish even more token off-white stories, such as *Crazy Rich Asians*. On the other side, the Belt and Road Initiative (BRI) and other neo-imperial projects have taken us to the far reaches of the globe and the Chinese cranium.

CODA

That's Rich!: Asian Americans Author(iz)ing *Crazy Rich Asians*

Like breeds like, especially those unlike who mimic in order to be liked—for survival and for advancement. As such, global culture fueled by Anglophone capitalism favors transnational artists practicing not only in English but also staying comfortably within an Anglo-American framework. Unfamiliar cultural elements serve as exotic spices to whet the palate rather than to overwhelm, to gag English speakers savoring novels and films on the Other. The exoticism comes across as a tease, an Oriental epigraph of sorts even if it permeates the opening chapters to titillate—before the Asian American or Anglo-Asian story "properly" begins. Alternately, Asian sights and sounds, oftentimes via immigrant or Asian, i.e., Asian Asian, characters, would periodically materialize to provide an ethnic or racial slant. These immigrant figures may well be figures of speech, the synecdoche of the Asian Other that is theoretically part of the Asian American or Anglo-Asian Self. These Anglo-American artists of Asian descent appear to function like bridges across cultures, insofar as the Anglophone culture remains the dominant frame of reference. Such bridges are oftentimes broken, though, as they rarely cross the intricacies of languages or cultures. Bi-lingualism and trans-culturalism are the trompe l'oeil achieved through strategic deployment of Romanized and italicized Asian words and cultural icons verging on stereotypes, as if Anglophone readers and viewers are entering an alien world, while they are treated to English and English only, with a modicum of disorientation over Oriental words and the Orient.

In our new millennium witnessing the rise of China, a good number of Asian American transnational cosmopolitan artists—writers, filmmakers, and actors—cash in on the stereotype of crazy rich Asians, a riff on the century-old cliché of an extravagant, overdriven Orient. As a gesture toward political correctness, such an elite culture, well-nigh neo-imperial in its flaunting of opulence and privilege, descends upon us without its blatantly racist twin of Oriental monstrous penury. Yet they are next of kin, the biblical filthy lucre having already stained gold with Freudian feces, such as Judas's thirty pieces of silver tainted by (self-)betrayal. Being crazy rich is as much envied as despised. Herein lies the genre's draw for America: the rich, entertaining, and ludicrous portrayal of Brand New Asians ultimately flips into, not to mince words, Same Old Ugly Chinese, all the more authentic because one of them, not us, is doing it to themselves. The box office success of Jon M. Chu's *Crazy Rich Asians* (2018), based on Kevin Kwan's 2013 novel, continues this millennial Asian American tradition of Tash Aw's *Five Star Billionaire* (2013), Val Wang's *Beijing Bastard* (2014), Daniel Hsia's *Shanghai Calling* (2012), and even Amy Chua's *Battle Hymn of the Tiger Mother* (2011). Rich it is for these Asian American artists to author and authorize a white-ish discourse of crazy rich Asians under the banner of multicultural diversity of an all-Asian fictitious universe and cast, and of minority self-representation. The catch is this, to rephrase Alistair Deacon's idiotic refrain from *As Time Goes By* (1992–2005), delivered with a slowing tempo and a knowing nod: there are Asians and there are ... Asians (read: crazy rich v. dirt poor; also read: Asian Asians v. Asian Americans). They may look alike to you and me, but they are worlds apart, literally.

The title *Crazy Rich Asians* exposes the definitional ambiguity of "Asian": Asian American or Asian Asian or both or neither. Owing to such obfuscation, people of Asian descent can ill-afford not to take it personally. Given the novel's and the film's popularity in the United States, can a mainstream audience of non-Asian descent avoid soul-searching over their sudden crush on those traditionally dismissed as "perennial aliens"? For either group, the feel-good romantic comedy may be symptomatic of a deep-seated unease with themselves in relation to the Asian Other, of an anxiety over the dimming West in relation to the brightening East.

On a rather fundamental level, "Asian" bifurcates into both a noun for the people and an adjective denoting Asianness. The slipperiness between the two is amplified by the abstraction of the latter. What exactly is Asianness? To tackle the "easy" part first: Asian Americans and Asians are not interchangeable. Americans of Asian descent are no different, legally and culturally, from Americans of European, African, and other descent, whereas Asians refer to the people in and from Asia. This results in the admittedly awkward, unwieldy contrast of Asian Americans versus Asian Asians. When Asian Americans proclaim themselves as Asian (note the adjective rather than the noun "Asians"), the shorthand self-designation telegraphs as much their ancestry as identity politics, as much their roots as their here and now. The choice of "Asian" initiates the pan-ethnic movement of Asian Americans in contradistinction to the majority Euro-Americans.

In the history of Asian American literature, Asianness has long been strategically essentialized to define the ethnic group's difference both from the majority group and from Asian Asians. To whites, Asian Americans announce that they are Asian, short for "of Asian extraction." To Asians, Asian Americans underscore the latter word of their erstwhile hyphenated identity. Asianness becomes a double-edged sword in the hands of Asian American writers: it is who they are and who they are not. The fluidity of "Asian" resembles that of a shape-shifting fetish. Asian American writers borrow it for self-labeling amongst themselves and for the mainstream society. On the other hand, they disavow it to demarcate themselves from Asian Asians. Asian Asians emerge in Asian American fiction as immigrant characters, mainly as (grand)parents from the Old World. The attachment to these immigrant parent characters is a matter of filiation. In the struggle for self-identity of the 1960s and 1970s, however, this affiliation triggers familial revolts tinged with guilt, even self-hate, which gradually settles into milder satire and New Age fusion of East and West in the following decades. Despite or because of its provenance from across the Pacific Ocean, the term "Asian" is both claimed and disclaimed by Asian Americans.

Consequently, Asian Asians constitute a trope for both Asian Americans' otherness vis-à-vis the white majority here at home and for Asian Americans' Americanness vis-à-vis Asians beyond our shore, out there. Yet this in and out, inclusion and exclusion, true and fake, morphs incessantly in the minority subconscious. After all, Asians exist amidst Asian Americans, while the adjective Asian, if not the noun, exists within the Asian American psyche. If Asian Asians are true Asians, then Asian Americans must be fake, which makes them, by default, true Americans. But if true (read: white) Americans deemed nonwhites from Asia as "perennial aliens," then does it make the minority true Asians? A multiple-choice question:

A) Asian Americans are neither white Americans nor Asian Asians.

B) Asian Americans are both American and Asian.

C) Asian Americans are nobody.

D) Asian Americans are Everyman and Everywoman.

E) None of the above.

F) All of the above.

G) Asian Americans are Asian American.

The last option begs the question of why bother to define Asian American in the first place, a mission impossible necessitated by the implied triangular relationship of American–Asian American–Asian unabashedly exploited by *Crazy Rich Asians*. Truth be told, this alleged triangle veils a Romanesque triumvirate at the tip of human resources in worldwide production and circulation. With the exception of a small number of movers and shakers at the pinnacle, 99 percent of Americans of Asian descent are neither crazy, nor rich, nor Asian. Rather, the powerful US publishing industry teamed up with Hollywood and a cohort of Westerners of Eastern descent to dream up an East, a "yellow" chick flick, pardon the expression, for global consumption, while having preciously little to do with either white Americans or Asian Asians.

Indeed, Americans of non-Asian descent and Asian Asians make but cameo appearances, if at all, in the story. Caucasians feature briefly in the opening "London 1995" sequence when racist hotel staff recommend Chinatown to the Asian-looking Singaporean Young family until they are apprised of the Youngs' new role as hotel owners. Asians are invariably maids, cooks, and gardeners at the Young estate, extras on the set without a single line. Despite its setting in Southeast Asia, the film features few "locals": two maids from the Thai royal court and, further afield, two turbaned Sikh guards (Nepali Gurhka guards in Kwan's novel). The absence of whites and Asians does not take away from the story's success in the United States, though. American mainstream readers and audience view *Crazy Rich Asians* as a spectacle on "them" in an us versus them divide, on those affluent transnationals crossbred by Chinese and Western capital and culture, speaking with a distinct Oxbridge accent. The warm reception by the American public manifests itself in the novel's top rating in *The New York Times* Best Seller list and, anecdotally, by my own experience.

When I went to Lansing's NCG Cinema to watch *Crazy Rich Asians*, there were two other Asian films catering to the large number of Asian, particularly Chinese, international students at Michigan State University (MSU): Hong Kong's *Golden Job* and China's *Cry Me a Sad River*, both financed by Chinese companies. A teen romance on Hunan Television with fifty-two episodes, *Cry Me a Sad River* has been turned into a film by Luo Luo, released on October 5, 2018, the very day I went to watch Jon M. Chu's Asian American romantic comedy. How can one explain that the first round of global distribution of *Cry Me a Sad River* should include this Midwestern college town of Lansing, Michigan, other than the existence of a critical mass of MSU's Chinese students with disposable income? This coincidence confirms, serendipitously, the image of well-heeled Asians, if not crazily so, ones with the capital, means of transportation, and the leisure to frequent the movie complex at an outlying mall at the edge of town. The audience of *Crazy Rich Asians* at the early matinee on October 5 consisted of approximately fourteen white retirees, with half a dozen more trickling in after the movie started, one of whom being African American. Is it a film that appeals primarily to seniors of the mainstream community, light-hearted enough to entertain a senior gathering, no different from an outing to local Chinese restaurants? Or is it simply a reflection of the demographics of moviegoers in relation to film genres? And how to read this white mainstream gravitation to the 1 percent jet-setting superrich not so much in their midst as in the never-never land called Singapore?

The ill-defined yet richly symbolic "Asian" in the title sums up the novelist's and the filmmaker's selling point. Both creators, along with the film's cast, are more Western than Asian, despite their Asian-looking faces, hence reconfirming the notion of strategic essentializing, if not appropriation, of Asianness. Kevin Kwan was born in Singapore and educated in British schools until the age of eleven, when the family migrated to the United States. Jon M. Chu the director is a Californian; Constance Wu (Rachel Chu) the female lead is a Virginian; Henry Golding (Nick Young) the male lead of mixed-race origin was born in Malaysia, who relocated to England at age eight; Michelle Yeoh (Eleanor) the Young matriarch was born in Malaysia and moved to England at age fifteen; Gemma Chan (Astrid Young Teo) the supporting actress hails from England; Awkwafina (Peik Lin Goh) the comic sidekick with her hair dyed blonde is a New Yorker from Queens; and more of the same. This cast of characters onscreen and behind the camera are all Anglo-American, with a smattering of early childhood and teenage experience in the privileged upper echelon of Asia, including the one who pens *Crazy Rich Asians*. All the "partners in crime" are us Asian Americans and Anglo-Asians, born and/or educated in the West, perpetrating in collusion an Asian—their—outrage of wealth porn against common decency. Asian Americans have succeeded in feigning Asianness, faking it, for real.

The plot goes like this. Daughter to a single parent of modest means, New York University Economics Professor Rachel Chu is in love with Nick Young, who has "Shanghaied" Rachel to his home country Singapore under the guise of keeping him company at a relative's wedding. Shanghaied in the sense of being abducted is not that far from the truth, for the quasi-royalty of the Young tycoon family remains concealed until Rachel finds herself, an "economy people," escorted to First Class on the transoceanic flight. "Shanghaied" further puns on the collaging of postmodern Singapore with the prewar, colonial Shanghai's International Settlement. The latter comes through in the interior décor of Singaporean mansions, costuming, and, most symbolically, the soundtrack and live performances of Shanghai's popular tunes of the 1930s and 1940s. One most famous song, "Shanghai in Nighttime," counterpoints the erstwhile Bund along the Huangpu River with the contemporary Singapore along the Strait of Malacca, both mirages blinking and undulating upside down at the water's edge.

This adventure to the "Far East" in Southeast Asia is inconceivable to a New Yorker like Rachel, who originally imagines the eastbound trip a short hop over the East River from Manhattan's East Village to Queens. Rachel's entry into the Young family estate further underlines, in her own hyperboles, her "poor ... low-class immigrant ... nobody" status—she is neither "low-class" nor an "immigrant," the latter often worn strategically as a badge of honor by second- or 1.5-generation Asian Americans. The exaggeration is probably caused by Rachel's faux pas, such as nearly downing a bowl of water intended for finger cleaning. The snobbishness of the Youngs and hangers-on constitutes in effect endless bullying, social media gossip, verbal taunts, physical abuse, and communal shunning, culminating in a bloody, gutted fish on Rachel's hotel bed with "Gold-digging bitch" graffitied on the French window nearby. The human instinct to rally around the underdog or Cinderella-esque Rachel means that her American individualism, personal ingenuity, and even scrappiness, would endear her to the audience, whatever the racial background. In Rachel, Americans see themselves, fallen in the face of the Young's old money from Old China and new elite culture from Oxford and Cambridge, yet about to rise again as is its Manifest Destiny, with or without Nick. The millennial geopolitics of Trumpian retrenchment meets the ascent of Xi Jinping's "China Dream"; American exceptionalism embodied by a beaten-down yet resilient Rachel would prevail, the film intimates, as it did over English colonialists.

The parallelism of China's hegemony today and Britain's yesterday is most apt, as the cultural forces converge in the role of Michelle Yeoh's Young matriarch Eleanor. Second in stature only to her mother-in-law or Nick's Ah Ma (granny), Eleanor poses the greatest hurdle to the romance, when she should be the one most sympathetic to Rachel on account of her own mistreatment as an outsider by the Youngs. First of all, Eleanor sacrificed her Cambridge study as a traditional Chinese wife would when she married Nick's father, a marriage without Ah Ma's blessing. Ah Ma objected to the match because Eleanor was not of the same social station, or not "*gagilang*" (or Kevin Kwan's "*gar gee nang*" [*Crazy Rich Asians* 198], "our own kind of people"), a Fukienese phrase now used against Rachel. A lady with unflappable dignity speaking in the King's/Queen's English, Eleanor rises above family squabbles. (Yeoh's Eleanor has purged Kevin Kwan's character of code-switching, since Chu has standardized— Anglicized or Americanized—the accent of the entire cast, except ethnic clowns ending every sentence with a prolonged *lah* in Fukienese-inflected Singlish.) So when she takes Rachel into her confidence apropos her own marital adjustment on the landing of the mansion's grand staircase, towering over the petite Rachel one step lower and caressing her cheek like a devoted maternal figure, viewers fully expect Eleanor to undergo a change of heart, to commiserate with someone with such a likeness to her younger self. This makes the curtness of her rejection—"you would never be enough"—so much more shocking, a dramatic plot twist that nearly evokes the trending image of Chinese tiger mothers of Amy Chua fame. Such a construct of Chineseness is fashioned, ironically, in perfect English by Yeoh's elocution and, a few years earlier, by Chua's egotistic, brazen diatribe in the so-called Chinese parenting tradition. Even Jon M. Chu's exquisite timing of cultural clashes of China and America is a tour de force, courtesy of his years of making Hollywood films. Chu predictably draws from the broader Asian American appropriation of the ambiguity of Asianness. In a quiet moment together, as Eleanor helps her son change out of the shirt spilled with Rachel's wine, Nick impresses upon Eleanor that "the first girl I brought back to Singapore is a Chinese Professor," which Eleanor corrects: "Chinese American." This rejoinder gains in symbolic capital as the "Chinese" mother and son share a moment of intimacy to purge "American" contamination, not just on Nick's shirt but in his mind. This formula of males' bared upper body of biceps and six-pack abs self-destructs as neither Eleanor nor Nick is Chinese: they are Hollywood.

The set of the grand staircase is one instance of Jon M. Chu's Asian American fusion of East and West. The grand staircase with its symmetrical structure stems from Western architecture, yet the landing is decorated on either side with a matching Chinese Lunar New Year spring couplet. Although the bottom halves are covered by railings, the first four words of each read "South North East West" (南北東西) and "Heaven Earth Sun Moon" (天地日月). Tellingly, Rachel hesitates over which side to take on the landing, where she is waylaid by Eleanor to deliver the Chinese coup de grâce to the American free spirit. Even the direction inscribed on the spring couplet is headed by the Chinese preference for the south, as the emperor's throne has traditionally been facing south, crystalized by the southside entrance to Beijing's Forbidden City. On the contrary, the West privileges the true north in the clockwise cardinal points of north, east, south, and west.

Rachel is understandably devastated. If not for her university classmate, the Singaporean Peik Lin Goh, and the Goh family's support, she would have given up. As opposed to the Southeast Asian aristocratic class of the Youngs, the Gohs are garish, tasteless nouveau riches bordering on ethnic clowns, a caricature fleshed out elsewhere by the horde of profligate sons and daughters partying on a transoceanic freighter ship. As opposed to the Oxbridge accent and pedigree of the Youngs, the Gohs speak in Americanisms. The father in fact switches between American slang and pidgin, while the mother delivers Singlish, mixing English and Singaporean Fukienese. A happy and supportive family perhaps, the Gohs are, nonetheless, regressive in the gender division of the husband playing with cultures and languages and of the wife nativized in her speech pattern. As cartoonish as the Gohs's flamboyant anime-inspired dress and hairdos, the filmmaker sets up a stark contrast between the Gohs's American English and the Youngs's British English. Although more stately, the Young household does not even have a patriarch, away throughout the film in Shanghai for business. While the Youngs apparently hail from China, their surname Young Anglicizes the Sinophone Yang. The old money from China has been rechristened Young, rhetorically rejuvenated and familiarized for the Anglophone culture. The Young-Yang word play denotes a mixed background, if not mixed blood as embodied by the Anglo-Malaysian Henry Golding. Despite the all-Asian cast, the white audience is still able to identify with a Chinese son so whitewashed that his face, physique, and last name put him, as they say, "in our corner."

Crazy Rich Asians' official trailer on YouTube shows Henry Golding displaying the engagement ring with which he is to propose to Rachel. The pea-sized diamond is level with two vaccine scars, each roughly of the same size, on Golding's left upper arm (Figure CODA.1). The film title's "Asian" suggests that trailer audiences are being treated to an Asian story that happens to Asians, whose wealth can be seen in the luxurious lagoon setting and the diamond ring. Yet Golding the alleged "Asian" is mixed race and educated in England, evident from his Oxbridge accent. This fake Asian sports, however, two "authentic" vaccine scars on his arm from a childhood in Malaysia at a time when inoculations against small pox and other diseases were required. Such Asian scarring will not strike home with a young American audience, who have no idea what those marks mean. The mixed-race actor and the rechristening of the family name as Young imply that too much Asianness is itself a blemish to be covered up. Ironically, a film that supposedly valorizes Chineseness turns to a mixed-race actor; a skin-deep reading of Nick Young's old wounds leads us down a rabbit hole that problematizes Asianness.

With her "American(ized)" allies of the Gohs, Rachel overcomes the "fall" from the grand staircase, only to crash again when Eleanor's private

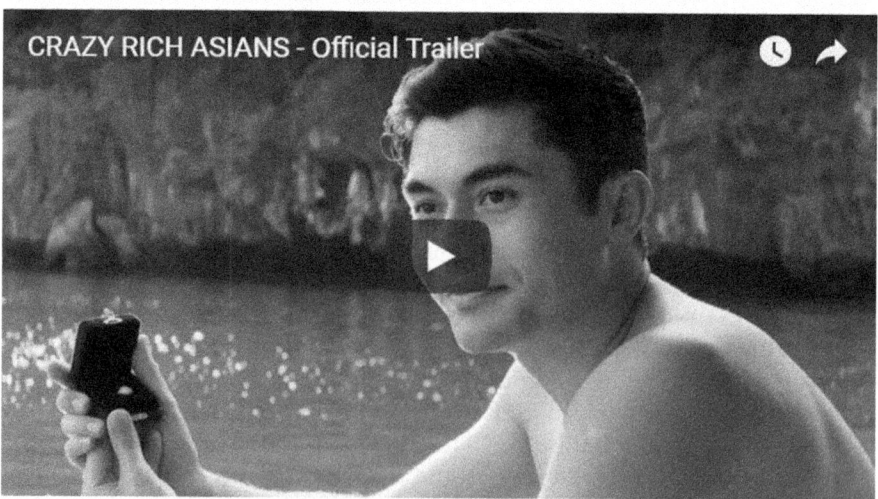

FIGURE CODA.1 Crazy Rich Asians, *Official Trailer.*

investigators uncover what appears to be Rachel's lies of her single parent household. It turns out that her mother's husband still remains in China. To lend her support, Rachel's mother flies out to Singapore at Nick's urging. She explains to Rachel that her husband was abusive, giving her no choice but to abandon the other man she truly loved in her flight to the United States for Rachel's sake, who would be discriminated against had she grown up in China. (Suffice to say that Kevin Kwan justifies the flight as more than fear of discrimination.) A juxtaposition to the Youngs's Chinese prestige and privilege, Rachel Chu's mother exposes its underside in the vein of patriarchal terror in Amy Tan's *The Joy Luck Club* (1989). The binary dichotomy of an aristocratic/aesthetic versus abhorrent/abject China, a good versus bad China, smacks of Orientalist extremes.

Rachel's final act that closes the film eerily circles back to Asian American literature's stock character of male gamblers. Granted only "a Chinaman's chance" in the United States, so to speak, Asian male characters eke out a living across this Promised Land, from Carlos Bulosan's Pinoy laborers to Louis Chu's New York Chinese bachelor community. Working-class laborers seek their fortune by betting with the only chip they have—their lives—in Old Gold Mountain, the Chinese name for San Francisco and for the United States at large, while dreaming of striking gold in the Sierra Nevada Mountains or in Chinatown's mahjong clubs. In keeping with her male forerunners, Rachel Chu the economics professor opens the film with a demonstration of "Game Theory," splashed across TV monitors in a New York University auditorium, by winning a hand in poker, beating her white, mustached opponent at the West's own game. She closes the film by deliberately losing another game of chance, a round of mahjong, to Eleanor to foreshadow her decision of relinquishing Nick, sparing him the painful choice between Old World family and New World Rachel. Rachel's sacrifice, reminiscent of her own at Cambridge, convinces Eleanor to give her blessing, quite a melodramatic twist. Rachel's retreat resonates with the Chinese tactic of *yituiweijin* (withdrawing in order to advance), uncannily enabling her to beat the East at its own game. Rachel's American straightforwardness joins hands with not only immigrant gambler tropes but also Asian-style letting go to manufacture a happy ending. Chu's finale is at variance with Kevin Kwan's cliffhanger to the first installment that leads to *China Rich Girlfriend* (2015) in his trilogy.

Rachel's ambidexterity in either game is borne out by the contrapuntal mise-en-scène. NYU's darkened auditorium focuses the floodlight on the two poker players as if at the bottom of an orchestra pit or a gladiators' dungeon. On the other hand, a mahjong match requires four, not to mention the open, sun-filled room, yet Eleanor is ensured of secrecy as the other two Singaporean women at the table are "half-deaf and they only speak Hokkien." As opposed to the sparring white masculinity at the outset, the banality of a subpar Orient, conveniently incommunicado, comes in handy to close the film with a bang. This disabled Orient comes to enable an Asian American coup, which reeks of "The Heathen Chinee" (1870), with the two Mahjong players' "smile that was," to quote Bret Harte's racist poem, "pensive and childlike," "childlike and bland"—infantilized. Bookended by a card game and a mahjong game, Jon M. Chu—Kevin Kwan, Constance Wu, and others, for that matter—has apparently won this hand, given the box-office hit of *Crazy Rich Asians*. Chu et al. have enriched the crazed spectacle and soliloquy by Asian America on an imaginary Asia, an ethnic "show and tell" for Anglo-America's eyes and ears. Those jealous eyes, green or otherwise, feasting on *Crazy Rich Asians*—all with the shadow of a sneer![1]

NOTES

Introduction

1 *The Story of English* describes Scot Lorimer's depiction of Standard English: "In the [Scottish] Lorimer's *New Testament* only the Devil speaks Standard English" (145).

2 See chapter 4, "Vincent Chin and Baseball: Law, Racial Violence, and Masculinity" in Sheng-mei Ma's *The Deathly Embrace* (2000).

3 For the flipping between duet and duel, see Sheng-mei Ma's *Sinophone-Anglophone Cultural Duet* (2017).

Chapter 1

1 As recent as 1986, Prince Philip, during a visit to China, quipped: "If you [a twenty-one-year-old British student Simon Kerby] stay here much longer, you will go home with slitty eyes."

2 The only place where the linguistic transference is noted occurs when Buck glosses the Chinese unit of distance "a *li* which is a third of a mile" (*The Good Earth* 54).

3 The dissociation of the body and the self/mind is an age-old Western narrative strategy to fashion the alien other as opposed to the white self. The racial other exhibits this split tantamount to schizophrenic affectlessness. In science fiction, aliens or robots show little emotion other than melancholia over the lack of emotions. In *Blade Runner* (1982), the robot Batty confides in the eye maker Chew, before killing him: "If only you could see what I have seen with your eyes"—indeed, a tête-à-tête between an Oriental supplier of spare parts and a robot who cannot claim his body as his own.

4 In contrast to Buck's praise of Luise Rainer's O-lan, Naomi Greene in *From Fu Manchu to Kung Fu Panda* (2014) believes that "Rainer's 'Chinese' mannerisms bring her performance to the brink of stereotype" (Greene 85).

5 See chapter 2, "To Anglicize and Angelize the Rape of Nanking," in Sheng-mei Ma's *Sinophone-Anglophone Cultural Duet* (2017).

Chapter 2

1   See Pierre Nora's *Les Lieux de mémoire* (1984).

2   See *Harold & Kumar Go to White Castle* (2004).

3   See Sander Gilman's *The Jew's Body* (1991), especially chapter 7 "The Jewish Nose: Are Jews White? Or, The History of the Nose Job," pp. 169–193.

4   See David Palumbo-Liu's *Asian/American* (1999), particularly chapter 3, "Written on the Face: Race, Nation, Migrancy, and Sex."

5   See "Introduction" to Sheng-mei Ma's *Alienglish* (2014).

6   See Gayatri Chakravorty Spivak's "Can the Subaltern Speak?"

7   See Kimberlé Williams Crenshaw's "Mapping the Margins," 375.

8   See Sheng-mei Ma's *Immigrant Subjectivities* (1998), particularly chapter 1, "Native Informants and Ethnographic Feminism in Asian American Texts."

Chapter 3

1   Anthony Horowitz resorts to the silk stereotype even in his title *The House of Silk: A Sherlock Holmes Novel* (2011). The title titillates with the Orientalist ring of the metaphor of "silk." Authorized by the Conan Doyle estate, this Holmes story crossbreeds Sherlock with Fu Manchu narratives. Fraught with menacing images of the other, Holmes was drugged at an opium den or The House of Silk in London's Limehouse District and framed for a murder.

2   Peter Messent in "American Gothic" believes that Hannibal's "monstrousness" moves Harris "beyond the borders of the detective genre into territories of the Gothic and Horror" (15). Messent links Jame Gumb in *The Silence of the Lamb* "to Frankenstein in the patchwork monster, his new feminine self" (15).

3   Stephen M. Fuller in "Deposing an American Cultural Totem" notes that in the 1990s, "Starling developed into an American cultural totem and feminist icon" (820). Yet the boundaries between hero and villain Harris maintains in the previous two books is collapsed in *Hannibal*, "thereby merging hero with antihero/villain" (822), leading "Harris [to] punish his audience for their shallow idolatry" (828).

4   Not unique to Thomas Harris's thrillers, Maggie Kilgour hypothesizes that "The detective story thus usually requires a simultaneous identification and opposition between detective and criminal … The detective's mode of exposure depends upon an underlying similarity between the two minds—an almost symbiotic understanding between them which enables the detective to intuit the criminal's moves" ("Dr. Frankenstein Meets Dr. Freud" 42).

5   Citing Freud, Maggie Kilgour in "The Function of Cannibalism at the Present Time" defines the oral stage of sexual development as "cannibalistic existence." The infant "has no sense of its own separation from the world: it is aware only

of the mother's breast, which it does not see as a separate object but, as it can be taken inside itself, as part of itself. The individual's original existence ... is thus described as a cannibalistic experience of fluid boundaries between self and world, who are joined in a symbiotic oneness" (244).

6 In "Objecting to Objectification," Greg Garrett cites *Red Dragon*'s opening epigraph, "one observes only things which are already in the mind," by Bertillon, where Garrett equates "Graham's 'gift'" with "a curse, a kinship of sorts with these killers ... Clarice's empathy works differently; she does not see things through the eyes of the serial killer who objectifies his victims. Her connection, instead, is to the victims" (7–8).

7 Conan Doyle in "Conan Doyle Tells the True Story of Sherlock Holmes's End" shares his "invention" of serial detective stories: "if one could write a serial without appearing to do so—a serial, I mean, in which each installment was capable of being read as a single story, while each retained a connecting link with the one before and the one that was to come by means of its leading characters—one would get a cumulative interest which the serial pure and simple could not obtain. In this respect I was a revolutionist" (xx).

8 Nicolas M. Williams notes in "Eating Blake, or an Essay on Taste": "Taste as a concept is itself subject to many ambiguities, not only the one Pierre Bourdieu notes in Kant in order to dispel it—'between the "taste of sense" and the "taste of reflection"'—but also the pervasive ambiguity that affects *both* the taste of the mouth and the taste of the mind, a confusion between subject and object, between taste as an attribute of the thing tasted and the taster himself/herself" (140). Williams proceeds to analyze that "In order to satisfy the paradoxical requirement of commodity production, that the commodity be 'the same yet different,' the category of the exotic provides just the right tang to a meal of leftovers, a diacritical accent (to change the metaphorical frame momentarily) over an otherwise unchanged word." This concept applies nicely to Chinglish's mutation of English to keep Chinglish exotic yet still the same.

   Barry Taylor, on the other hand, advances the notion that Harris "define[s] Lecter through an oxymoronic implosion of definitions: brilliant scientist and bestial madman, a psychiatric case-study whom, as a psychiatrist himself, ridicules the models which his captors apply to him, the serial-killer who is consultant to the police. More fundamentally, Lecter confounds the monstrous and the civilized, the violence of nature and the refinements of culture, the raw and the cooked" ("The Violence of the Event" 219–220).

9 Tony Williams in "From *Red Dragon* to *Manhunter*" explicates the painting as "Dolarhyde sees himself as Blake's Red Dragon standing above the woman who symbolizes the feminine side of himself he wishes to subdue. But these repressed emotional drives return with a vengeance in the form of the castrating super-ego of his abusive grandmother seeking punitive control even after death" (106).

10 Coincidentally, the protagonist of *Little Shop of Horrors* (1986) also comes by the vampiric plant at the floral shop "Chang's," run by a Chinese proprietor.

Chapter 4

1   Cay Van Ash and Elizabeth Sax Rohmer's *Master of Villainy* (1972)
     documents how Sax Rohmer attributes his literary success: "I made my
     name on Fu Manchu because I know nothing about the Chinese! ... I know
     something about Chinatown. But that is a different matter" (72).

2   See Edmund Burke's *A Philosophical Enquiry into the Origin of our Ideas of
     the Sublime and Beautiful*, particularly chapter 7, "On the Sublime."

3   "The Bamboo-Tree" is coined more or less for rhyming purposes in Judy
     Garland's number in *Meet Me in St. Louis* (1944). This song and dance is
     reprised in Steve Martin's *The Man with Two Brains* (1983). As opposed to the
     motifs of revenge and romance of "the Rose-Tree," "the Bamboo-Tree" is more
     for exotic entertainment.

4   Ruth Mayer in *Serial Fu Manchu* (2014) advances the notion that Fu
     Manchu's "camp appeal" comes from its serial "spread" (3). Mayer describes
     "a semantics of spread" in "Fu Manchu's volatility and intangibility—his
     expertise at masquerade, make-believe, infiltration, and impersonation, which
     renders him at the same time impossible to locate and ubiquitous" (6). The
     spread gives Fu Manchu a "machinic" momentum (6). But Mayer stresses
     "the 'looped' quality of serial phenomena" (7). Specifically, Mayer holds an
     idea similar to the "viral China" in terms of "the recurring imputation that the
     Chinese entered the Western world in the form of a uniform, robotic 'invasion'
     of 'flood': faceless, impervious to pain and hardship, enduring, impassionate,
     and *infectious*" (22; italics mine).

5   See Walter Benjamin's *Illuminations* (256).

6   See chapter 3, "Zen Keytsch: Mystery Handymen with Dragon Tattoos," in
     Sheng-mei Ma's *Alienglish* (2014).

7   Semiotician Ferdinand de Saussure in *Course in General Linguistics* (1916)
     proposes that any sign that communicates consists of the signifier (the word as
     well as the sound of the word) and the signified (the thing the word refers to).

Chapter 5

1   See Donna Haraway's "The Cyborg Manifesto."

2   Eric G. Wilson notes the paradox of the melancholic android: "The android
     is fully sacred, sacer: consecrated and accursed" (19). He describes "The
     source of mechanisms" as "sacred obsession: the holy yet accursed longing for
     eternity—endless life, painless death" (3).

3   See Arthur Conan Doyle's "The Sign of the Four" for the reference to Sherlock
     Holmes's cocaine and hypodermic syringe in the "Morocco case" on the
     "mantelpiece" (3). See "The Last Bow" for the reference to "the east wind
     coming, Watson" (1155).

4   The English dubbing of the Major by Mary Elizabeth McGlynn did a disservice by changing the cause of the static from "that time of the month" to the matter-of-fact "a loose wire," hence missing the original irony between human and machine.

5   This human touch of vulnerability has been de rigueur in film noir to allow the audience to identify and empathize with the gumshoe, who is otherwise too cool and self-contained to be one of us. Humphrey Bogart's Marlow finds his hand trembling and his brows beaded with sweat after a meeting with his nemesis in *The Maltese Falcon* (1941). A contrast to Bogart's nonchalance, these moments epitomize how the body betrays the mind in that the heart races, the pulse quickens. The sweat and the tremor signal rising heat, despite the cool front the gumshoe puts up.

6   Asian cinema seems populated by such sighs. The Major's eroticized sigh in silence evokes another silent appeal in Wong Kar-wai's *In the Mood for Love* (2000), where Tony Leung, forlorn after having lost his love, confides into a wall hole at an Angkor Wat temple. Leung's character is so repressed that he could only find his voice as a tourist away from Hong Kong. But even so, his whispering is entirely mute to the audience, captured in a long take slowly distancing itself from the shot of his back.

7   See "Picture of the Priest Dainin Killing the Girl Umegae" and "Picture of the Lonely House on Adachi Moor," in Eric van den Ing and Robert Schaap's *Beauty and Violence* (1992).

8   Via his puppet character Batou, Oshii refers to Chikamatsu's bunraku play (puppet theater) "The Love Suicides at Amijima."

9   This is in effect what Chua Beng Huat observes with respect to Japan's TV dramas: "Japanese audiences tend to see in the struggles of less developed Asia a sense of nostalgia for a past which the Japanese have lamentably lost. Japan's present is economically these lesser developed people's future, while the latter's present is Japan's past" ("East Asian Pop Culture" 235).

10 See chapter 3, "Mazu's Touch, Taiwan Nezha, and Crying," and chapter 4, "Globalization's Bottom: Subtitle and Switch in Wang Yu-Lin's Taiwanese Dialect Films," in Sheng-mei Ma's *The Last Isle* (2015), particularly the analyses of Taiwan's folk festivals and parades in two films: *Island Etude* and *Din Tao*.

11 Human-cyborg conflicts can motivate various sci-fi scenarios, such as HBO's *Westworld* (2016–2018) revolving around a futuristic theme park populated by cyborg hosts for paying guests bent upon satisfying their wild West fantasies. This TV series is a remake of the film *Westworld* (1973). The Anglo-American obsession with Asian femininity playing the triple roles of nanny/mummy/baby recurs. Some recent examples include Lucy Liu's Joan Watson, the sober companion to the addict Sherlock in *Elementary* (2012–2018), and Gong Li's Mrs. Murasaki, stepmother and samurai coach to a young Hannibal Lecter in *Hannibal Rising* (2007).

Chapter 6

1   See "Downtown Houghton" [Image No.: No Neg 10–18-2005–001], Michigan Tech, July 26, 2006, https://cchi.mtu.edu/copper-country-image-detail?duid=a316fd9b-25b2-4e00-9b3d-3f80376fc823&width=1242&height=732&nid=15863. Accessed Dec. 1, 2016.

2   Mark Twain in *Roughing It* (1872) notes Chinese laundrymen in the American West as well, specifically in Virginia City, Nevada: "The chief employment of Chinamen in towns is to wash clothes …. A very common sign on the Chinese houses was: 'See Yup, Washer and Ironer'; 'Hong Wo, Washer'; 'Sam Sing & Ah Hop, Washing'" (291). The nonsensical names to American eyes are less important than the trade they ply.

3   See chapter 2 "Walt Disney's Swiss Family Robinson: Family Entertainment and Imperialist Ideology," in Sheng-mei Ma's *The Deathly Embrace* (2000).

4   The assembled Lee Ling Laundryman "in action," see "Lee Ling – Chinese Laundry Man," *Brian Batista's Opposite Machine*, May 18, 2010, http://artistavision.blogspot.com/2010/05/lee-ling-chinese-laundry-man.html. Accessed Dec. 1, 2016.

5   For the Abercrombie and Fitch T-shirt, see Sheng-mei Ma's "Whitewashing Chinese Laundryman" 10–15.

6   For the Hoover advertisement, see Sheng-mei Ma's "Whitewashing Chinese Laundryman" 10–15.

7   For the background of xenophobic "The Chinese Must Go" movement, see John and Selma Appel's "Sino-Phobic Advertising Slogans: 'The Chinese Must Go.'" See also the website "Illustrating Chinese Exclusion" on, among other subjects, Thomas Nast's cartoons in *Harper's Weekly*. For the turn-of the-last-century use of trade cards, see Thomas Beckman's "Japanese Influences on American Trade Card Imagery and Design."

Chapter 7

1   Albert J. La Valley's "Traditions of Trickery" explicates the paradox of reception in the fantasy genre: "Though all movies confront us with the simultaneous sense that we are seeing something real and the realization that it is only a movie, only images, science fiction and fantasy films in their most spectacular moments show us things which we immediately know to be untrue, but show them to us with such conviction that we believe them to be real" (144). This certainly applies to CGI morphs. Vivian Sobchack in "At the Still Point of the Turning World" focuses on the paradox in a slightly more judgmental way: "so quickly clichéd and yet remains so surprisingly 'uncanny' as the digital 'morph'" (131).

2 In "Speaking (of the) Dragon," chapter 5 in my *Sinophone-Anglophone Cultural Duet* (2017), I have discussed alchemical transformations in *Beowulf*'s dragon.

3 Or the other way around? Is a dream the dreamer's subconsciousness, as Freud claims? Is a life a dream's variation, leitmotif, as Leslie Cheung sings in *A Chinese Ghost Story* (1987)? Is a footnote hypertextual subconsciousness? Is a text a footnote's avatar? Can we add a footnote to a footnote? Can we sleep and dream of ourselves sleeping and dreaming of having a dream?

4 Marsha Kinder's "From Mutation to Morphing" follows Freudian interpretation of dream transformations: "its dreamwork codes of condensation and displacement ... with its endless chain of substitutions" (68).

Chapter 8

1 Howard W. French in *Everything Under the Heavens* (2017) calls Xi's China Dream "his so called Military Dream" (272). Scholars more in line with Xi's agenda attributes the China Dream to the traditional concept of *Tianxia* (under the heaven), devoid of French's irony. For example, Li Zhang and Zhengrong Hu write in "Empire, *Tianxia* and Great Unity": "The cultural strategy of 'going out'" in 2006 entails "the setting up of branches of Chinese media abroad, the showing of clips promoting the Chinese national image in New York's Times Square, the founding of Confucius schools, the export of cultural products such as films ... and exchange programmes for culture and education" (197). Arguably, Zhang and Hu would see Huallywood films as Beijing's soft power aiming for peace and harmony inherent in the traditional concept of *Tianxia*.

2 See chapter 1 "Sino-Anglo-Euro Wolf Fan(g)s from Jiang Rong to Annaud" in Sheng-mei Ma's *Sinophone-Anglophone Cultural Duet* (2017).

3 The best example of the importance of food in Chinese culture may well be the popular TV program *A Bite of China* for three seasons (舌尖上的中国, aired in 2012, 2014, and 2018). For Mao-induced famines, see Wang Ruowang's *Hunger Trilogy* (1991).

4 Beyond food, clothing is also an important feature of his labor camp experience. His two ironic "little inventions" of mending his shoes "with a wire and rubber tire" and socks with patches (260–261) are eerily similar to Vladek Spiegelman mending Nazi boots and "organizing" cigarettes to curry favors in Art Spiegelman's *Maus* (1986, 1991) based on the testimony of his father, a Holocaust survivor.

5 Marina Svensson coins "sousveillance" in "Connectivity, Engagement, and Witnessing on China's Weibo" to empower Chinese social media Weibo as "a platform for spectatorship, performativity, witnessing, sousveillance" (50). Sousveillance is defined as "inverse surveillance" by social media users to monitor government policies (55). Svensseon evidently disagrees with critics who "dismiss civic engagement in the form of clicking, sharing, and liking on

Twitter and Facebook as 'clicktivism' or 'slacktivism'" and who see social media as a "safety valve and outlet for 'feel-good' activism or clicktivism" (49, 50).

6   James Reilly in "Going Out and Texting Home" provides the context for *Wolf Warrior*'s rescue mission of overseas Chinese. Since the "Going Out" policy, "more than 60 million Chinese citizens traveled abroad" in 2012 and "more than 5 million Chinese nationals work abroad," including "in undeveloped and turbulent regions" (182). When a crisis occurs, it becomes a test of China's global role. In 2006, Beijing reacted to anti-Chinese riots in the Solomon Islands and executed its "first international air evacuation of [312] overseas Chinese" (181). Reilly argues that Chinese netizens' social media exerted pressure on the government to rescue those Chinese. Furthermore, Reilly hypothesizes that "Images of Chinese citizens being whisked away to safety aboard Chinese planes or boats are used by the party-state to portray itself as a powerful and benevolent regime" (181). Reilly adds: "Concern with China's international reputation, bureaucratic drivers (such as the military's interest in operations overseas), and enhanced capacity for extraction and protective actions, and, most important, the dramatic expansion in Chinese citizens and investment aboard have all contributed to this policy shift" (181).

Chapter 10

1   "Where are you from?" and "How can you speak English so well?" are two questions from mainstream Americans most dreaded by Asian Americans, no matter how many generations removed from the ancestral land, so long as they are not mixed-race. Trail-blazing Asian American historian Ronald Takaki testified to that on the opening page of *Strangers from a Different Shore: A History of Asian Americans* (1989). Takaki recalled that when he had attended a midwestern college, he had been invited for "dinner for foreign students" and often asked by "fellow students and even my professors" regarding "how long I had been in America and where I had learned to speak English." To which, Takaki replied: "In this country ... I was born in America, and my family has been here for three generations" (3). Takaki was a sansei, with a family history longer than some of his white interlocutors. Author Helen Zia chronicles a similar experience: "Growing up in the 1950s as one of the few Chinese-American kids in my New Jersey town, I was so often told to 'go back where you came from'" ("My Mother's Secret" 8). If only this were happening in the last century! Gene Luen Yang's *American Born Chinese* (2006) satirizes a Mayflower Elementary School teacher for introducing the San Francisco-native protagonist as having come from China. Born in the United States and speaking English like any other kid, my daughter, on the first day of her elementary school, was waylaid by the English as a Second Language teacher and directed summarily to enter the ESL classroom rather than that of Ms. Miller, her first-grade teacher and a family friend. My six-year-old daughter's look of shock and confusion had been seared into my memory, as I stood outside the school's glass door.

2   For the quintessential Japanese sensibility, see Natsume Sōseki's *Kokoro*
    (1914).

3   For a discussion on Jen's *The Love Wife*, see chapter 7, "Italic and
    Indiscernible Asianness in Asian Diaspora Literature," in Sheng-mei Ma's
    Diaspora Literature and Visual Culture: Asia in Flight (2011).

Coda

1   The concluding sentence refers to Iago: "O, beware, my lord, of jealousy; / It
    is the green-eyed monster which doth mock / The meat it feeds on" (*Othello*
    3.3.165–167).

WORKS CITED

3-Iron. Directed by Kim Ki-duk, performances by Seung-Yun Lee, Hee Jae, and Hyuk-ho Kwon, Sony Pictures, 2004.

Appel, John, and Selma Appel. "Sino-Phobic Advertising Slogans: 'The Chinese Must Go.'" *The Ephemera Journal*, vol. 4, 1991, pp. 35–40.

As Time Goes By. Performances by Judi Dench, Geoffrey Palmer, and Philip Bretherton, BBC, 1992–2005.

Auster, Paul. *Oracle Night.* Henry Holt, 2003.

Aw, Tash. *Five Star Billionaire.* Spiegel & Grau, 2013.

Bakhtin, M. M. *The Dialogic Imagination.* Edited by Michael Holquist, translated by Caryl Emerson and Michael Holquist, University of Texas Press, 1981.

Baldwin, Alec, and Kurt Andersen. *You Can't Spell America Without Me: The Really Tremendous Inside Story of My Fantastic First Year as President Donald J. Trump (A So-Called Parody).* Google Books, 2017.

Beckman, Thomas. "Japanese Influences on American Trade Card Imagery and Design." *The Ephemera Journal*, vol. 5, 1992, pp. 35–49.

Beebe, Roger Warren. "After Arnold: Narratives of the Posthuman Cinema." *Meta-Morphing: Visual Transformation and the Culture of Quick-Change.* Edited by Vivian Sobchack, University Minnesota Press, 1999, pp. 159–179.

Benedict, Ruth. *The Chrysanthemum and the Sword: Patterns of Japanese Culture.* Houghton Mifflin, 1946.

Benjamin, Walter. *Illuminations.* Translated by Harry Zohn, Schocken, 1969.

Benjamin, Walter. "Theses on the Philosophy of History." *Illuminations*, translated by Harry Zohn, Schocken, 1969, pp. 253–264.

Beowulf. Directed by Robert Zemeckis, performances by Ray Winstone, Crispin Glover, and Angelina Jolie, Paramount, 2007.

Beowulf. Translated by Seamus Heaney, illustrated by John D. Niles, New York: Norton, 2008.

Beowulf and Grendel. Directed by Sturla Gunnarsson, performances by Gerard Butler, Hringur Ingvarsson, Spencer Wilding, and Stellan Skarsgård, Movision, 2005.

Beowulf: Return to the Shieldlands. Directed by James Dormer, ITV, 2016.

Bishop, Claire Huchet. *The Five Chinese Brothers.* Illustrated by Kurt Wiese, Coward-McCann, 1938.

A Bite of China (舌尖上的中国). China Central Television (CCTV), 2012, 2014, and 2018.

Black Magic. Directed by Phil Rosen, performances by Sidney Toler and Mantan Moreland, Monogram, 1944.

Blade Runner. Directed by Ridley Scott, performances by Harrison Ford, Rutger Hauer, and James Hong, Warner Bros., 1982.

"The Blind Banker." *Sherlock*, season 1, episode 2. Directed by Euros Lyn and Paul McGuigan, performances by Benedict Cumberbatch, Martin Freeman, and Gemma Chan, BBC, 2010.

The Bridge. Performances by Sofia Helin, Rafael Pettersson, and Dag Malmberg, Filmlance International AB, seasons 1–4, 2011–2018.

Broken Blossoms. Directed by D. W. Griffith, performances by Lillian Gish, Richard Barthelmess, and Donald Crisp, D. W. Griffith Productions, 1919.

Buck, Pearl S. "The Chinese Novel." Nobel Lecture delivered before the Swedish Academy, December 12, 1938, Stockholm. John Day, 1939.

Buck, Pearl S. *Dragon Seed.* John Day, 1941.

Buck, Pearl S. *The Good Earth.* 1931. Washington Square, 2004.

Buck, Pearl S. *The Living Reed.* John Day, 1963.

Buck, Pearl S. *My Several Worlds.* Pocket Book, 1954.

Buck, Pearl S., translator. *All Men Are Brothers (Shui Hu Chuan).* John Day, 1933.

Bukatman, Scott. "Taking Shape: Morphing and the Performance of Self." *Meta-Morphing: Visual Transformation and the Culture of Quick-Change.* Edited by Vivian Sobchack, University of Minnesota Press, 1999, pp. 225–249.

Bulosan, Carlos. *America is in the Heart.* 1943. University of Washington Press, 1973.

Burke, Edmund. *A Philosophical Enquiry into the Origin of our Ideas of the Sublime and Beautiful.* 1757. Oxford University Press, 2008.

Chang, Jade. *The Wangs vs. the World.* Houghton Mifflin Harcourt, 2016.

Charlie Chan in the Chinese Cat. Directed by Phil Rosen, performances by Sidney Toler, Joan Woodbury, and Mantan Moreland, Monogram, 1944.

Charlie Chan in the Secret Service. Directed by Phil Rosen, performances by Sidney Toler, Mantan Moreland, and Arthur Loft, Monogram, 1944.

Chikamatsu Monzaemon. "The Love Suicides at Amijima." *Four Major Plays of Chikamatsu*, translated by Donald Keene, Columbia University Press, 1961, pp. 17–208.

Chin, Frank. "The Year of the Dragon." *Two Plays by Frank Chin.* University of Washington Press, 1974, pp. 67–142.

China Salesman (Deadly Contract 中國推銷員*).* Directed by Tan Bing, performances by Dong-xue Li, Mike Tyson, and Janicke Askevold, Beijing Juhe (聚合), 2017.

A Chinese Ghost Story. Directed by Siu-Tung Ching, performances by Leslie Cheung, Joey Wang, and Wu Ma, Miramax, 1987.

Cho, Margaret. *I'm the One That I Want.* Ballantine, 2002.

Choudaha, Rahul. "Are International Students 'Cash Cows'?" *International Higher Education*, no. 90, Summer 2017, pp. 5–6.

Chronicles of the Ghostly Tribe. Directed by Lu Chuan, performances by Mark Chao, Jin Chen, and Li Feng, Chuan Films, 2015.

Chu, Louis. *Eat a Bowl of Tea.* 1961. Lyle Stuart, 1990.

Chua, Amy. *Battle Hymn of the Tiger Mother.* Penguin, 2011.

Chua Beng Huat. "East Asian Pop Culture." *Genre in Asian Film and Television: New Approaches*, edited by Felicia Chan, Angelica Karpovich, and Xin Zhang, Palgrave Macmillan, 2011, pp. 222–245.

Conan Doyle, Arthur. "Conan Doyle Tells the True Story of Sherlock Holmes's End." *The Big Book of Sherlock Holmes Stories*, edited by Otto Penzler, Vintage, 2015, pp. xix–xxii.

Conan Doyle, Arthur. "The Last Bow." *The Complete Sherlock Holmes*. Doubleday, 1953, pp. 1143–1155.

Conan Doyle, Arthur. "The Man with the Twisted Lip." *Sherlock Holmes: Selected Stories*. Oxford University Press, 2014, pp. 162–183.

Conan Doyle, Arthur. "The Sign of the Four." *Sherlock Holmes: Selected Stories*. Oxford University Press, 2014, pp. 3–101.

Conan Doyle, Arthur. "A Study in Scarlet." *The Complete Sherlock Holmes*, pp. 1–62. https://sherlock-holm.es/stories/pdf/a4/1-sided/cnus.pdf. Accessed May 22, 2014.

Conn, Peter. *Pearl S. Buck: A Cultural Biography*. Cambridge University Press, 1996.

Crazy Rich Asians. Directed by Jon M. Chu, performances by Contance Wu, Henry Golding, and Michelle Yeoh, Warner Bros., 2018.

Crenshaw, Kimberlé Williams. "Mapping the Margins: Intersectionality, Identity Poitics, and Violence against Women of Color." *Critical Race Theory: The Key Writings that Formed the Movement*, edited by Kimberlé Williams Crenshaw, Beil Gotanda, Gary Peller, and Kendall Thomas, The New Press, 1995, pp. 357–383.

Crouching Tiger, Hidden Dragon. Directed by Ang Lee, performances by Yun-Fat Chow, Michelle Yeoh, and Ziyi Zhang, Columbia TriStar Home Video, 2000.

Cry Me a Sad River. Directed by Luo Luo, performances by Min Ren, Yunlai Xin, and Ruonan Zhang, Beijing Enlight Pictures, 2018.

Dai Sijie. *Balzac and the Little Chinese Seamstress*. Translated by Ina Rilke, Alfred A. Knopf, 2001.

Dai Sijie, director. *Balzac and the Little Chinese Seamstress*. Performances by Xun Zhou, Kun Chen, and Ye Liu, Empire Pictures, 2002.

Defoe, Daniel. *Robinson Crusoe*. W. Taylor, 1719.

Dragon Seed. Directed by Harold S. Bucquet and Jack Conway, performances by Katharine Hepburn, Walter Huston, Aline MacMahon, and Turhan Bey, MGM, 1944.

Eble, Kenneth. *Pearl S. Buck*. Twayne, 1980.

Elementary. Created by Robert Doherty, performances by Jonny Lee Miller, Lucy Liu, and Aidan Quinn, CBS, seasons 1–6, 2012–2018.

Eliade, Mircea. *The Forge and the Crucible*. Harper, 1956.

Engels, Frederick. "On Authority." 1872. *Marx-Engels Reader*, translated by Robert C. Tucker, Norton, 1978, pp. 730–733.

Ex Machina. Directed by Alex Garland, performances by Alicia Vikander, Domhnall Gleeson, and Oscar Isaac, Universal, 2015.

Extraordinary Mission. Directed by Alan Mak and Anthony Pun, CMC Pictures, 2017.

Fanon, Frantz. "The Negro and Language." *Black Skin, White Masks*. 1952. Translated by Charles Lam Markman, Grove, 1968, pp. 17–40.

Franz, Marie-Louise von. *Alchemy: An Introduction to the Symbolism and the Psychology*. Toronto: Inner City, 1980.

French, Howard. *China's Second Continent: How a Million Migrants Are Building a New Empire in Africa*. Alfred A. Knopf, 2014.

French, Howard W. *Everything Under the Heavens: How the Past Helps Shape China's Push for Global Power*. Alfred A. Knopf, 2017.

Freud, Sigmund. "Mourning and Melancholia." *Collected Papers Vol IV. Papers on Metapsychology and Papers on Applied Psycho-analysis*. Hogarth Press, 1953, pp. 152–170.

Freud, Sigmund. "The Interpretation of Dreams." *The Basic Writings of Sigmund Freud*, translated by A. A. Brill, Modern Library, 1995. https://books.google.com/books?id=OcYXHtLccZUC. Accessed Jan. 2, 2017.

Freud, Sigmund. "The Uncanny." *Collected Papers*, translated by James Strachey, Hogarth, 1953, vol. 4, pp. 368–407.

Fuller, Stephen M. "Deposing an American Cultural Totem: Clarice Starling and Postmodern Heroism in Thomas Harris's *Red Dragon, The Silence of the Lambs*, and *Hannibal*." *The Journal of Popular Culture*, vol. 38, no. 5, 2005, pp. 819–833.

Garrett, Greg. "Objecting to Objectification: Re-Viewing the Feminine in *The Silence of the Lambs*." *The Journal of Popular Culture*, vol. 27, no. 4, Spring 1994, pp. 1–12.

Gilman, Sander L. *The Jew's Body*. Routledge, 1991.

Golden Job. Directed by Kar Lok Chin, performances by Ekin Cheng, Jordan Chan, and Michael Tse, Well Go USA Entertainment, 2018.

Greene, Naomi. *From Fu Manchu to Kung Fu Panda: Images of China in American Film*. University of Hawaii Press, 2014.

Ha Jin. "Exiled to English." *Sinophone Studies: A Critical Reader*, edited by Shu-mei Shih, Chien-hsin Tsai, and Brian Bernardset, Columbia University Press, 2013, pp. 108–114.

Ha Jin. *A Free Life*. Vintage, 2007.

Ha Jin. *A Good Fall*. Vintage, 2009.

Hammett, Dashiell. *The Maltese Falcon*. 1929. Vintage Crime, 1992.

Hannibal. Executive Producer Bryan Fuller, performances by Mads Mikkelsen and Hugh Dancy, NBC, seasons 1–3, 2013–2015.

Hannibal. Directed by Ridley Scott, performances by Anthony Hopkins, Julianne Moore, and Gary Oldman, MGM Studios, 2001.

Hannibal Rising. Directed by Peter Webber, perfromances by Gaspard Ulliel, Rhys Ifans, and Li Gong, Dino De Laurentiis Co., 2007.

Haraway, Donna. "A Cyborg Manifesto: Science, Technology, and Socialist-Feminism in the Late Twentieth Century." 1984. *Simians, Cyborgs, and Women*, Routledge, 1991, pp. 149–181.

Harker, Jaime. *America the Middlebrow: Women's Novels, Progressivism, and Middlebrow Authorship between the Wars*. University of Massachusetts Press, 2007.

Harold & Kumar Go to White Castle. Directed by Danny Leiner, performances by John Cho and Kal Penn, Endgame Entertainment, 2004.

Harris, Thomas. *Hannibal*. Delacorte, 1999.

Harris, Thomas. *Hannibal Rising*. Delacorte, 2006.

Harris, Thomas. *Red Dragon*. Penguin, 1981.

Harris, Thomas. *The Silence of the Lambs*. St. Martin's Press, 1988.

Harte, Bret. "Plain Language from Truthful James." James R. Osgood & Co, Boston, 1871. http://twain.lib.virginia.edu/roughingit/map/chiharte.html. Accessed Nov. 1, 2018.

Hiroshima Mon Amour. Directed by Alain Resnais, performances by Emmanuelle Riva, Eiji Okada, and Stella Dassas, The Criterion Collection, 1959.

Hodges, Graham Russell. *Anna May Wong: From Laundryman's Daughter to Hollywood Legend*. Palgrave Macmillan, 2004.

Horowitz, Anthony. *The House of Silk: A Sherlock Holmes Novel*. Little Brown, 2011.

Humans. Performances by Gemma Chan, Katherine Parkinson, and Lucy Carless, BBC and AMC TV, seasons 1–3, 2015–2018.

The Hunchback of Notre Dame. Directed by Wallace Worsley, performances by Lon Chaney, Patsy Ruth Miller, and Norman Kerry, Universal Pictures, 1923.

The Hunger Game. Directed by Gary Ross, performances by Jennifer Lawrence, Josh Hutcherson, and Liam Hemsworth, Lionsgate, 2012.

In the Mood for Love. Directed by Wong Kar-wai, performances by Tony Leung and Maggie Cheung, Block 2 Pictures, 2000.

"Illustrating Chinese Exclusion." https://thomasnastcartoons.com/2014/04/01/every-dog-no-distinction-of-color-has-his-da/. Accessed Dec. 25, 2018.

Ishiguro, Kazuo. "A Family Supper." *The Penguin Collection of Modern Short Stories*, edited by Malcolm Bradbury, Penguin, 1987, pp. 434–442.

Ishiguro, Kazuo. *A Pale View of Hills*. 1982. Vintage, 1990.

Ishiguro, Kazuo. *An Artist of the Floating World*. 1986. Vintage, 1989.

Ishiguro, Kazuo. *Never Let Me Go*. Knopf, 2005.

Ishiguro, Kazuo. *Nocturne*. Knopf, 2009.

Ishiguro, Kazuo. *The Buried Giant*. Knopf, 2015.

Ishiguro, Kazuo. *The Remains of the Day*. 1989. Knopf, 1990.

Ishiguro, Kazuo. *The Unconsoled*. Knopf, 1995.

Ishiguro, Kazuo. *When We Were Orphans*. Knopf, 2000.

Jacobs, Joseph, editor. *English Fairy Tales*. David Nutt, 1890.

Jen, Gish. *The Love Wife*. Penguin, 2004.

Journey to the West. Directed by Stephen Chow, performances by Zhang Wen, Qi Shu, and Bo Huang, Bingo Movie, 2013.

Journey to the West: The Demons Strike Back. Directed by Tsui Hark, performances by Kris Wu, Kenny Lin, and Chen Yao, Stars Overseas, 2017.

Kiarostami, Abbas, director. *Like Someone in Love*. Performances by Rin Takanashi, Tadashi Okuno, and Ryo Kase, IFC Films, 2012.

Kilgannon, Corey. "He Irons, She Stitches." *The New York Times*, Jan. 15, 2016. http://www.nytimes.com/2016/01/17/nyregion/laundry-service-in-new-york-city-brooklyn-san-toy.html?_r=0. Accessed Jan. 15, 2016.

Kilgour, Maggie. "Dr. Frankenstein Meets Dr. Freud." *American Gothic: New Interventions in a National Narrative*, edited by Robert K. Martin and Eric Savoy, University of Iowa Press, 1998, pp. 40–53.

Kilgour, Maggie. "The Function of Cannibalism at the Present Time." *Cannibalism and the Colonial World*, edited by Francis Barker, Peter Francis Hulme, and Margaret Iversen, Cambridge University Press, 1998, pp. 238–259.

Kim, Suki. *The Interpreter*. Picador, 2003.

Kinder, Marsha. "From Mutation to Morphing." *Meta-Morphing: Visual Transformation and the Culture of Quick-Change*, edited by Vivian Sobchack, University of Minnesota Press, 1999, pp. 59–80.

Kingston, Maxine Hong. *The Woman Warrior: Memoirs of a Girlhood Among Ghosts*. Knopf, 1976.

Kingston, Maxine Hong. *Tripmaster Monkey: His Fake Book*. Knopf, 1989.

Kitamura, Katie. *A Separation*. Riverhead, 2017.

Kunnemann, Vanessa. *Middlebrow Mission: Pearl S. Buck's American China*. Blelefeld, Transcript Verlag, 2015.

Kwan, Kevin. *China Rich Girlfriend*. Doubleday, 2015.

Kwan, Kevin. *Crazy Rich Asians*. Doubleday, 2013.

Kwan, Kevin. *Rich People Problems*. Doubleday, 2017.

La Valley, Albert J. "Traditions of Trickery: The Role of Special Effects in the Science Fiction Film." *Shadows of the Magic Lamp: Fantasy and Science Fiction in Film*, edited by George Slusser and Eric S. Rabkin, Southern Illinois University Press, 1985, pp. 141–158.

Larsson, Stieg. *The Girl with the Dragon Tattoo*. Translated by Reg Keeland, Vintage, 2005.

Lee, Chang-rae. *Aloft*. Riverhead, 2004.

Lee, Chang-rae. *Native Speaker*. Riverhead, 1995.

Lethem, Jonathan. *Gun, with Occasional Music*. Harcourt, 1994.

Lethem, Jonathan. *Motherless Brooklyn*. Doubleday, 1999.

Lewis, Barry. *Kazuo Ishiguro*. Manchester University Press, 2000.

Leyerle, John. "The Interlace Structure of *Beowulf*." *Beowulf: A Verse Translation*, edited by Daniel Donoghue, Norton Critical Editions, 2002, pp. 130–151.

Liem, Deann Borshay, director. *First Person Plural*. NAATA, 2000.

Lim, Louisa. *The People's Republic of Amnesia: Tiananmen Revisited*. Oxford University Press, 2014.

Little Shop of Horrors. Directed by Frank Oz, performances by Rick Moranis, Ellen Greene, and Vincent Gardenia, Warner Home Video, 1986.

Liu, James J. Y. *The Chinese Knight-Errantry*. Routledge, 1967.

Ma, Ling. *Severance*. Farrar, Straus and Giroux, 2018.

Ma, Sheng-mei. *Alienglish: Eastern Diasporas in Anglo-American Tongues*. Cambria Press, 2014.

Ma, Sheng-Mei. *Diaspora Literature and Visual Culture: Asia in Flight*. Routledge, 2011.

Ma, Sheng-mei. *Immigrant Subjectivities in Asian American and Asian Diaspora Literatures*. State University of New York Press, 1998.

Ma, Sheng-Mei. *Sinophone-Anglophone Cultural Duet*. Palgrave Macmillan, 2017.

Ma, Sheng-Mei. *The Deathly Embrace: Orientalism and Asian American Identity*. University of Minnesota Press, 2000.

Ma, Sheng-mei. *The Last Isle: Contemporary Film, Culture and Trauma in Global Taiwan*. Rowman & Littlefield International, 2015.

Ma, Sheng-mei. "Whitewashing Chinese Laundryman." *The Ephemera Journal*, vol. 21, no. 3, May 2019, pp. 10–15.

The Maltese Falcon. Directed by John Huston, performances by Humphrey Bogart, Mary Astor, and Gladys George, Warner Bros., 1941.

The Man with Two Brains. Directed by Carl Reiner, performances by Steve Martin, Kathleen Turner, and David Warner, Warner Bros., 1983.

Manhunter. Directed by Michael Mann, performances by William Petersen, Brian Cox, Kim Greist, and Joan Allen, De Laurentiis Entertainment Group, 1986.

Maugham, W. Somerset. *The Painted Veil*. 1925. Penguin, 1952.

Mayer, Ruth. *Serial Fu Manchu: The Chinese Supervillain and the Spread of Yellow Peril Ideology*. Temple University Press, 2014.

McConnell, Frank. "Born in Fire: The Ontology of the Monster." *Shadows of the Magic Lamp: Fantasy and Science Fiction in Film*, edited by George Slusser and Eric S. Rabkin, Southern Illinois University Press, 1985, pp. 231–240.

Meet Me in St. Louis. Directed by Vincente Minnelli, performances by Judy Garland, Margaret O'Brien, and Mary Astor, MGM, 1944.

Messent, Peter. "American Gothic: Liminality and the Gothic in Thomas Harris's Hannibal Lecter Novels." *Dissecting Hannibal Lecter: Essays on the Novels of Thomas Harris*, edited by Benjamin Szumskyj, McFarland, 2008, pp. 13–36.

Mojin: The Lost Legend. Directed by Wuershan, performances by Kun Chen, Angelababy, and Qi Shu, CKF Pictures, 2015.

The Monkey King: Havoc in Heaven's Palace. Directed by Pou-soi Cheang, performances by Donnie Yen, Yun-Fat Chow, and Aaron Kwok, Global Star, 2014.

The Monkey King 2. Directed by Pou-soi Cheang, performances by Aaron Kwok and Gong Li, Filmko Films, 2016.

Moon, Krystyn. *Yellowface: Creating the Chinese in American Popular Music and Performance, 1850s–1920s*. Rutgers University Press, 2005.

Nora, Pierre. "Between Memory and History: Les Lieux de Mémoire." *Representations*, vol. 26, Spring 1989, pp. 7–24.

Nora, Pierre. *Les Lieux de Mémoire*. Gallimard, 1984.

Operation Mekong. Directed by Dante Lam, performances by Joyce Wenjuan Feng, Baoguo Chen, and Xudong Wu, Distribution Workshop, 2016.

Operation Red Sea. Directed by Dante Lam, performances by Yi Zhang, Johnny Huang, and Hai-Qing, Well Go USA Entertainment, 2018.

Palumbo-Liu, David. *Asian/American: Historical Crossings of a Racial Frontier*. Stanford University Press, 1999.

Park, Patricia. *Re Jane*. Viking, 2015.

Qiaobi Detergent Commercial. 2016. https://www.youtube.com/watch?v=OQL5p3HRR24. Accessed Dec. 12, 2017.

Qiu Xiaolong. *Death of a Red Heroine*. Soho, 2000.

Rao Pingru. *Our Story: A Memoir of Love and Life in China*. 2013. Translated by Nicky Harman, Pantheon, 2018.

Red Dragon. Directed by Brett Ratner, performances by Anthony Hopkins, Edward Norton, and Ralph Fiennes, Universal Pictures, 2002.

Reilly, James. "Going Out and Texting Home: New Media and China's Citizens Abroad." *The Internet, Social Media, and a Changing China*, edited by Jacques deLisle, Avery Goldstein, and Guobin Yang, University of Pennsylvania Press, 2016, pp. 180–199.

Roh, David S., Betsy Huang, and Greta A. Niu, editors. *Techno-Orientalism: Imagining Asia in Speculative Fiction, History, and Media*. Rutgers University Press, 2015.

Rohmer, Sax. *The Insidious Dr. Fu-Manchu*. Methuen, 1913.

Ryall, Chris. *Beowulf*. Illustrated by Gabriel Rodriguez, based on the screenplay by Neil Gaiman and Roger Avary, IDW Publishing, 2007.

Said, Edward. *Orientalism*. Pantheon, 1978.

Saul, Stephanie. "As Flow of Foreign Students Wanes, U.S. Universities Feel the Sting." *The New York Times*, Jan. 2, 2018.

Saussure, Ferdinand de. *Course in General Linguistics*. 1916. Columbia University Press, 2011.

Shadows. Directed by Tom Forman, performances by Lon Chaney, Marguerite De La Motte, and Harrison Ford, B. P. Schulberg Productions, 1922.

Shanghai Calling. Directed by Daniel Hsia, performances by Le Geng, Daniel Henney, and Sean Gallagher, China Film Co., 2012.

The Shanghai Express. Directed by Josef von Sternberg, performances by Marlene Dietrich and Anna May Wong, Paramount, 1932.

Shapiro, Sidney, translator. *The Outlaws of the Marsh (Shui Hu Zhuan)*. By Shi Nai'an and Luo Guanzhong, Classic Literature Collection (WorldLibrary.org). http://uploads.worldlibrary.net/uploads/pdf/20130423230739the_outlaws_of_the_marsh_pdf.pdf. Accessed Jan. 28, 2017.

Sherlock Holmes and the Baker Street Irregulars. Directed by Julian Kemp, performances by Jonathan Pryce, Bill Paterson, Anna Chancellor, and Alice Hewkin, BBC, 2007.

Sherlock Holmes and the Case of the Silk Stocking. Directed by Simon Cellan Jones, performances by Rupert Everett, Nicholas Palliser, Neil Dudgeon, and Michael Fassbender, BBC, 2004.

Shih, Shu-mei, Chien-hsin Tsai, and Brian Bernardset, editors. *Sinophone Studies: A Critical Reader*. Columbia University Press, 2013.

Shirow, Masamure. *Ghost in the Shell*. Kodansha, 1989.

The Silence of the Lambs. Directed by Jonathan Demme, performances by Anthony Hopkins and Jodie Foster, Orion Pictures, 1991.

Siu, Paul C. P. *The Chinese Laundryman: A Study of Social Isolation*. New York University Press, 1984.

Sobchack, Vivian. "At the Still Point of the Turning World: Meta-Morphing and Meta-Stasis." *Meta-Morphing: Visual Transformation and the Culture of Quick-Change*, edited by Vivian Sobchack, University of Minnesota Press, 1999, pp. 131–158.

Sobchack, Vivian. *Screening Space: The American Science Fiction Film*. Rutgers University Press, 1997.

Soderbergh, Steven, director. *Contagion*. Performances by Matt Damon and Kate Winslet, Warner Home Video, 2011.

Sōseki, Natsume. *Kokoro*. 1914. Translated by Edwin McClellan, Gateway, 1957.

Speedy. Directed by Ted Wilde, performances by Harold Lloyd, Ann Christy, and Bert Woodruff, Harold Lloyd Corporation, 1928.

Spiegelman, Art. *Maus: A Survivor's Tale*, part 1, *My Father Bleeds History*. Pantheon, 1986.

Spiegelman, Art. *Maus: A Survivor's Tale*, part 2, *And Here My Trouble Began*. Pantheon, 1991.

Spivak, Gayatri Chakravorty. "Can the Subaltern Speak?" *Marxism and the Interpretation of Culture*, edited by Lawrence Grossberg and Cary Nelson, University of Illinois Press, 1988, pp. 271–313.

Svensson, Marina. "Connectivity, Engagement, and Witnessing on China's Weibo." *The Internet, Social Media, and a Changing China*, edited by Jacques deLisle, Avery Goldstein, and Guobin Yang, University of Pennsylvania Press, 2016, pp. 49–70.

Swinton, Alma W. *I Married a Doctor: Life in Ontonagon, Michigan from 1900 to 1919*. Marquette, MI: Swinton, 1964.

The Swiss Family Robinson. Directed by Ken Annakin, performances by John Mills, Dorothy McGuire, James MacArthur, Janet Munro, and Sessue Hayakawa, Walt Disney, 1960.

Takaki, Ronald. *Strangers from a Different Shore: A History of Asian Americans*. Little, Brown, 1989.

Tan, Amy. *The Hundred Secret Senses*. Putnam, 1995.

Taylor, Barry. "The Violence of the Event: Hannibal Lecter in the Lyotardian Sublime." *Postmodern Surroundings*, edited by Steven Earnshaw, Rodopi, 1994, pp. 215–230.

Teo, Yugin. *Kazuo Ishiguro and Memory*. Palgrave Macmillan, 2014.

The Thief of Bagdad. Directed by Raoul Walsh, performances by Douglas Fairbanks, Julanne Johnston, Snitz Edwards, and Anna May Wong, United Artists, 1924.

Thien, Madeleine. *Do Not Say We Have Nothing*. Norton, 2016.

Thurner, Arthur W. *Strangers and Sojourners: A History of Michigan's Keweenaw Peninsula*. Wayne State University Press, 1994.

Tianxiabachang. *Ghost Blows Out the Candle* (*Guichuideng* 鬼吹灯). Anhui Wenyi Publisher, 2006.

Tsiang, H. T. *And China Has Hands*. (出番記). R. Speller, 1937.

Tsui Hark, director. *Detective Dee and the Mystery of the Phantom Flames*. Performances by Andy Lau, Tony Ka Fai Leung, Chao Deng, and Carina Lau, Cinedigm Entertainment Group, 2010.

Tsui Hark, director. *Young Detective Dee and Rise of the Sea Dragon*. Performances by Carina Lau, Chien Sheng, Mark Chao, Well Go USA Entertainment, 2013.

Twain, Mark. *Roughing It*. 1872. Holt, Reinhart and Winston, 1953.

Underworld. Directed by Len Wiseman, performances by Kate Beckinsale, Scott Speedman, and Shane Brolly, Lakeshore Entertainment, 2003.

Van Ash, Cay, and Elizabeth Sax Rohmer. *Master of Villainy: A Biography of Sax Rohmer*. Tom Stacey, 1972.

Van Den Ing, Eric, and Robert Schaap, editors. *Beauty and Violence: Japanese Prints by Yoshitoshi 1839–1892*. Society for Japanese Arts, 1992.

Van Gulik, Robert Hans. *Sexual Life in Ancient China: A Preliminary Study of Chinese Sex and Society from ca. 1500 BC till 1644 AD 1961*. Brill, 2003.

Van Gulik, Robert Hans. *The Chinese Gold Murders*. Harper, 1959.

Van Gulik, Robert Hans. *The Gibbon in China: An Essay in Chinese Animal Lore*. Brill, 1967.

Van Gulik, Robert Hans. *The Lore of the Chinese Lute: An Essay in the Ideology of the Ch'in*. 1940. Sophia University Press, 1968.

Van Gulik, Robert Hans, translator. *Celebrated Cases of Judge Dee* (Dee Goong An). 1949. Dover, 1976.

Van Gulik, Robert Hans, translator. *T'ang-yin pi-shih* (Parallel Cases from under the Pear Tree). Brill, 1956.

Waley, Arthur, translator. *Monkey (Xiyouji)*. By Wu Cheng'en. Grove, 1943.

The Wandering Earth. Directed by Frant Gwo, performances by Jing Wu, Chuxiao Qu, Guangjie Li, Netflix, 2019.

Wang Dulu. *Hetie Wubu Qu* (The Crane and the Steel 1938–1944), vol. 1, *Hejing Kunlun* (The Crane's Cry Echoes through Mt. Kunlun). Hong Kong: Tiandi (Cosmos), 2001.

Wang Dulu. *Hetie Wubu Qu* (The Crane and the Steel 1938–1944), vol. 2, *Baojian Jinchai* (The Sword and the Gold Hairpin). Taipei: Chungli, 2000.

Wang Dulu. *Hetie Wubu Qu* (The Crane and the Steel 1938–1944), vol. 3, *Jianqi Zhuguang* (The Qi of the Sword, the Light of the Pearl). Hong Kong: Tiandi (Cosmos), 2001.

Wang Dulu. *Hetie Wubu Qu* (The Crane and the Steel 1938–1944), vol. 4, *Wohu canglong* (Crouching Tiger, Hidden Dragon). Taipei: Vista, 2001.

Wang Dulu. *Hetie Wubu Qu* (The Crane and the Steel 1938–1944), vol. 5, *Tieji yinping* (Iron Steed, Silver Vase). Hong Kong: Tiandi (Cosmos), 2001.

Wang Ruowang. *Hunger Trilogy*. Translated by Kyna Rubin, M. E. Sharpe, 1991.

Wang, Val. *Beijing Bastard*. Penguin, 2014.

The Warrior's Way. Directed by Sngmoo Lee, performances by Dong-gun Jang, Kate Bosworth, and Geoffrey Rush, Rogue, 2010.

Welles, Orson, director. *The Lady from Shanghai*. Performances by Orson Welles and Rita Hayworth, Columbia Pictures, 1947.

Westworld. Directed by Jonathan Nolan and Lisa Joy, performances by Evan Rachel Wood, Jeffrey Wright, Ed Harris, and Anthony Hopkins, HBO, 2016–2018.

Westworld. Directed by Michael Crichton, performances by Yul Brynner, Richard Benjamin, and James Brolin, MGM, 1973.

Whissel, Kristen. *Spectacular Digital Effects: CGI and Contemporary Cinema*. Duke University Press, 2014.

The White Countess. Directed by James Ivory, produced by Ismail Merchant, screenplay by Kazuo Ishiguro, performances by Natasha Richardson, Ralph Fiennes, and Hiroyuki Senada, Sony Pictures, 2005.

Williams, Nicholas M. "Eating Blake, or an Essay on Taste: The Case of Thomas Harris's 'Red Dragon'." *Cultural Critique*, no. 42, Spring 1999, pp. 137–162.

Williams, Tony. "From *Red Dragon* to *Manhunter*." *Dissecting Hannibal Lecter: Essays on the Novels of Thomas Harris*, edited by Benjamin Szumskyj, McFarland, 2008, pp. 102–117.

Wilson, Eric G. *The Melancholy Android: On the Psychology of Sacred Machines*. State University of New York Press, 2006.

Wolf Warrior. Directed by Jing Wu, performances by Jing Wu, Nan Yu, Dahong Ni, and Scott Adkins, Well Go USA Entertainment, 2015.

Wolf Warrior 2. Directed by Jing Wu, performances by Jing Wu, Frank Grillo, and Celina Jade, Well Go USA Entertainment, 2017.

Wong, Cynthia F. *Kazuo Ishiguro*. Northcote House, 2000.

Wu Cheng'en. *Monkey (Hsi-yu chi)*. Translated by Arthur Waley. Grove, 1943.

Wu Cheng'en. *Xiyouji (Monkey)*. Tainan, Taiwan: *Diyi* (First) Bookstore, n.d. Print.

Wu Zetian sida qi'an (Four Strange Cases of Wu Zetian). Shanghai Guji Publishers, 1902. http://ctext.org/wiki.pl?if=gb&res=487050. Accessed May 2000.

Wyss, Johann David. *The Swiss Family Robinson, or, Adventures of a Shipwrecked Family on a Desolate Island.* 1812. T. Nelson and Sons, 1872.

Xiu Xiu: the Sent-Down Girl. Directed by Joan Chen, performances by Xiaolu Li, Lopsang, and Zheng Qian, Stratosphere Entertainment, 1998.

Yang, Gene Luen. *American Born Chinese.* First Second, 2006.

Yang Jiang. *Six Chapters from My Life "Downunder."* 1981. Translated by Howard Goldblatt, University of Washington Press, 1983.

Yang Jiang. *Womensa'er.* Taipei: Shibao wenhua, 2003.

Yoshihara, Mari. *Embracing the East: White Woman and American Orientalism.* Oxford University Press, 2003.

Yu, Anthony C., translator. *Journey to the West (Xiyouji).* By Wu Cheng'en. University of Chicago Press, 1980.

Yu Hua. *To Live.* 1992. Translated by Michael Berry, Random House, 2003.

Yun, Jung. *Shelter.* Picador, 2016.

Zhang, Li, and Zhengrong Hu. "Empire, *Tianxia* and Great Unity: A Historical Examination and Future Vision of China's International Communication." *Global Media and China*, vol. 2, no. 2, 2017, pp. 197–207.

Zhou Haohui. *Death Notice.* Translated by Zac Haluza, Penguin, 2014.

Zia, Helen. "My Mother's Secret." *The New York Times*, January 20, 2019, p. 8.

INDEX

Lightning Source UK Ltd.
Milton Keynes UK
UKHW021812051219
354810UK00005B/258/P